BRINGING LAW HOME

ARTICULATIONS STUDIES IN RACE,
IMMIGRATION,
AND CAPITALISM

EDITORS
Cedric de Leon
Pawan Dhingra

BRINGING LAW HOME

Gender, Race, and Household Labor Rights

KATHERINE EVA MAICH

STANFORD UNIVERSITY PRESS
Stanford, California

Stanford University Press
Stanford, California

Library of Congress Cataloging-in-Publication Data

Names: Maich, Katherine Eva, author.
Title: Bringing law home : gender, race, and household labor rights / Katherine Eva Maich.
Other titles: Articulations (Stanford, Calif.)
Description: Stanford, California : Stanford University Press, 2025. | Series: Articulations | Includes bibliographical references and index.
Identifiers: LCCN 2024055121 (print) | LCCN 2024055122 (ebook) | ISBN 9781503642201 (cloth) | ISBN 9781503643239 (paperback) | ISBN 9781503643246 (ebook)
Subjects: LCSH: Household employees—Legal status, laws, etc.—Peru—Lima. | Household employees—Legal status, laws, etc.—New York (State)—New York. | Women household employees—Legal status, laws, etc.—Peru—Lima. | Women household employees—Legal status, laws, etc.—New York (State)—New York. | Women household employees—Peru—Lima—Social conditions. | Women household employees—New York (State)—New York—Social conditions.
Classification: LCC K1841.H68 M35 2025 (print) | LCC K1841.H68 (ebook) | DDC 344.747/10176164—dc23/eng/20241121
LC record available at https://lccn.loc.gov/2024055121
LC ebook record available at https://lccn.loc.gov/2024055122

Cover design: Lee Friedman
Cover art: Based on icons by parkjisun for The Noun Project
Typeset by Newgen in Minion Pro 10

The authorized representative in the EU for product safety and compliance is: Mare Nostrum Group B.V. | Mauritskade 21D | 1091 GC Amsterdam | The Netherlands | Email address: gpsr@mare-nostrum.co.uk | KVK chamber of commerce number: 96249943

To my parents, who taught me that the sky is the limit

To Eva and Eric, with all my love

CONTENTS

LIST OF FIGURES AND TABLES

FIGURES

TABLES

ACKNOWLEDGMENTS

Writing this book was truly a collective effort—a reflection of mentorship and support woven together over many years. I am deeply grateful to so many people who invested in me and my ideas, and who helped bring this book to fruition.

My time at Berkeley was formative and filled with discussion, encouragement, constructive criticism, and global thinking. Raka Ray's wisdom, thoughtfulness, and sociological insights have made this journey deeply meaningful. Raka taught me to believe in myself to my core and she taught me to be a sociologist; she kept me on track, inspired me with her intellectual energy, and made every step of the research process feel so worthwhile. This book would have been impossible to imagine without her, and our conversations over the years are on these pages. Kim Voss' thoughtful insights and critiques helped me to shape my interests in the sociology of labor early on, and Barrie Thorne's immediate warmth and expansive intellectual depth was influential. I was lucky to begin conversations with Laura Enríquez, as her thoughtful guidance was formative for shaping my understanding of Latin American politics and social movements. Jonathan Simon helped me see the potential for the law in my own work with attention to the way it shapes the workers' lives, and I am grateful to his welcome connections between social theory, literature, and film. Michael Burawoy taught me to be persistent and thoughtful as an ethnographer, and I am also grateful for feedback and support from Cristina Mora, Cybelle Fox, Armando Lara Millán, Mara Love-man, and Leslie Salzinger.

I was lucky to cross paths and establish community with many talented scholars at Berkeley, including Marcel Paret, Eli Friedman, Jennifer Carlson, Abigail Andrews, Barry Eidlin, Ryan Calder, Mike Levien, Tianna Paschel, Fidan Elcioglu, Adam Reich, Gabe Hetland, Elif Lostuvali, Ofer Sharone, Ryan Centner, Margo Mahan, Freeden Oeur, Fithawee Tzeggai, Tara Gon-salves, Paula Uniacke, Jonah Stuart-Brundage, Ben Shestakofsky, Jessica Compton, Michaeljit Sandhu, Alex Roehrkasse, Jessica Schirmer, Aya Fabros, and Karolina Mikołajewska-Zając.

The "Team Raka" collective, then and now, has been a source of intellectual discovery and cross-cohort bonding over the years, all thanks to Raka Ray's mentorship. I am lucky to have worked with and learned from Dawn Dow, Nazanin Shahrokni, Abigail Andrews, Jenny Carlson, Kimberly Kay Hoang, Gowri Vijayakumar, Kate Mason, Jordanna Matlon, Sarah Anne Minkin, Kemi Balogun, Katie Hasson, Carter Koppelman, Joy Hightower, Gill Gual-tieri, and Louise Ly. Ana Villarreal and Kara Young were early friends in the program and trusted sources of sociological reflection as we made our journey together. Sun Kim's insights and encouragement have pushed my work for-ward significantly and Sujin Eom offered critical legal insights to my work. I am grateful to both for their intellectual honesty and friendship. Marcel Paret is a remarkable listener who can take a rough draft and somehow turn it into gold by distilling two to three clear, good ideas from a jumbled concoction of thoughts. I am grateful for the time he invests in others, and his belief in my work has been very influential. I have admired Astrid Ackerman since I met the amazing Ackerman family in its entirety, and I remain always impressed by Jennifer Siqueira with our writing and running solidarity. I am thankful to Zachary Levenson and Elise Herrala for their love of social theory, unpar-alleled wit, writing and grading sessions, and deep friendship through thick and thin. And I am lucky to count Edwin Ackerman and Graham Wilson Hill as wonderful colleagues who are shining sociologists but even better friends. They are the closest thing to brothers that I have, and they have helped me finish this book in more ways than they know.

Studying at the UMass Labor Center was formative for shaping my in-tellectual interests in gender, work, and labor. I am grateful to the engaged faculty there for supporting my developing research trajectory, including

Stephanie Luce, Paula Chakravartty, Eve Weinbaum, Tom Juravich, Jasmine Kerrissey, Ann Ferguson, Joyce Berkman, Nancy Folbre, Dan Clawson, Dale Melcher, and Harris Freeman. Cedric de Leon has been incredibly supportive and encouraging of this book and my work overall. I'm thrilled to have a place in his Articulations series with Pawan Dhingra through Stanford University Press. But the most valuable thing to come out of my time at UMass was meeting my best friend of nearly twenty years, Clare Hammonds. She is a brilliant, grounded scholar with a critical eye and a selfless determination. We first taught together in 2006 and have been talking through our ideas ever since. Our writing retreats in the Catskills and Poconos, halfway between Northampton and State College, sustained me as we crunched the fall leaves and revised our papers together. And now it seems fitting that another key mentor, Carolina Bank Muñoz, has joined the UMass Sociology Department. Her support and encouragement of my work has been crucial throughout the last decade, and my success feels very much bound up with her enthusiastic support.

Sofía Mauricio was instrumental to my fieldwork in Peru as she welcomed me to La Casa de Panchita and opened the doors to experience Lima in a new way. Our law workshops, walks through the city, and dinners together helped me understand Lima and the struggles of its domestic workers in context, and Sofía continues to be a role model in her dedication to domestic workers. Josefina Medina inspired me in the hot kitchen, while valuable conversations with Blanca Figueroa and Agata Zumaeta Figueroa sharpened my research. I also want to thank Johana Reyes Quinteros, José Alberto Ramírez, Carlos Ramírez Guevara, Ana Mónica, and Lizbeth Moreno Salomé for their cooperation and hospitality. Daniela Ortiz and Nicolás Kisic Aguirre were generous in sharing their artistic designs and architectural analyses around inequalities in household labor with me. Victoria Maraví, whose quick wit, sociological mind, and linguistic prowess enabled me to more readily situate my work, did excellent work as my research assistant. I am grateful to the talented Peruvian artists Victor Delfín and Jesús Ruiz Durand for their work, and appreciate Jesús Ruiz Durand generously allowing his art to be shared in this book. Friendships with María Paz Gómez Karadza, Natalie and Azaad Mohamed, Lunia Vera, Gabriela Blohm, Vassnia Nizama, Lilian Quispe, Benexy Gandullia, Heather Platter, and Diana Suttin sustained my fieldwork and made Lima feel like a home away from home.

During the research I conducted in New York City, KC Wagner took me under her wing at the Cornell University Worker Institute; her energy, engaged politics, and willingness to draw connections between people and ideas continue to inspire me. Gene Carroll's kindness made the city a little more accessible, while conversations with Alice Berliner warmed the winter days we spent together. Linda Burnham's generous support of my work took me far, as she reached out to friends and contacts in the city on my behalf, as did Jill Shenker, Ai-jen Poo, and others at the National Domestic Workers Alliance. Christine Lewis's poetry, honesty, and willingness to share her spirit and enthusiasm for my project profoundly shaped it. Robert and Alexis Gutiérrez and Roberto and Rosie Gutiérrez shared their Brooklyn neighborhoods with me, and I am thankful for their encouragement of this book.

I am greatly indebted to the many domestic workers in Lima and New York City who shared their lives and their working experiences with me over the course of this research. They shaped this book in a profound way through their bravery and honesty, taking time out of their busy lives to answer my questions and reflect on challenging moments. Their struggles and strength remain an inspiration to me. At the founding congress of the International Domestic Workers Federation in Montevideo, Uruguay, I was lucky enough to meet Jennifer Natalie Fish, Eileen Boris, and Mary Romero who, along with Premilla Nadasen, Evelyn Nakano Glenn, Rhacel Parreñas, Erynn Masi de Casanova, María Elena Valenzuela, and Mary Goldsmith, have pushed me as scholars and mentors to hone my focus on global and comparative approaches to domestic worker rights.

Thanks to Peter Evans and Chris Tilly, I joined UCLA's Experiences Organizing Informal Workers research team in 2013, which allowed me to work with and learn from the brilliant Elizabeth Tang, Fish Ip, Adriana Paz, Myrtle Witbooi, Carmen Britez, June Barret, Daphne Ip, Shirley Price, Adelinda Díaz Uriarte, Ai-jen Poo, Antonia Peña, Jill Shenker, and other leaders in the global domestic worker movement. Claire Hobden and I met at the Justice in the Home conference at Barnard College in 2014, and she has been a friend and source of wisdom since. Chris Tilly has been a generous mentor and a role model of incredible work ethic, integrity, and focus. He and Marie Kennedy remain a source of inspiration and support, and I hope to follow their example through my contributions to academia more broadly.

I was fortunate enough to present developing material from this book at a number of universities, including Cornell, MIT, Penn State, Illinois, UPenn, Washington, Penn State, Virginia, and Notre Dame. There and at related conferences, many colleagues engaged with my work and offered useful feedback, including Shannon Gleeson, Jenn Bair, Kevan Harris, Jamie McCallum, Virginia Doellgast, Kate Griffith, Michael McCarthy, Rina Agarwala, Gretchen Purser, Jennifer Chun, Ryan Lamare, Dan Graff, Susan Silbey, Paul Osterman, Erin Hatton, and Katherine Benton-Cohen. Mary and Greg Downes and Candace Feck also gave important feedback. Before her untimely death, Laurie Edelman offered key commentary on my work in various stages. Scholars from the Latin American Studies Association (LASA) Labor Studies Section offered important insights on my research, and I especially appreciate Cecilia Senen, Ana Miranda, Jean François Mayer, Carlos Salas, Leda Pérez, Rodolfo Elbert, Pablo Pérez-Ahumada, Maggie Gray, Lucila D'Urso, Laura Moisa, and Omar Manky.

At Penn State, I would like to thank my colleagues Sarah Damaske, Mark Anner, Paul Clark, Elaine Farndale, Elaine Hui, Dan DiMaggio, Michael Maffie, Kathy Sexsmith, Hazel Velasco Palacios, Alicia Decker, Sarah Brothers, Hilary Wething, Kristina Brant, Leif Jensen, Forrest Briscoe, Cyanne Loyle, Luis Mendoza, Cara Adrian, Cate Bowman, Becky Tarlau, Manuel Rosaldo, Matthew Fisher-Daly, Kate Ragon, and Rak Piyanontalee. I especially appreciated support from the School of Labor and Employment Relations, the Center for Global Workers' Rights, the Women's, Gender, and Sexuality Studies Department, and the Faculty Writing Program. The friendship and solidarity with Mary Bellman, Lee Szymkiewicz, Cody Stephens, and Sasha Coles made my time at Penn State so meaningful, and I will miss them dearly. I was fortunate enough to work with excellent research assistants through the Labor and Global Workers' Rights Program: Sergio Saravia, Saulo Galicia Vidal, Bashiratu Kamal, Mikael Ruukel, Anya Popovych, Allison Petonic, Muzummal Afzal, and Mercy Nabwire, and through the UMass Labor Center, Olivia Geho and Rafael Botello. Sergio Saravia in particular went above and beyond with crucial research assistance and editorial deftness during the final stages of this manuscript.

Central PA was a great place to live during important transitions in my life. I am grateful to John and Susan Pettengill, who kept me running, writing, and motivated while at Penn State. They are the kind of generous, caring professionals and parents I hope to emulate. Meghan Colley became a friend and confidante, offering me respite whenever I was lucky enough to sit in her warm corner chair overlooking Calder Way. Dr. Jamie Miller and Dr. Sue Lincoski took wonderful care of my first baby, my gentle giant of a golden retriever, Samuel Leonard. Sam sat curled up next to me during the revisions and editing of this manuscript, keeping me company on so many long nights. And during travel for fieldwork and conferences, Jackie Lepore and Dustin Neumann took Sam in as family, adding a little golden to their big-dog crew. They also helped prepare Sam to become a big brother to Eva while this book came together, taking care of him after I gave birth. Katie Nurmi dazzled us with such a winning personality, spirited devotion to animals and marginalized youth, and willingness to clean with grace, dignity, and humor. Katie was there for us during many family transitions, and for that, we will always be grateful. And Eric and I are thankful for our Bellefonte friends, the members of the Moose Lodge #206, the Elks #1094, and the VFW Post #1600. They welcomed Eric, me, and (eventually) Eva with open arms and shuffleboard games, truly making us feel at home.

In my brief time so far in the Sociology Department at Texas A&M, many faculty members have been supportive of this book and my overall research trajectory, including Nadia Kim, Mary Campbell, Chaitanya Lakkimsetti, Theresa Morris, Harland Prechel, Defne Over, Ernesto Amaral, Pat Rubio Goldsmith, Heili Pals, Alex Hernandez, Emilce Santana, Rob Mackin, and Kevin Barge. However, Nancy Plankey-Videla stands out among them all, as her line edits, generous engagement and incisive comments guided this manuscript to completion and brought out its best.

Conducting the research for this book would not have been possible without the support of the American Association of University Women's American Fellowship, the Inter-America Foundation Grassroots Research Fellowship, and the Andrew W. Mellon Foundation's Latin American Sociology Fellowship. At Berkeley, the Center for Latin American Studies, the Institute for Governmental Studies, the Center for Race and Gender, the Graduate Division, and the Department of Sociology's Lowenthal Fellowship offered generous funding that helped shape my research and writing. I am also grateful to Berkeley Connect and to the Center for the Study of Law and Society's Berkeley Empirical Legal Studies Fellowship through Berkeley Law School.

The brilliant Marcela Maxfield of Stanford University Press was fabulous to work with, as she understood my ideas from the start and worked tirelessly to push this book forward. Justine Sargent was a wonderful editorial assistant, and I am infinitely grateful to them both, as Stanford University Press became the perfect home for this book. An earlier version of selections from Chapter 3 was published in *Critical Cities: Ideas, Knowledge, and Agitation from Emerging Urbanists, Volume 4*, co-edited by Deepa Naik and Trenton Oldfield, and an earlier version of Chapter 5 was published in *Political Power and Social Theory*, co-edited by Michael McCarthy and Barry Eidlin.

Finally, I dedicate this book to my family because I could not have done any of this without them. My parents, Paul and Jessica Maich, are so hard-working, selfless, generous, and inspiring. They give so much of themselves to their three daughters and their three granddaughters, and we are the better for it. They are also genuinely incredible people to spend time with, and they nurtured me with great questions, wonderful meals, and endless support throughout the process of writing this book and the many years of research leading up to it. My sisters, Emily and Hilary, have believed in me every step of the way with this project and with everything else in my life, and they also kept me motivated and feeling loved. My nieces Fiona, Stella, and Ellie are so smart and creative, and they are already wonderful cousins to my daughter Eva.

I was lucky enough to have my two sets of grandparents alongside me for a great deal of my life. William and Marie Maich were so proud of me, my sisters, and our cousin Will, and loved us all fiercely. Leonard and Jo Ann Isban's commitment to family and hard work remain an inspiration, and my grandfather, a voracious reader, read any of my work that I shared. I only wish that I could have finished this book before he passed away. My godmother, Patricia Eva Maich, cares so much about our family, is the founder of the Scary Movie Team, and skillfully found a way to always be encouraging of this book. My godfather, Michael Isban, went to great lengths and many dinners at Kinkaid's to help me to stay grounded and focused, and to see the light when things were challenging along the way. I am grateful to my aunt and uncle, Sue and Greg Payne, who have been supportive of my professional accomplishments. Aunt Betty and Aunt Lori have been enthusiastically rooting for this book for a long time. Will and Annie Maich continually cheered me on, and I know that Peter and Mary Ellen Maich would also be happy that this book is finished.

Young and Yun Sook Lee were crucial in supporting our growing family as they cooked incredible food to sustain us and took care of Eva. They are role models of great work ethic, discipline, and resilience, and I love being their daughter-in-law. Judy, Tim, Jason, and Melissa Miller have welcomed me with open arms, helped us with moving and caring for Eva, and continue to impress me as loving and supportive family members.

I could not have finished this book without the steadfast support and constant encouragement of my husband, Eric Young Lee. He kept our beautiful baby daughter Eva entertained and happy for hours through concert time and other fun, creative Appa activities so that I could finalize this manuscript. You inspire me to be my best, 자기야, and I love you. And to my little one, Eva June, who lights up my life and gives me great hope for the future.

ONE CONCEPTUALIZING THE HOME AS A SITE OF WORK, AS A SITE OF LAW

In Ousmane Sembène's 1966 film *La Noire de . . .* (*Black Girl*), a young Senegalese woman sits patiently on the corner among other maids and nannies awaiting employment, who chatter in the hot afternoon sun. An upper-class French woman approaches the corner, hair smoothly wound and tucked back with a pin, high heels clicking on the broken asphalt of the Dakar street. A rush of women moves toward her, arms up, clamoring voices asking to be chosen. The camera is suddenly full of hands and palms grabbing; the employer steps back and winces, momentarily flustered. She pauses and glances over at Diouana, still sitting quietly, thin wrists extended coolly in front of her, and with a slight nod, quickly summons her. "Oui, madame," Diouana murmurs softly, moving past the other women and falling into step with her employer. Based on Diouana's display of reserve and poise, she is *chosen*; she has been selected to move to the French Riviera to work for the French couple, caring for their home and, later, their children. As the title of the film suggests, she is "someone's Black girl"; she is not her own.

I purposefully begin this book's introduction with a cinematic vignette from fifty years ago about a country that is not the subject of this study for a number of reasons. First, Sembène's film takes as its main character the domestic worker Diouana; rather than an incidental character in scenes of a maid bustling in the kitchen or passing through the background of the lives of others, she is central.

We see where she comes from, how and why she leaves her home, the promise of work, and what awaits her in France. Second, the film visually depicts many of the characteristics of the essence of domestic work, including its intersecting hierarchies of race, class, and gender. I explore these dynamics in two cities that are distinct from Dakar, and yet simultaneously reveal important parallels that characterize the universality of this industry as it plays out in various formations globally. Third, we see Diouana's life initially transformed by her job and later taken by it, as she slips into a deeper and deeper depression, becomes catatonic, and finally, slits her throat in her employer's bathtub. Her tall, elegant body is positioned awkwardly for the first time, arms bent like growing branches stretched out against the pristine white porcelain.

La Noire de . . ., then, serves a dual purpose here for the book. First, it clearly shows the *vulnerability* of domestic workers, a commonplace trope used both in the sociological research and in the scant, but growing, public discourse around this occupation. Diouana is isolated in someone else's home in someone else's country, where she is separated from her family, language, and culture. She is subjected to poor treatment by her employers and lacks the resources to leave. She is, quite clearly, a victim, just as domestic workers are typically cast, and just as many experience and field in their working lives.

Yet in Sembène's unflinching portrayal of Diouana's rise and decline, of the potential represented by the job that eventually leads to her end, she is the only character presented as having a solution. Second, then, is the way in which *La Noire de . . .* presents Diouana's "way out," or means of escape, as highly *personal*. Diouana's life working inside of a home in Dakar and her death working inside of a home in the French Riviera—and all that happens in between, including her agreement to leave and travel to another country, the poor working conditions paired with an increase in job duties she experiences upon arrival, and her resultant vulnerable status as an immigrant—fall completely outside the bounds of formal rules or regulation. Her death, this last act of plotted agency to escape her poor treatment, is displayed as the ultimate rebuttal of her employers, who must now tend to her body and clean up all signs of her corporeal existence. They slowly empty the drawers of her neatly folded clothes on a sunny day in the French Riviera, and as they contact her family in Dakar, they must remember that Senegal exists. Diouana has severely reversed the power dynamic inside of the home, as her actions now control their behavior and command a response. Sembène skirts dangerously close to romanticizing the precise moment when Diouana appears most powerless, and yet her fiercely held coolness cautions us against cheering her on and challenges us as silent witnesses to see her personal decision as a show of strength.

In this way, the film speaks to the ubiquity of the industry of domestic service through its portrayal of a relatively mundane reality: wealthy employers visually size up and then select a young woman to leave behind all that she knows and relocate to a new place, where things do not go well. Its dramatic ending similarly echoes the less common, yet still present, cases of extreme exploitation that shape how the industry is understood more broadly today: employers are cast as antagonistic, greedy, and one-dimensional at best, if not violent and hostile at worst, while workers remain hapless victims who are trapped in someone else's life. And drawing attention to those cases is important, as they continue to occur globally. The far-too-frequent recent incidents of domestic worker deaths and abuses in Beirut (Su 2017), Hong Kong (Ives 2016), Singapore (O'Brien 2015), London (Leghtas 2014), and Kuwait (Ewe 2023), to just name a few, only prove the point further.

Yet presented by Diouana's final, calculated performance to close the film on her own terms, we have a different narrative around domestic service—one that explores the labor relations of *power* and the *personal* embedded in the home as a site of work. However, this narrative is also telling for what it does *not* include or explore, for what is exposed as being absent from Diouana's life, and death, as a migrant domestic worker of the informal economy—the law, or any gesture at legal regulation designed to govern the conditions of her work, categorize what she does as legitimate work, grant her a specific set of protected labor rights, and recognize her as a real worker. Labor law is not missing only from Diouana's highly personal relationship of inequality with her employers, however. In fact, its absence is characteristic of most domestic workers' employment situations, as out of the estimated number of 76 million domestic workers globally, 80% are informal, nearly 30% are excluded completely from labor protections and only 10% enjoy coverage under general labor laws to the same extent as other workers (ILO 2013:50; ILO 2015; Seiffarth, Bonnet, and Hobden 2023). And even in sites where political struggle has brought about said law to recognize and regulate this specific employment relationship in the home, its highly personal nature persists.

The book insists upon a departure from the narrative of the *absent* law, then, and instead takes the *presence* of law as its core focus and area of inquiry. Due to the long-standing, entrenched nature of the dominant discourse around the home as somehow being *separate* from work, it is by definition more difficult to draw attention to the labor performed there. It follows, then, and as domestic workers' years of concentrated organizing and mobilizing for labor rights and recognition across various countries and contexts show, that it is that much more difficult to bring labor rights home for those responsible for the household labor.

SITUATING LABOR RIGHTS AT HOME

Bringing Law Home asks, given the place of the home as constitutive of the private sphere, how do we regulate it as a workplace? What does it mean to have "labor rights at home" and what limits to labor legislation exist there? When the state steps in to (finally) regulate this group of workers in the informal sector, what possibilities and potential problems result? How does the implementation and specifics of legislation come to bear on the lives of those it attempts to protect, offer benefits to, or bring into social and political inclusion as *real workers*? And finally, once the law is there, the book strives to show how its presence through a recognized employment relationship shapes the lives of the very domestic workers it was designed to protect, as well as the space of the home itself, and with what consequences.

To answer these questions and explore their implications, I focus on two recent pieces of domestic worker legislation through a Global North/South comparison set between Lima, Peru, and New York City. Both of these large, urban centers of migration were the sites of sustained household worker organizing which resulted in distinct, measurable outcomes—the implementation of state-granted legislation offering unprecedented protections and benefits to domestic workers, finally bringing them into political inclusion after a long period of historical exclusion. To study these laws and their effect upon the lives and working conditions of the very domestic workers they were designed to regulate, I spent 10 months conducting ethnography in Lima and 9 months in New York City, and also conducted 120 in-depth interviews with domestic workers in both cities. Additionally, I analyzed legislative transcripts about the laws themselves, and incorporated demographic survey data on the population of domestic workers in the two capitals.

The book thus contributes to and expands upon sociological literatures on domestic work, labor informality, and the global nature of household labor in several ways. The literature on paid domestic work has long acknowledged the difficulties of organizing workers and, to a lesser degree, of regulating with labor rights in an industry based in the home. Yet, I argue that the difficulties arise from the historical organization of labor in the home itself, which is fundamentally an ordering of gender and racial subordination. Historically, we know that the household has been challenging to regulate, given that it is protected as special, private, and exceptional, and we also know little about efforts to bring rights into this space for the workers within it. My work intervenes in the unresolved debate around domestic work being categorized as exceptional, or "other than work," due to its location in the isolated, individualized home. I show how efforts to regulate that space as a site of labor often prioritize the household over the worker and view the worker as an extension of the home itself, thus preserving a social hierarchy which codifies extant structural vulnerability for domestic workers. While there is no single, universal "home," then, when examined as a place of work, it is a rich site from which to observe, analyze, and theorize historical continuities which persist today, even when there is labor legislation present.

Second, my work sheds light on efforts to formalize employment relationships that exist inside of the home by grappling with determinants such as labor informality and immigration status. I explore how these factors shape the legally regulated employment relationship between household workers and employers, moving beyond superficial explanations of enforcement. In turning this attention to the private sphere of the home, I also move forward our understanding of law as a site of power through which dynamics of gender, race, and marginality are negotiated.

The book contributes a grounded, micro-level analysis of these labor laws in practice as they govern the household as a site of labor, and this focus on labor rights in the home poses an exception to literature on workplace rights that has glanced over the home.

A key premise of my study is the central importance of the home itself as a *site*. Similar to Giddens' (1984) notion of *locale*, which he theorizes as signifying a physical space that provides a context through which people interact with each other and the social world, I use *site* in order to show the specificity as well as the universality of the concept of home, in addition to the sociospatial ramifications of the physical design in practice. I consider the home as a conflicted site of ideological production, of social hierarchies, of work, and of law. The home as a site occupies a contradictory location in the global, but especially the Western, imaginary (Watson 1986).

Long protected by the doctrine of individual private property, the home has historically been associated with a kind of "sacred refuge" mythology, as a space to be protected from the public interference of the outside world. The privacy of the home often masks the social relations of intimacy, power, love, and exploitation that take place inside of it, as domestic workers reproduce family life and the ideologies of home by cleaning, cooking, and caring for those who live there. Because of the entrenched nature of this dominant discourse around the home as *separate* from work, it is by definition more difficult to draw attention to the labor performed there. Decades of scholarly research on domestic service have made this clear, resulting in exclusionary consequences for domestic workers that have come to shape how we think about the industry itself as beyond the law. I ask, given the place of the home as constitutive of the private sphere, how do we regulate it as a workplace? How do we bring legislated labor protections into the home?

A third way that my book draws upon and contributes to extant literature on global domestic worker organizing involves its case selection that brings both internal and external migrants into comparative focus. Examining workers who have immigrated to another country to seek work, as compared to workers who have migrated to their own capital to do the same, grants important purchase on our understanding of their particular forms of structural vulnerability and the extent to which efforts to regulate domestic work must consider that im/migrant vulnerability. Previous scholarship has largely focused on industrialized countries' reliance on imported domestic workers, as Ray and Qayum (2009) point out, while research on domestic work in Latin America (Chaney and Garcia Castro 1989; Gill 1994) has shifted away from its former focus on studies of internal migrants (10). My approach, however, shifts back to a central focus on the structural vulnerability of Peruvian internal migrant workers, providing analytical leverage to examine Southern labor on its own terms as I build on the specific shape and texture of existing relationships between workers and employers in the Peruvian home. Additionally, it brings Lima into conversation with New York City, a fixture of the Global North and the site of many previous studies of domestic work. While there is much asymmetry in their political, historical, and social contexts, then, my research reveals a similar outcome in both New York City and Lima, as I show that the industry's historic roots in colonial and racialized relations shape its legal regulation and thus reproduce those inequalities in practice.

In Lima, household workers waged a decades-long political struggle to win the Peruvian Household Workers' Law. However, it grants few rights, fails to codify a minimum wage, and legalizes discrimination against household workers, complicating an employment relationship already shaped by social hierarchies of race, ethnicity, class, gender, and geography. I show how the law extends to household workers only half of the labor protections afforded to other occupations, shaping a labor regime of what I call "colonial domesticity" inside Lima's contemporary homes through three sets of practices. Later in the book, I show the ways that colonial domesticity is *spatially* manifested via segregation of workers' living quarters, *embodied* through workers' racially coded uniforms, and *temporally* legislated as efforts to draw boundaries around time reveal the impossibility of regulating the working day inside the household.

Domestic workers similarly organized and mobilized for years to bring about the Domestic Workers' Bill of Rights in New York City. However, I find that the law grants only negligible protections: one day of vacation and language around obligatory overtime pay for workers. In fact, it was stripped of its strongest provisions, including the right to collectively bargain, a termination clause, a standard contract, and a living wage, for it to be passed into law in 2010. I argue that the law deliberately eschews language around immigration, thus establishing what I call "immigrant domesticity" instead of improving working conditions. The law circumscribes the rights of domestic workers in three ways: it *institutionalizes* dependency by shouldering employers with the onus of immigration-status enforcement, it is *inconsistent* because it subjects workers to their employers' whims by failing to create a standardized contract, and it engenders *informality* by permitting private employer networks to shape labor market access and thus skirt formal regulations concerning hiring and firing.

Beyond knowing that the household has proved a difficult and reluctant arena for social change for those who work inside it, however, we know very little about how laws that attempt to regulate the home actually do or do not work, and why. Separately and together, then, my fieldwork from both sites sharpens our understanding of how, despite important legislative victories for domestic workers, the home has not yet been democratized. In the following sections, I explore how my research engages with and understands labor law, the home as a concept and as a site of work, and the industry of domestic service and workers' particular struggles to organize for labor rights.

CLASSIFICATION STRUGGLES: LINKING LAW AND LABOR RELATIONS

This book argues that to fully understand what it means to consider the home as someone's site of work, we must also understand it as a site of *law*. This is a considerably different understanding of "law" than the usual broad, legalistic definition. Through my research and fieldwork, I specifically employ an understanding of the ambiguous term "law" to refer to labor law for household workers, either at the national level as in Peru or at the state level as in New York. In the case of New York's Domestic Workers' Bill of Rights and in other countries, the bulk of its legal protections either 1) narrow the exemptions of one or more previous labor laws or 2) abolish the law's previous categorical exclusions and, thus, enable the law to cover domestic workers. All eighteen of the Peruvian law's tenets are written expressly concerning the working lives and conditions of labor for domestic workers and for their employers, while in New York, the law only implicitly references employers.

Yet in both sites, this type of legislation resembles a collection of labor protections that identify and codify the rights and responsibilities prescribed by an *employment relationship*. The International Labour Organization (ILO) defines the employment relationship as a "universal notion which creates a link between a person, called the 'employee' (frequently referred to as 'the worker') with another person, called the 'employer' to whom she or he provides labour or services under certain conditions in return for remuneration" (ILO 2003:2). This "link" is key, as it establishes a legal connection that binds the two parties together and designates a particular set of responsibilities and obligations.

Chen (2012) similarly notes that both historically and globally, the employment relationship has been the central legal concept around which labor law has attempted to grant rights and protections to workers (13). As we see through classification struggles, who can and cannot be defined as either an employee or an employer holds important consequences, especially with respect to worker rights and protections. Chen explains the categorical importance of these terms, referencing the growing population of workers in the informal economy:

> Historically, labor law, labor statistics, and labor organizing have all centered on the notion of a recognized employer–employee relationship. But in addition to self-employed workers, increasingly, many wage or salaried workers are no longer in a clearly recognized employer–employee relationship. These two groups are generally referred to as "informal workers" in developing countries and "nonstandard" workers in developed countries. (2012:67)

Yet if labor law was historically set up to address a recognized employer-employee relationship, how are we to understand the employment relationship between the most vulnerable workers—those who are not in a clearly recognized relationship? Martha Fineman (2009) theorizes the term *vulnerable* as capturing a "universal, inevitable, enduring aspect of the human condition that must be at the heart of our concept of social and state responsibility," (8) as she attempts to wrest it free from its "limited and negative associations" (8). I consider the term *structural vulnerability* in the book, by which I similarly understand it as an "encompassing" concept, yet one that in my study remains rooted in the precise, structural conditions of the work and the social relations that surround and compel domestic service. I locate my definition of structural vulnerability, then, as one that is adhered to the conditions and nature of the work itself and that is reflective of the historical social relations in which that labor is embedded. In the industry of domestic service, structural vulnerability is real, lived out, and imbued in the isolated conditions and practices of subservience. Law and vulnerability, then, are inextricably bound up with each other.

Classification struggles also exist within workers themselves. Due to the multiple stigmas associated with domestic work and the location of the work itself, workers themselves often wish to disassociate themselves from their job. The fundamental misrecognition of domestic work as not being "real" work or a "real" job and rather naturalized and gendered is a pervasive narrative in New York City, in Lima, and elsewhere, as other scholarship on paid domestic labor has found (Fine 2007; Hondagneu-Sotelo 2001). This poses another challenge to bringing labor rights and legal protections into the home. Janice Fine (2007) discusses a typical interaction at a worker center in New York City, involving an organizer asking a domestic worker about her employment status. "Do you work?" the organizer inquires. And though she is a domestic worker, she answers, "No, I work in a house" (2007:218). The notion of "becoming" or "being" a domestic worker is fraught for many women, then.

"Present in the Memories of Things and People": Reading the Law

Laws operate within social context, and they speak through and to each other, often attempting to correct or right what one law has left out or misrecognized. Boaventura de Sousa Santos (1987) explains as he references literary critic Harold Bloom, "laws misread [reality] in order to establish their exclusivity" (281). Sousa Santos (1987) elaborates:

> Since law and society are mutually constitutive, the previous labour laws, once revoked, nevertheless leave their imprint on the labour relations they used to regulate. Though revoked, they remain present in the memories of things and people. Legal revocation is not social revocation. (281)

In this sense, laws never "un-do" what was once before; instead, they rewrite and reinscribe, and yet the regulations and social relations of years past still exist, as they are overridden yet ever present. One way that I recognize this in the book is by attempting to employ a mode of reading and analyzing the law that follows Said's (1994) notion of *contrapuntal reading*. One way to think about contrapuntal reading is to consider all that the specific text is saying or arguing, as well as what was left out or left behind from the narrative. Said articulates this concept as a manner of interpreting the text that destabilizes itself before it gets too sure of itself and ventures too far afield with particular conclusions; it is accountable in an important way because of its *a priori* recognition of various perspectives being represented and questioned through the text itself. In *Culture and Imperialism* (1994), he remarks:

In reading a text, one must open it out both to what went into it, and to what its author excluded. Each cultural work is a vision of a moment, and we must juxtapose that vision with the various revisions it later provoked . . . (67)

Yet this is not some pluralistic account, either, as engaging in contrapuntal reading of the law for my analysis, then, recognizes the field of power in which law is produced. In this way, it is not just a mode of reading but also a mode of giving voice and recognition to historical moments that shaped the law itself yet are often overlooked. Both "what went into it" and what was excluded, then, are recognized by Said, who notes that "texts are not bounded by their formal historic beginnings and endings" (1994:66). In this sense, then, I attempt to expose those linkages and connections through bringing history to bear upon my analysis of the content of the two laws in the book. I take their contemporary form as very much a *result of* and an *extension from* the previous decrees, ordinances, and laws that came before.[1] Additionally, in extending out from the text itself, I also look to read the law as a cultural work, and thus to recognize its social interactions, and the way it remains present in the memories of people and things (Sousa Santos 1987).

TOWARD THEORIZING THE HOME AS A SITE OF LAW

In Austin Sarat's (1990) article, ". . . The Law is All Over," he explores how the unquestioned authority of law and its complex bureaucratic processes of administration can hold an unwelcome and looming presence for some vulnerable, marginalized populations. The social protections of reform law can, at times, entangle its recipients who cannot interpret the law on their own terms or contest its meaning. Sarat illustrates an important perspective here regarding the law's position in structuring everyday life, especially for marginalized, vulnerable communities who are assigned a particular legal category which they may find confining rather than liberating. It prescribes what Sarat (1990) calls a "particular legal consciousness" as the lives of members of these communities are organized by a specific legal regime; he notes that the very act of being governed by such a law is one of the myriad ways the state exercises power over the poor (347). Furthermore, this kind of legal governance in practice constructs and makes visible a particular kind of subjectivity, as those groups negotiate dynamics of power and resistance within their social world, where the "law is all over" (347).

Yet the law *at work* is not all over—or at least not present in sites of labor that are not recognized as such, including the home. Scholarship on employment law and the workplace (Albiston 2006; Krieger, Best, and Edelman 2015; Schultz 1992; Zheng, Ai, and Liu 2017) seeks to understand, and challenge, gendered and racialized discrimination at work, and yet it tends to rely upon a fairly narrow and traditional definition of the workplace itself. In their recent work that shows how workplace discrimination law surprisingly perpetuates the very inequality it attempts to stamp out, Berrey, Nelson, and Nielson (2017) note, "Law and society scholarship illuminates how law-in-action, as opposed to law-on-the-books, shapes the realization of rights" (13). However, in this understanding, law-in-action appears to only shape rights that can be realized in particular kinds of sites of labor.

All is not harmonious for workers and their employers in these other, more recognized workplaces, of course. Burghgrave (2017) speaks to the lack of transparency and privatized forms of governance in the typical American workplace in an interview with Elizabeth Anderson. To this point, Anderson lays out how she understands the stark power dynamic between U.S. workers, employers, and their rights (or lack thereof) at work:

> Employers in the United States wield an extraordinary amount of power over their employees. In the workplace, workers can be surveilled by their employer, compelled to work long hours, and even denied bathroom breaks. . . . In most parts of the U.S., employers can legally terminate employees for being "too attractive," for having the wrong political affiliations, and for choosing a particular sexual partner. When American workers go to work, they enter a world marked more by unaccountable hierarchy than democracy and freedom. (Burghgrave 2017)

For domestic workers, as well as for workers in more recognized sites of labor, the law is not all over and it may even be used as a tool of control against workers themselves. As the book explores, it is difficult to regulate labor rights at work in the space of the home, and yet it is also key to remember that some of these workplace struggles are shared across contexts. There are indeed more parallels between the home and other sites of work than one might initially think.

However, domestic workers have been legally constructed to remain beyond the bounds of labor regulation, and as I will explore in later chapters, this is yet another further reflection of the specific and structurally vulnerable social world in which they are embedded (Sarat 1990:347).

Yet law can mean many things—it can categorize, discriminate, prioritize, and recognize, all actions which in sometimes conflicting and contradictory ways can, as Sally Engle Merry (1991) notes, "contribute to the construction of a new consciousness, a new set of understandings of persons and relationships" (892). Domestic workers are on one hand positioned inside, privy to the "life of the home" and all that happens there, and yet on the other outside, historically excluded from labor protections and benefits precisely because of their labor's location (Palmer 1995). By comparing two legislative efforts that regulate the home as a site of labor, my work takes on the question of law and its power to include after a long history of exclusion. In her essay entitled "Ethnographies of Law," Eve Darian-Smith (2004) argues that the task of the ethnographer must be "[r]ecording on-the-ground personalized experiences of the law, and abstracting from these memories and narrations of identity and collectivity in order to better grasp historical contexts of struggles over power" (2004:553). In this book, I explore the *limits of law* and its myriad (un)intended consequences, reflecting upon law as a set of multiple meanings, especially when regulating the home as a site of paid labor.

Can the law grant recognition categorically to domestic workers? How, when, and under what conditions does labor law *de jure* become labor law *de facto*? Laws are both products of social relations and constitutive of them, and so they vary in the ways they categorize, grant, or strip away privilege and rights. Additionally, we know that the law interacts with dynamics of other social relations embedded in the home—but what does, or could, Merry's "new set of understandings of persons and relationships" look like? What shape must these efforts take in order to regulate the highly specific site of the household? And what would it look like to embrace that model of legal regulation and rights for such a historically informal occupation, perpetually looked down upon as not "real" work? More simply put, can we legislate vulnerability away?

Laura Beth Nielson (2004) responds to these questions in part when she delivers a critical empirical approach to the *work of rights* and the *work rights do* that urges a scholarly turn to examine "social settings." Rather than looking to formal legal institutions, she advises law and society and socio-legal scholars to analyze rights in their actual social context where we can observe potentially beneficial or detrimental social effects (74). By doing so, we can better start to understand under what conditions certain rights work differently for certain people, and why. In considering rights as legal constructs ready to be marshaled for a larger social cause or movement, then, as with domestic workers, we must first recognize that there is significant inequality among those who have knowledge of their rights to begin with, those who have the ability to access said rights, and those with a decent probability of encountering even a modicum of success when attempting to do so (75). In assessing how these two particular labor laws create a labor regime inside of the home, then, I examine if the law gestures toward the production of domestic workers-as-workers, or if it instead fosters conditions of perpetual servitude.

I also move between three related elements of law in my analysis of what the law *makes* of those it regulates inside of the home. First, its *limits*: there is a general lack of awareness about household worker rights and very rare enforcement; second, its *contradictions*, as both laws grant household workers significantly fewer benefits than other formally recognized workers in the U.S. and in Peru; and third, its *failures*, as I find and encounter inherent complications in legally regulating the home as a site of work (Minow 1987:1867). The Comparative Law Appendix brings to light these stark differences in the laws themselves, and I lay out these differences in Table 1.1. In this summary chart, which compares the terms of their particular benefits, protections, and conditions side by side, the New York law is noticeably weaker than the Peruvian law. And yet the New York law also set an important precedent in the context of the U.S., and served as a legislative springboard for other states to follow. The Comparative Law Appendix goes into further exploration of each piece of legislation.

TABLE 1.1 Comparative Overview of Legislation in Lima and New York City

	NYC: DOMESTIC WORKER BILL OF RIGHTS, 2010	LIMA: HOUSEHOLD WORKERS' LAW, 2003
Contract Provisions	N/A	Contracts can either be written or verbal
Wage Provisions	Enforces the New York State minimum wage	N/A: No minimum wage language; salary is decided by "mutual accord" between both parties
Limitations on the Working Day	8-hour working day	8-hour working day, 48 hours/week maximum
Rest-Time Provisions	1 day of rest per week	1 day of rest per week

(Continued)

TABLE 1.1 *(Continued)*

	NYC: DOMESTIC WORKER BILL OF RIGHTS, 2010	LIMA: HOUSEHOLD WORKERS' LAW, 2003
Vacation Provisions	After an entire year of employment, 3 days of paid vacation per year	After an entire year of employment, 15 days of paid vacation per year
Overtime Provisions	Overtime at 1.5x pay rate after 40 hours/week for live-out workers and 44 hours/week for live-in	Overtime for working recognized holidays, 1.5x pay, or the ability to trade in the holiday for a different day off
Workplace Discrimination Protections	Protection against workplace discrimination based on race, gender, sexual orientation, national origin, disability, marital status, and domestic violence victim status	Protection against a serious offense, such as violence or other forms of abuses
Scope of Coverage	Technically applies to citizens of the United States, legal permanent residents, immigrants with temporary protected status, and undocumented workers	Applies to all household workers; scope is defined by job duties rather than citizenship or documentation status
Termination Provisions	N/A	15 days' notice of termination for both parties, the employer and the worker
Bonus Provisions	N/A	½ month's pay in July and December each year
Longevity of Service and Loyalty to Employers	N/A	½ month's salary for each year of service to the same employer
Food and Shelter Provisions	N/A	Employers are obligated to provide food and shelter corresponding to the economic level of the household for live-in workers
Education Provisions	N/A	Employers are obligated to provide access to education for live-in workers
Retirement Provisions	N/A	Pension and social security access

Source: Author.

With these two laws I study in mind, Figure 1.1 demonstrates the process I argue takes place in both research sites. When a historic labor law attempts to regulate the space of the home, which is already characterized by its particular structural conditions for domestic workers there due to its historically racialized and gendered labor relations, it results in the production of one of two types of vulnerability. I map out a sense of how this process works in Lima and in New York City below.

Figure 1.1 demonstrates the production of a particular *kind* of structural vulnerability in both of my comparative cases. This is important because context matters; rather than glossing over the industry of domestic service, and therefore domestic workers, as universally vulnerable, the specific configuration of cultural, social, and economic factors that structure the industry in each site and create particular, situated vulnerabilities should be recognized. I use the term "outsider" for two related reasons that speak to geography and a sense of belonging.

The first is that workers are consistently reminded that they are not "from here" and that they are "foreign," which is particularly ironic in New York City, a city that prides itself on its historical immigrant narrative. The second sense of "outsider" holds a deeper implication of marginality and exclusion that is tied to the work itself and to the site of that labor. As much of the scholarship on paid domestic work has shown, domestic workers play a key role in constructing family life and the household and as such are "insiders" within

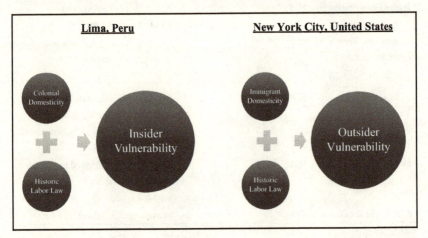

FIGURE 1.1   The Production of Insider and Outsider Vulnerability through Labor Regulation of the Domestic Sphere. Source: Author.

that space, and yet due to their role being a contractual one of employment, they are never truly considered to be a part of it.

I argue that the Household Workers' Law in Peru is undermined by the racialized colonial legacy, which constitutes Indigenous and mestiza domestic workers as perpetual servants, while the Domestic Workers' Bill of Rights in New York City is undermined by the racialized history of citizenship, which prevents immigrant domestic workers from accessing the law. In Lima, I find that the historic labor law meets particular limits when attempting to regulate the space of the home, where a labor regime of what I call "colonial domesticity" remains alive and well. I argue that this interaction produces *insider vulnerability*, as internal migrant workers mostly live in, where they have little privacy and are subject to employers' lingering colonial fantasies and particular whims.

In New York City, I find that the historic labor law meets particular limits when attempting to regulate the space of the home, where a labor regime of what I call "immigrant domesticity" continues to position immigrant workers as outside of the law. This regime exacerbates precisely what is most structurally vulnerable about this population of workers in context. I argue that this interaction produces *outsider vulnerability*, as workers are constantly reminded of the threat of deportation. In a surprising way, then, in two very different settings, labor law specifically designed to protect the employment relationship of domestic work codifies structural vulnerability inherent to the industry, producing insider and outsider vulnerability.

Few scholars, and fewer sociologists, however, have taken up Nielson's call to consider the implications of labor rights for domestic workers in grounded social settings, however. Shireen Ally's (2009) research on post-apartheid labor legislation in South Africa is a fascinating examination of a highly mobilized domestic worker population, as workers took to the streets demanding legal inclusion during the country's first democratic elections of 1994. However, the South African example is an outlier, as it remains too exceptional of a case due to those labor protections being written into the country's new constitution. Merike Blofield's (2012) comparative study of domestic worker legislation across Latin America offers a useful overview of the region, though she remains interested in political process rather than lived outcomes and social context. Lesley Gill's (1994) often overlooked ethnography of Aymara domestic servants in La Paz, Bolivia, responds to that contextual call, revealing the

racial dynamics of household labor practices set inside the Andean neocolonial context, yet it took place years prior to any efforts to regulate the relations of labor inside the Bolivian home. The poorest country in South America
and the only one with an Indigenous majority, highly unequal Bolivia would
later become the first country to enact national domestic worker legislation
(Blofield 2012).

We know, then, very little about what happens when workers actually win
these types of laws and protections, and even less regarding how workers experience labor rights at home. This is precisely where my work intervenes to
show—surprisingly—how the law actually codifies the vulnerability inherent
to the occupation, with particular consequences in each city. What the law
in practice reveals is, in fact, a profound story of vulnerability. Yet as with
Diouana's narrative, this story is structurally located as stemming from the
historical organization of labor inside of the home and codified through the
successful quest to bring labor rights there.

IDEAS OF HOME: PERPETUATING THE
PAST, PERPETUATING THE PRESENT

Paid and unpaid household labor takes place every day inside of the homes of
Lima, New York City, and virtually every city globally, and yet as a site, the
home is severely undertheorized as a workplace. Mary Douglas (1991) writes
of the home as a "self-organizing system" wherein takes place the "realization
of ideas," while Simone de Beauvoir (2015) famously said that "[f]ew tasks are
more like the torture of Sisyphus than housework," mentioning that it "makes
nothing" and "simply perpetuates the present" (438). Here, I show that labor
practices and the organization of labor also serve to perpetuate the past, one
that is etched with lingering racial legacies around coloniality and immigration that continue to limit legal reforms and labor rights for those who work
inside of the home. This section examines some of the important contradictions of home and yet also brings forward recognition of its possibilities for
organizing, mobilizing, and politics, making room to "bring the law home."

Often those responsible for the reproduction of family life inside of the
home, domestic workers move between the multiple meanings and contradictions of the Western liberal "public/private" split, which has been falsely
dichotomized as distinct, oppositional, and gendered (Arendt 1958). The effort

to separate the market from family life and the home dates back to the nine-teenth century during a series of legal debates over the value of household labor (Siegel 1994; Zelizer 1994). These decisions ignored the economic con-tribution of women's work inside of the household, and thus certain groups of race- and class-privileged women started to earn "outside" income, while household labor and its contributions to the market were left unconsidered (Zelizer 1994).

For women who left the home to venture into male-dominant factory life, however, this was far from a seamless transition. Milkman (1987) and Kessler-Harris (1981), among others, have documented the early difficulties women faced in those workplaces, both on the shop floor and in joining labor unions. Milkman's work on economic mobilization during World War II also shows how, rather than "breaking down barriers" around jobs that were coded as men's or women's work, similar boundaries that continued patterns of oc-cupational segregation were mapped onto new types of factory labor that had not been previously gender coded as such.

These gendered categories reinforced the notion that it was exceptional for women to work outside of the home; this kind of new economic advancement for women as wage earners was viewed as what Milkman calls only a "tem-porary extension of domesticity" that was reinforced by an assumption they would return to their "place" of the home following the war (1987:50).

Part of what this shows, then, is that though groups of women were enter-ing the formal labor market in unprecedented ways in a time of great economic and political change, little social change was happening correspondingly in relation to the separate-spheres mythology and to the emphasis on women as responsible for the ongoing domestic work of the home. Scholarship on the sociology of gender has continued to examine this trend in years since and has continued to find similar staying patterns in the gender division of labor at home. Hochschild (1989) called this phenomenon "the Stalled Revolution," and a great deal of work since has continued to understand, explain, and in-terrogate this question in various contexts. The questions and focus of this book similarly are built upon the premise of the home as gendered and the burden of its maintenance squarely foisted onto women. The other key part of this equation, then, is the continual perpetuation of shifting those labor duties onto other groups of more marginalized women via a class- and race-based hierarchy. As noted by Glenn (1992) and a large body of research since, this labor has for the most part *not* been transferred onto men but has instead remained part of a gendered domain of care work, reproductive labor, and domestic work, ridden with emotional labor and contained instead in the private sphere of the home.

Feminist scholars have long critiqued this differentiation of spheres, especially with regard to property, marriage, and family relations, though the assumptions around a division between public and private activities remain (Davidoff 2003; Hayden 1981; Munro and Madigan 1999). Indeed, feminist theorists and writers have explored the home as gendered and interpreted its historical role as oppressive, as merely a prison in which women are entrapped and sequestered from the outside world (Chopin 1899; Perkins Gilman 1892). A valorizing of this concept rose to prominence during the early nineteenth century as a kind of "domestic ideology" that positioned women as moral leaders inside of the home, though their relative power was sharply muted beyond its boundaries. Through a series of lectures, Virginia Woolf (1929) famously urged for a "room of one's own" for women as subjects of their own lives, noting that both literal and figurative space would allow women the autonomy to produce better work. As many feminist scholars of color (Collins 1986; Rollins 1985; Romero 1992) have pointed out, however, a prominent class- and race-based universalism influenced these narratives since they usually portrayed a white, middle-class female subject. However, the point holds here regarding the centrality of home and its deeply gendered nature that continues to play out dichotomously between public and private sphere.

Thavolia Glymph (2008) also troubles the notion of the household as private through her research on the social relations of plantation lifestyles in the U.S. South during slavery. She examines the gendered dynamics of violence and power between white slave-owning plantation wives and Black enslaved women themselves, disputing the notion of some kind of feminine alliance existing through a shared bond under patriarchy and paternalism (3). Pointing out how this narrative has for too long falsely obscured the modes of power which shaped both groups of women's lives quite differently, she argues that the plantation household was deeply public for the enslaved people and servants who—by default—witnessed the private and personal lives of the plantation owner's family members and were subjected to their whims via their structural positioning (43).

Situating the practice of domestic work in the U.S. context draws a parallel with slavery because of the similar organization of labor, but also because of the very continuity of the unquestioned, supposed privacy and discourses of ownership that structure the identity of the generalized household to this day. Glymph's (2008) work also points out the important distinction between family members or paid workers doing what Bridget Anderson (2000) calls "the dirty work" of the home, and yet within familial relationships, the racial and gender division of household labor also continues to matter in deciding who does what both in- *and* outside of the home. Additionally, it also shapes the way that we understand, organize, and value the people whom we, or whom our friends and family and colleagues, pay to do this work, as well as the work itself.

Bringing forward a nuanced analysis, Iris Marion Young (1997) valorizes the home as the place where we become ourselves:

> I am not ready to toss the idea of home out of the larder of feminist values. Despite the oppressions and privileges the idea historically carries, the idea of home also carries critical liberating potential because it expresses uniquely human values. Some of these can be uncovered by exploring the meaning-making activity most typical of women in domestic work. (124)

Young importantly sees the centrality of housework here, though she privileges certain tasks over others when she compares the minutiae of cleaning bacteria from a bathroom as opposed to the "more meaningful" act of dusting off mementos preserved inside of the home (1997:191). Both pertain to the notion of cleanliness as linked to the process of making order from chaos (Douglas 1966), yet the latter preserves a sense of identity and, as I argue, reproduces the notion of family life and the household itself. Rather than delve into validating particular tasks over others within the category itself, however, I attempt to highlight the intrinsic value of the labor overall that is associated with *domestic work*, *domestic service*, and *household work* as I move between those categories interchangeably within this manuscript.

In an important way, hooks (1990) sees a value in the home due to its ability to foster community and serve as a political space of dignity and resistance for African American women and other marginalized groups. She explores the construction of what she calls *homeplace* as a safe political harbor that is located outside of the dominant, often quietly racist and exploitative social structures and can thus be visionary, especially for members of historically oppressed communities. She notes, "For when a people no longer have the space to construct homeplace, we cannot build a meaningful community of resistance" (388). Taken together then, I follow Young's (1997) sense of domestic work as a meaning-making activity and hooks (1990) in recognizing the home—and the *homeplace*—as a site of political agency, one that is certainly worth not turning our back on.

While the construct of home has been acknowledged by these various literatures, the meaning and implications of the organization of labor there has not yet been fully explored. My research here does not delve into the myriad cultural meanings of home and their consequences, as that is beyond the scope of this project, yet it is important to have laid out some of the theorizing and thinking about all that the home contains, and all that does not "usually" belong there—including law and labor protections for those who work inside its walls. Instead, I focus on the home as a site of work and a site of law, with attention to the spatial layout, segregation, and social interactions that take place inside the home for domestic workers. How we inhabit and experience the world, then, offers an important distinction in feeling *at* home as opposed to simply being in some/one's home. For domestic workers, home takes on a different meaning, as many of those I interviewed have lived and worked longer in someone else's home (and in the case of New York City, someone else's country) than they ever did in the place where they were born. Home, for many of these workers, is a distant memory or a deep yearning for what was left behind. In Woodside, an ethnically diverse neighborhood in Queens with a large Nepali immigrant population, home is routinely fashioned on Sunday afternoons when Nepalese nail-salon workers and domestic workers share their cooking after health and safety trainings at Adhikaar, their community organization. Therefore, pointing to various conceptions of home is assuredly a part of the analysis, as it is a part of structuring how domestic workers experience, cope, and thrive through doing their work.

Given the place of the home as constitutive of the private sphere, how do we regulate it as a workplace? How do we bring legislated labor protections into the home? This book attempts to explore the spatial and legal dimensions inherent to this understanding of the home that shapes its particularity as a site of labor and law. In my fieldwork in New York City and Lima, I move away from the home as only a place of oppression or containment and instead point to the *potential* and the *possibilities* that are encapsulated there, even though it remains a highly private space fraught with contradictions and tension.

HISTORICIZING AND SITUATING DOMESTIC WORK

The book builds upon a large multidisciplinary body of scholarship that has focused on the intersectional inequalities of class, caste, gender, race, and ethnicity embedded within the domestic employer-worker relationship in varying contexts, and yet has failed to fully theorize how those relationships change when legally regulated, and in what ways those laws then shape anew the household. Yet due to the entrenched nature of the dominant discourse around the home as *separate* from work, it is by definition more difficult to draw attention to the labor performed there. Domestic work as a category blurs the lines between public and private, home and work, and service and servitude (Hondagneu-Sotelo 2001; Qayum and Ray 2003; Rollins 1985; Romero 1992). The labor relations that constitute domestic work are shaped by social hierarchies of race, ethnicity, class, gender, and nation for the more than seventy-six million domestic workers employed in homes globally (Seiffarth, Bonnet, and Hobden 2023). The majority of those workers are women, though as previous scholarship shows, the gender differential depends upon the particular context and there are notable exceptions (Bartolomei 2010; Martínez and Lowrie 2009; Qayum and Ray 2010; Sarti 2010).[2]

Over the last several decades, scholars of domestic work have analyzed internal dynamics of labor exploitation faced by workers paid to clean, cook, and care inside another's home (Hondagneu-Sotelo 2001; Hondagneu-Sotelo and Riegos 1997; Rollins 1985; Romero 2011). These accounts draw attention to the key obstacles inherent to this specific—or, more problematically, "exceptional"—type of labor, however, including the isolation and individualization intrinsic to the home as a site of labor, the gendered and racialized nature of the work, and the ideologies of family and care that appropriate and mask a highly unequal class relationship (Glenn 1992; Jiang and Korcynski 2016; Nadasen 2015; Ray and Qayum 2009; Romero 2011).

This category of labor traces its origins to the labor practices of slavery and colonialism lived out through racialized, sexualized, and economic relations of domination (Rollins 1985; Dill 1988; Glenn 1992; Mullany 2014). As Burnham and Theodore (2012:3) note in their comprehensive overview of the industry, domestic work has *always* been a feature of life in the United States, dating back to enslaved, indentured, and only nominally "free" women workers during colonial times, and thus has consistently remained a devalued and marginalized—though ever-present—occupation (Ally 2009; Bunster and Chaney 1985; Dill 1988; Nadasen 2015; Parreñas 2001). My work thus attempts to reveal some of that which has long been obscured through the heavy presence of historical "master narratives" around imperialism and colonialism as played out through the service encounters during and after slavery. I build upon that shift (Ballantyne and Burton 2005; Fox-Genovese 1988; Genovese 1976) to recognize and analyze the operation of power in sites that are typically thought of as private and separate, such as the home, revealing the continued difficulties of formalizing labor rights for those who work there.

Early historical scholarship that considered the home seriously focused on *homework*, or waged work performed inside of the home itself (Allen 1989; Benson 1989; Boris 1989), generated empirical research on waged work performed inside of the home. Boydston (1994), however, is an exception to this trend, as she charts women's domestic labor in their own homes as key to the industrialization movement in the United States prior to the Civil War, while Kessler-Harris' (1981) classic text give us a historical overview of the different kinds of work women did to maintain and manage the household itself, including hiring servants to shoulder the burden (35).

In recent decades, a great deal of scholarship has examined the ethnic, racial, and nation-based hierarchies embedded in domestic workers' working relationships to their often native-born, white employers (Chang 2001; Glenn 1992; Hondagneu-Sotelo 2001; Duffy 2007; Romero 1992). Another key area has focused on debunking constructed racial justifications that historically served to slot women into particular positions of low-wage, low-prestige service work (Duffy 2007; Glenn 1991). Other scholarship has sought to challenge the powerful rhetoric through which domestic workers' labor is devalued as casual (Tuominen 2003) and the resultant uncomfortable, odd positionality of being treated "like one of the family" when employed as a domestic worker inside of the home (Bapat 2014; Childress 1956; Burnham and Theodore 2012). And yet, they are not, given their status as an employee there.

In an effort to preserve their own comfort and entitlement to power, however, many employers try to obscure the structural positionality of the person working inside of their home. Alice Childress (1956) perhaps most famously demonstrated this through the working lives and experiences of Mildred and Marge, African American domestic workers in New York City, in *Like One of the Family*. In the first chapter, Mildred's white employer, Mrs. C, has company over and remarks to her friend directly in front of Mildred, as she cleans:

> "We just love her! She's like one of the family and she just adores our little Carol! We don't know what we'd do without her! We don't think of her as a servant!" (Childress 1956:2)

In Collins' (2001) analysis of Childress' story, she points out the importance of the qualifier *like*; Mrs. C decides what family is, who it includes, and the particular ranking of its members. The fact that Mildred can be *like* a family member, though not an *actual* one, signals that she is fundamentally lesser. Second, it reveals a problematic, binary classification system that operates in the home—one is either a family member or a servant—which excludes Mildred and obscures the work that she does. Furthermore, her even being talked about as such by Mrs. C completely overlooks Mildred's own biography, family, and identity. Along with her labor, the story of Mildred's life is able to be purchased for a set rate on a daily basis by Mrs. C, who promptly negates it and maps it onto her own, dominant narrative. Thus, we see how a racialized and classed hierarchy is both built and then reified through daily life inside of the home. The home acts as a site of ideological production, and those who propagate such ideas also naturalize them. Yet the contradictory ways in which domestic workers are "thought of" has profound consequences for how they and their labor are or are not recognized as legitimate.

Part of this book's broad goal, then, is to build upon the long-standing effort to recognize domestic work as real work, and as such, to demonstrate how the industry's continuing informality partly stems from the home not being considered a site of work, or a site of labor rights for those who work there. Without recognized categories in which to organize domestic work as "deserving" of those rights, further issues of ambiguity continue to plague the occupation. The most pressing and long-standing consequence resulting from a lack of proper occupational categories for this kind of work is that it has been excluded from traditional labor protections long extended to other occupations. This stems in part due to domestic work's highly racialized and gendered nature, its location based within the expressly feminized realm of the home, and its personal nature (Chang 2001; Glenn 1992; Palmer 1995; Perea 2011; Wrigley 1995).

The Long-Organized "Unorganizable"

Due to early decisions to categorize their work as outside of labor regulations, household workers were long glossed over as "unorganizable." However, Nadasen's (2015) historical account of African American household worker organizing in Atlanta, New York City, Detroit, Washington, D.C., and other cities from the 1950s through the 1970s demonstrates otherwise. May (2011) similarly reveals the intricate political mobilizations around labor and social reforms in early twentieth-century New York City. Both historical accounts clearly show that Black domestic workers and other domestic workers of color in the United States organized, often quite successfully, for decades prior to broader recognition (Das Gupta 2008; Ford 2004; Middaugh 2012). Yet while much of this research recognizes that some of the underlying assumptions about why it is difficult to organize household workers are reflected in why it is difficult to regulate their work by law as well, these accounts do not fully theorize the importance of the structural organization of the home itself. Due to being positioned inside of the home and hidden from public scrutiny, domestic workers often fall victim to severe exploitation, and though abuse is widespread, only the most egregious cases tend to draw public attention (Gonzalez and Leberstein 2010; Zarembka 2003).

Significant labor mobilization by domestic workers has taken place globally over the last two decades; these efforts have recently been made to broaden, extend, or create anew labor protections and benefits that most other occupations enjoy, both in the U.S. and globally. These demands take various contextual shapes and utilize particular resonant frames across worker struggles. Related sociological and historical literature on household worker organizing and mobilization in varying contexts of informality (Ally 2009; Boris and Nadasen 2008; Swider 2006; Tomei 2011) has showcased its rich, comparative history through examples across various regions, including Asia, the Middle East, and Europe (Blofield 2012; De Regt 2010; Jiang and Korcynski 2016; Ray and Qayum 2009). Domestic workers nationally and globally have harnessed legal and political exclusions into a platform from which to navigate new pathways and trajectories, though currently only 10% of domestic workers globally access labor rights coverage equivalent to other workers (Seiffarth, Bonnet, and Hobden 2023). However, their long-standing exclusion from the mainstream labor movement has not hindered workers' efforts to improve their working conditions and seek respect and recognition on the job. In the case of the

United States, Nadasen (2015) notes how that very exclusion granted them independence and creativity that required a more nuanced approach. As such, workers drew upon the very traits that employers valued in them, such as their importance to the household and their intimate association with family life, as leverage in negotiations with their employers (Nadasen 2015:105).

And important, historic organizing on the global scale or what Adelle Blackett (2019) calls a "transnational challenge to international labor law," has taken place over the last decades, resulting in the first set of global labor standards for domestic workers, the International Labour Organization's Convention 189: Decent Work for Domestic Workers (Blackett 2019). Longtime domestic worker advocate and activist Jennifer N. Fish (2017) thoughtfully explores the grassroots organizing and social movement's success and challenges in organizing for C189 and its ratification in her book, *Domestic Workers of the World Unite!* Yet even with such a strong and thriving social movement, many domestic workers still struggle for labor rights and worker protections on the job.

Indeed, household work—whether performed by servants, slaves, children, or wives—has a storied history in many parts of the world and especially in highly unequal Latin America, the region with the world's most inequitable income distribution (Kuznesof 1989; Lautier 2003; Skop and Peters 2007). With nearly one out of every five female wage workers employed in household work, it is the largest single source of employment for women in Latin America, and nearly 20% of the world's domestic workers are employed across Latin America and the Caribbean (ILO 2022). And though Peru has reduced poverty overall in the last twenty years, seven out of ten Peruvians still currently live in poverty, and the percentage only increases in rural settings, which prompts continued migratory flow from the provinces to the capital (Rubiano-Matulevich 2023). In Peru, the wealthiest 20% of the population earn 13 times more than the poorest 20%, and the practice of hiring household workers is nearly ubiquitous among the middle and upper classes, which serves as a key example of the staying power of classed and racialized inequality throughout the region since colonial relations (CIED 2007).

Focusing specifically on the practice of domestic work in the Latin American context, early scholarship examined its historical legacies of slavery and colonialism, including employer expectations around sexual access (Blondet 1987; Kuznesof 1989; Chaney and Garcia Castro 1989) and the construction of gender and class within ethno-racialized servant-employer relationships across the region (Bernardino-Costa 2011; Casanova 2013; García 2013; Gill 1994). While the majority of these studies speak to the racial dynamics between employers and employees set against the background of the gendered, domestic space of the home, however, few venture further to think both historically and contemporarily about the organization of labor there, as the home is spatially and, often, legally separated from the outside world (Coleman 2016).

While a number of studies about Peruvian domestic workers have been published in the last several decades, Figueroa (2003) argues that they remain disconnected from any kind of social policy that truly addressed the situation of these women in Lima. The most famous of these generative accounts, *Simplemente Explotadas: El Mundo de las Empleadas Domésticas de Lima*, brings together case studies, demographic data, social theory, and history as it continues to stand out as the most comprehensive portrayal of domestic service in Lima from this era (Rutté García 1973). Akin to what Quijano (2000) theorizes regarding the "coloniality of power," which I address later, Rutté García argues that while the precise colonial arrangement of servitude has, for the most part, ended, much of the collective mindset around superiority, status, and hierarchy has directly continued (116).

Yet stepping back, Raffaella Sarti (2014), in her comprehensive overview of the global industry of domestic work, notes that for at least two centuries domestic servants have been fighting for rights in much of the same way through various contexts. For instance, she finds a reoccurring historical trend as domestic workers must, over and over, continually assert that they *are*, in fact, workers (Sarti 2014:310). And yet, noting the continuity in the struggle itself dating back to the French Revolution, Sarti calls for a specific theoretical framework to be developed that connects global history with domestic service (310).

Here, I build toward that idea by locating the global history of racialized colonial practices and racialized immigration patterns in my two field sites, knitting together an understanding of how social and historical forces shaped the organization of labor inside of the home and those who work there. Sarti ties this understanding back to the "servant problem" and earlier conversations that predicted the decline and potential eradication of paid domestic work (Martin and Segrave 1985). Yet with my work I echo Tronto (2002), especially the call to imagine alternatives to "hiring domestic servants" (311).

I extend this to shift away from a focus on *ending* the practice and instead shift to a focus on rigorous, empirical evidence on ways to successfully understand the work of the home as real, and deserving of formal labor-law recognition and regulation. This is tied to my emphasis on understanding the home as a site of work, and a site of law—how do relationships in the home change when they are legally regulated? What consequences arise, and how are social relations changed, especially given that it is a gendered and racialized space? This is new terrain for the sociology of work, law and society, and the global domestic workers' movement in many ways.

With both of my cases, then, I argue that we must take into account the racialized colonial legacies and racialized immigration practices that order—and serve to naturalize—exploitative relations between domestic workers and their employers as well as shape the organization of labor inside of the home. This is a particularly important finding in light of significant recent national and global domestic worker organizing. Sarti (2014) points out, however, that the industry of domestic work has, historically, had a global dimension, and that global dimension is even more pronounced today (312). And as Saskia Sassen noted at Barnard College's Justice in the Home conference, the first gathering of its kind solely devoted to conversations around domestic work, however, "Global never means the whole world, by the way—it's a very strategic term" (2014). By selecting two strategic cases, I demonstrate both the universal need to bring labor rights to the home and the complications that result from doing so in two distinct contexts that speak to the dimensions of household work through a Global South/North comparison.

SITUATING THE RESEARCH CONTEXT

Following the way that Raka Ray and Seemin Qayum (2009) situate their study of domestic work as embedded in historical relations, my two cases show the extent to which formerly colonial and currently capitalist economies still shape the industry of domestic work in each country. The nature of the industry has strong parallels between Lima and New York City, and yet it is organized very differently in each city due to a particular colonial past that codifies what I call colonial domesticity in Peru and a specific racialized past that codifies immigrant domesticity in New York City. My project examines the effects of the law in these two major global cities where I find, despite their strikingly different social contexts, the law in practice produces outcomes that are actually quite similar; I find that the deep origins in colonial and racialized relations of this occupation shape its legal regulation, thus reproducing those inequalities in practice.

Why Lima and New York City?

Lima occupies an important, and at times contradictory, place in the Peruvian imaginary, just as does New York City in relation to the rest of the United States. New York City is iconic and reigns as a continuous site of immigration in the U.S., then and now, ridden with both immigrant-minded infrastructure and ethnic conflict. Yet in Chapter 5, I position New York City as a palimpsest, as a city that has been literally "rubbed smooth, again" as its current iteration is written over that which came before, with only traces remaining. In this way, to thrive in New York City is only possible through a deeper, collective process of beginning anew. Its history matters in shaping the current political, economic, and social context of the city, but it is not displayed in an obvious way.

Lima could not be any more different in this respect, as its colonial past is visually noted in its architecture both stylistically from an earlier era and in its modern apartments whose designs continue to feature small maid's quarters. As Kelley (2001) points out, though the city is prone to earthquakes and has, thus, been torn down and rebuilt anew in different forms, it has not been done so in a way that ever truly expunged its colonial architectural rule of the past (62).

Lima, as a site of concentrated power, maintains a fraught relationship to the rest of the country and has been understood in varying and overlapping moments as both a representative of the entirety of Peru through its ethno-racial diversity geographically situated in one place, and at times as quite the opposite (Higgins 2005:17). It is blamed for being "too European," highly Westernized, not "Peruvian enough," and not the "real Peru," which Miguel González Prada famously defined in 1888 as consisting instead of the "masses of Indians living on the Eastern slopes of the mountains," rather than those of Spanish and European ancestry living on the coast (Osorio 2008:146; Rivera 2016:385). The severe disparity between Lima and its surrounding provinces is not just imagined in the cultural or literary realm of the nation, however. The sharp divide continues today around access to health care, sanitation, education, employment, and other key services, with serious consequences for Peru's estimated 45% Indigenous population, as their life expectancy is a striking 30 years shorter in the highlands than in Lima (Hufstader 2010).[3]

Lima and New York City both hold nearly nine to ten million densely packed residents, act as key financial meccas for their region of the world, and have been shaped by historical and contemporary patterns of migration and immigrant populations. Both cities were the site of sustained organizing for household worker laws that passed within seven years of each other. And while the engagement of domestic service as a practice of status definition and class boundary maintenance takes place by employers in both cities, this varies by class in each context. Yet Peru is noticeably more centralized than the United States, with over a third of the entire country's population residing in the capital. New York City, however, is only one major metropolitan area within the U.S. and, furthermore, it is only one of a number of sites of historical and contemporary domestic worker organizing, as Atlanta, Los Angeles, and San Francisco, among others, have also long been strongholds of the burgeoning movement in the U.S. The demand for domestic workers also differs by city—while Lima is steeped in generational patterns of domestic servitude, as even working-class families employ domestic workers, hiring a maid or nanny remains a mark of at least some amount of wealth in New York City, though increasing inequality has recently led to greater normalization of hiring domestic workers, and especially nannies. Dual-earner middle- to upper-middle-class families can afford to do so, though the practice is less common overall and not nearly so widespread among all but the poorest classes, as it is in Lima.

Lima's population is more stable than that of New York City, and its various generations tend to remain based in the capital for their working lives, as strong regionalism and stigma is directed against those from anywhere outside of the capital. Peru has no true "second" city to draw people away from Lima; the closest approximation is Arequipa, though it only boasts one million people to Lima's population of nearly ten times that amount. In the United States, population shifts are much more frequent among younger and middle-aged professionals. Many large metropolitan areas and suburbs draw young couples out of New York City, especially after having children, and thus many of the city's domestic workers find themselves seeking work in a cyclical manner every two to three years.

Another significant contrast between the cities is the difference in who actually performs domestic work. Though there are exceptions, Lima is highly *homogenous* in terms of a particular profile: mestiza women and Indigenous Quechua and Aymara peasants from the provinces, internal migrants who work for employers of European descent in the capital. Using data from the National Household Survey (ENAHO) on living conditions and poverty of the National Statistics Institute (INEI) in Peru, Pérez and Llanos (2022) have shown that domestic workers are mostly internal migrants, meaning they live and work in a province different from the one in which they were born (51.4%). Furthermore, while the overall migrant population has increased in Lima in recent years due to an influx of Venezuelan migration, in 2018 only 3.4% of the Venezuelan employed population in Peru worked as domestic workers, increasing just slightly to 4% in 2022 (INEI 2022).

New York City is highly *heterogeneous*, with differences based on country of origin, language, cultural tradition, and immigration status. New York City's domestic worker movement is vibrant, diverse, and highly organized. I spoke with women from more than ten countries in New York City, and while all were currently domestic workers, they had previously been employed as engineers, government workers, baby nurses, and schoolteachers. While some Peruvian domestic workers I spoke with were taking nursing, culinary, beauty or dental-school classes, the vast majority had not completed secondary school and thus not held professional positions prior to finding work as a domestic worker. And as Erynn Masi de Casanova (2019) has skillfully noted, a great deal of research written in English over the last 20 years on domestic work has tended to focus on international migrants (3), but in fact that population only represents 17% of global domestic workers (Casanova 2019; ILO 2016). Thus, New York City's highly international population of domestic workers represent an important microcosm and subset of the broader global population, as compared to Peruvian domestic workers, who fall squarely within the majority 83% of internal migrants.

Additionally, Lima's law is administered by the centrally located Ministry of Labor and Work, whereas in New York City, the Department of Labor administers the law through Albany, so there is a distance and disconnect between where the politics are decided and the hub of the city where the politics are actually lived out. And importantly, Peru only recently transitioned to democratic rule after Fujimori in 2000, and was plagued by violence and unrest throughout the 1980s and into the 1990s (Boesten 2010). Finally, work-ers in Lima tend to *live in*, while New York City's domestic workers generally *live out*, which is a key point of distinction in my findings.

Table 1.2 illustrates several of these key comparative points from both cities. In this way, then, the sites are reflective of starkly different political histories. And yet, in their current social context, it is even more telling that regulation of the industry in both cities results in a similar outcome.

Additionally, studying the exact same thing in two very distinct sites with their own particular social patterns provides the possibility to destabilize tak-en-for-granted, naturalized thinking in each. Those ways of thinking have been solidified into various forms, as they shape the social policy and insti-tutions whose practices interpellate us, or hail us in a way that recognizes us

TABLE 1.2   Features of the Industry of Domestic Work in Lima and New York City

FEATURES OF THE INDUSTRY OF DOMESTIC WORK		
	LIMA	NEW YORK CITY
Worker/Employer Characteristics	Indigenous (Quechua and Aymara) women and young girls, internal migrants	Immigrant, multi-ethnic population, Caribbean/ West Indian, Filipina, South Asian, Latin American
	Mestizo/Limeño employers of all classes	Diverse multi-ethnic employers of middle-upper and upper classes
Number of Workers/Overall Population	Est. 500,000	Est. 200,000 to 600,000
	10 million residents	8–9 million residents
Living Situation	Workers live in (*cama adentro*)	Workers live out (*cama afuera*)
Date + Administration of Legislation	June 2003, Ley Número 27986: Ley de los Trabajadores del Hogar	November 2010, Domestic Worker Bill of Rights
	National law; Ministry of Labor and Employment in Lima	Statewide law; New York State Department of Labor in Albany

Source: Author.

as subjects (Althusser 1971). However, they are routinely ridden with racist, sexist, xenophobic, and nationalist narratives that play out in our daily interactions and are often left unquestioned. The scholarship on the industry as a whole, taken together with the lived experiences of domestic workers as understood through in-depth interviews and ethnography, demonstrates the ways that gender, race, and class have not only shaped what kind of worker is thought to be "appropriate" for doing the work itself but also the shifting yet ever-present set of categorical legal exclusions. This effectively excludes this entire group of women workers from coverage under the most basic worker legislations in most countries. Part of what I show here in a unique way is that these two pieces of legislation are both a product of those underlying ideologies and instrumental in their continued practice and relevance.

Methods

In both sites, I conducted the bulk of the research during a central, primary research phase consisting of nine contiguous months living in first Lima and then New York City, after which I then returned for a follow-up field revisit of two additional months in each city. I made sure to schedule both the central field research phases as well as the field revisits in alternating fashions, so that for nearly twenty-four months between 2012 and 2014, I moved to Lima, then to New York City, then back to Lima, and finally back to New York City again. This allowed me to deepen my analysis over time spent in each city as well as to sharpen the comparative observations upon returning to each site and confirming the key substantive differences. Over the course of my fieldwork I was involved in conducting research for the UCLA-based research network, "Experiences Organizing Informal Workers Global Research Network." As part of that research, those twenty-four months were punctuated by trips to document the International Domestic Workers Federation (IDWF) Congress in Uruguay and an IDWF regional meeting in Hong Kong, which also shed useful comparative light on my research.

In Lima, I conducted ten months of ethnography and seventy-two in-depth interviews between September 2012 and February 2014.[4] Over the course of the research, I volunteered at a household workers' center in Lima, where I participated in and later taught a weekly three-hour household workers' law workshop. I interviewed workers actively looking for employment through the worker center as well as others I met outside of it, by either speaking with them in public parks, establishing contact at the Peruvian Ministry of Labor and Employment Promotion (Ministerio de Trabajo y Promoción del Empleo, or MTPE) conferences, or via snowball sampling to reach workers through personal networks in Lima. Interviews lasted from thirty minutes to over two hours, and all were recorded, transcribed, and translated from Spanish into English by me and by a hired research assistant, a Limeña linguistics student, Victoria Maraví. Additionally, I wrote frequent memos based upon ethnographic field notes and interview summaries in order to analyze larger patterns arising in my data.

Household workers I spoke with ranged in age from 18 to 75, with the majority between their late twenties and late forties. This squares with current and often difficult to acquire data on household workers, as Bastidas Aliaga (2012) found that more than two-thirds, or 68%, of Peruvian household workers were between the ages of 14 and 29, while 22% fell between 30 and 45 years old (82).[5] Nearly all were born outside of the capital, and many spoke Quechua or Aymara as their first language, with Spanish as their second. To supplement my research, I also examined publications from the worker center, local media coverage and newspaper articles, and a demographic database of more than 1,200 women who accessed the worker center in 2013. The worker center was generous in sharing these resources with me after my many months working to establish a rapport there, after I had demonstrated my commitment to understanding the law and its social consequences in Lima.

I also had informal conversations with dozens of employers, and I spoke more in depth with a number of employers whom I befriended while living in Lima. I purposefully sought out and attended various social events and activities throughout the city to try to encounter a range of perspectives and positions from their side of the employment relationship. While some employers understood me as someone they could either complain or "vent" to about their frustrations with their household worker, many other employers were genuinely interested in the project and in what I was learning through my interviews. Employers were also important to my study because many more of them (as compared to household workers) are Limeño, meaning that many of them and their families grew up in the city and know it well. The violence of the twenty-year-long internal armed conflict, and especially the several bombings and attacks that took place throughout Lima, are still very much in the city's imagination. Employer friends would describe the palpable fear during the height of Sendero Luminoso's attacks in the early 1990s, drawing from their own experiences. Several times when I was walking with employer friends during a particularly quiet moment on the street, they would notice and point out how unique that sought-after silence is, but especially was, during the conflict and its immediate aftermath. These personal conversations and their reflections added important social and political context to my understanding of the recent history of Lima, as well.

In New York City, I conducted nine months of ethnography and collected fifty-two in-depth interviews between May 2013 and July 2014. Additionally, I analyzed policy documents from the New York Department of Labor along with organizational materials and research reports from Damayan Migrant Workers Association, Adhikaar, Domestic Workers United (DWU), and the National Domestic Workers Alliance (NDWA). I also volunteered with NDWA and its citywide coalition events, and I affiliated with Cornell University's Worker Institute in Manhattan as a visiting scholar, which facilitated access to a number of domestic worker organizations throughout the city.

I conducted interviews across all of New York City's boroughs, save for Staten Island. Interviews in Queens and Brooklyn were usually at the home of the respondent or in her neighborhood, while those conducted in Manhattan were always while domestic workers were working. Manhattan is where the bulk of employers live and where wealth is highly concentrated in the city, and though 20% of New Yorkers live below the poverty line, the top 5% of Manhattanites earned more than USD 860,000 when I was living there in 2014 (ESRI 2016). I shadowed my respondents at work if they were amenable, and so our interviews took place in a number of Manhattan locales, including coffee shops, public parks, toddler sing-a-longs, the New York Public Library's story hours, and on public transportation. My interviewees ranged in age from 26 to 62 years of age and had immigrated to the U.S. from the Philippines, Nepal, Tibet, Mexico, Guatemala, Colombia, Peru, Uruguay, Barbados, Saint Vincent and the Grenadines, Trinidad and Tobago, and Jamaica. While conducting interviews, I did not directly ask my respondents about their immigration status, but instead asked where they were born and when they began working in New York City. And as I began to see the growing importance of immigration in my New York City-based fieldwork, I interviewed legal staff from immigrant advocacy groups and urban justice groups working with informal workers.

I made a deliberate decision to exclude college students and European au pairs from my sample. These women constitute a small and short-term portion of the population of New York City's domestic workers, which, when paired with their drastically elevated class, immigrant, and ethno-racial status, positions them as distinctly privileged compared to those for whom caring, cooking, and cleaning has become a lifelong career with few other options. However, the one exception included in my interviews is a U.S.-born nanny who is a worker-activist aligned with one of the prominent domestic worker organizations, though I do not draw from our conversation in the book.

OVERVIEW OF THE BOOK

To fully theorize the home as a site of work, then, we must begin by theorizing it as a site of law. This book explores this question empirically, as I draw from qualitative data to situate the household as such in two cities with recent labor regulation. In *Chapter 1: Conceptualizing the Home as a Site of Work, as a Site of Law*, I first introduce my sites, their histories, and their demographics. I then ask, What does it mean for our understandings of the home itself when the law permeates its space, granting protections to those who work inside of it? I engage with law and society literature on worker categories, classification struggles, and the nature of a defined, protected employment relationship. I ask, If labor law was historically set up to address a recognized employer-employee relationship, how are we to understand the employment relationship between the most vulnerable workers—those who are not in a clearly recognized relationship? Martha Fineman (2009) understands the term *vulnerable* as capturing a "universal, inevitable, enduring aspect of the human condition that must be at the heart of our concept of social and state responsibility," (8) as she attempts to disentangle it from its "limited and negative associations" (8). I consider the term *structural vulnerability* in this book, by which I similarly understand it as an "encompassing" concept, yet one that in my study remains rooted in the precise, structural conditions of the work and the social relations that surround and compel domestic service. I locate my definition of structural vulnerability, then, as one that is adhered to the conditions and nature of the work itself and that is reflective of the historical social relations in which that labor is embedded. In the industry of domestic service, structural vulnerability is real, lived out, and imbued in the isolated conditions and practices of subservience. Law and vulnerability, then, are inextricably bound up with each other.

Can we legislate away the vulnerability inherent to domestic work—and when trying, what do the limits of labor legislation reveal about the industry itself, and about the way that labor has historically been organized inside of the private sphere of the home? While the literature has acknowledged the difficulties of organizing workers and, to a lesser degree, of regulating an industry based in the home, I argue that the difficulties arise from the historical organization of labor in the home itself, which is fundamentally an ordering of gender and racial subordination. Thus, the following chapters show this, with attention to the spatial, social, and legal relations of the home.

Chapter 2: Architecture of Access: Race, Space, the City, and the Peruvian Colonial Imaginary demonstrates how the development, urbanization, and concentration of wealth in Lima, Peru, has structured (both historically and contemporarily) the industry of household work. This chapter also pays attention to how race played out historically in Peru, as an interconnected part of what I call a *dual-centralization process* that connects to a geographically based and culturally understood stigma against Peruvian internal migrants from the provinces. I draw on Aníbal Quijano (2000) and Marisol de la Cadena (1998) to examine the "silent racisms" taking place across the country, meaning those exclusions made legitimate through biological determinism and superior attitudes (144). I show how indigeneity maps onto geography in the country, with attention to architecture and space as mediators of discrimination as seen through a focus on the construction of the city of Lima and its current sprawling metropolitan status. The racialized colonial legacy undermines the law as it constitutes Indigenous domestic workers as perpetual servants. Additionally, this chapter lays out the relevant Peruvian historical and political context that shaped the timing and tenets of the law itself, situated in relation to former decrees passed in earlier decades.

With *Chapter 3: Insider Vulnerability: Constructing Colonial Domesticity inside Lima's Homes*, I delve into the 2003 Peruvian Household Workers' Law in lived-out practice through content analysis of the law, ethnography, and interviews. I find that the Peruvian law extends to household workers only half of the labor protections afforded to other occupations, and argue that the law codifies preexisting inequalities by shaping a labor regime of "colonial domesticity" that is enacted through *body*, *space*, and *time* inside Lima's contemporary homes. I show how these enclosed, constrained physical and symbolic spaces reproduce a racialized, gendered, and classed hierarchy of social inequality through a lack of privacy and historical expectations of sexual access. Emphasizing the colonial ordering of the home and its lingering effects upon democratic labor legislation for this distinctive kind of devalued labor reveals both the continuity from the colonial era and a new analytical lens through which to understand the law's lack of purchase. Stepping back, I show that the Peruvian case provides an opportunity from which to theorize coloniality as deeply embedded in and constitutive of contemporary relations of servitude, revealing important distinctions in how we more broadly understand power, domination, and inequality embedded in the home as a workplace.

I then turn to flesh out the parallel story in my comparative case of New York City in Chapters 4 and 5. *Chapter 4: From Slavery to Service: Continuing Struggles to Regulate Domestic Worker Rights in the United States* accomplishes three key tasks needed to understand the meaning behind the consequences of the 2010 Domestic Worker Bill of Rights. First, it provides historical context to the industry of domestic work throughout the United States, with a focus on New York City. Second, it explores domestic workers' racialized legal exclusion story, examining the origins of the law-making itself and its deliberate intentions to categorically legislate around them. Importantly, New York's "them" also shifted from being a majority population comprised of Black women to one of immigrant women, which is reflected in what the law does and does not legislate. This chapter also asks what we should expect of the law, and discusses what we know about efforts to formalize and standardize the industry of domestic work. Finally, the rest of the chapter turns to the organizing that led to the law itself, and then addresses the provisions that were lost in its final iteration. This provides the necessary context for an informed understanding of the findings regarding how this particular labor law regulates the home that follows in the next chapter.

With *Chapter 5: Immigrant Domesticity: Producing Outsider Vulnerability in New York City*, I further explore the outcome of the law in action, as after nearly a decade of concentrated organizing by various domestic worker organizations, unions, and progressive faith groups, the resultant Bill of Rights is significantly weakened compared to its original intended provisions. I find that the law grants negligible protections and deliberately eschews language around immigration, thus codifying "immigrant domesticity" instead of improving working conditions. This chapter shows how the law circumscribes the rights of domestic workers in three ways: domestic vulnerability *institutionalizes* dependency by shouldering employers with the onus of immigration-status enforcement, it is *inconsistent* because it subjects workers to their employers' whims by failing to create a standardized contract, and it engenders *informality* by permitting private employer networks to shape labor market access and thus skirt formal regulations concerning hiring and firing. However, there is hope in cultural change. I discuss two important symbolic understandings that have emerged from the Bill of Rights, and here I show how workers identify a *cultural change* as a broader collective win rather than an individual benefit, as well as a newly sharpened *political language*, rejecting racist claims and asserting power and pride on the job.

Finally, the conclusion, *Chapter 6: Toward New Sites of Labor, Toward New Labor Rights*, reflects upon how regulation of the home fails to fully account for its specificity as a site of labor, thus preserving a social hierarchy and, consequently, creating further structural vulnerability for domestic workers. I revisit the concept of structural vulnerability and look to the future of domestic workers organizing and mobilizing taking place both nationally and globally, and the growing care-work economy. I then explore the main arguments of the book again and return to both laws in Lima and New York City to think through the overall analysis, and point to new developments in the Peruvian Household Workers' Law. Finally, I discuss the implications of my work for efforts to regulate the growing informal economy as well as legislate inclusion for formerly marginalized groups in their struggles for labor rights, speaking to creative possibilities for bringing the law and labor into the home.

A *Methodological Appendix* follows that offers a reflexive analysis of my ethnography and my positionality within the research, while the *Comparative Law Appendix* details the tenets of each of the two central laws I examine in practice throughout the course of the book.

TWO ARCHITECTURE OF ACCESS

Race, Space, the City, and the
Peruvian Colonial Imaginary

A tall, thin, dark-haired and light-skinned woman steps into a well-decorated, expensive drawing room. A step behind her, a shorter, dark-haired, darker-skinned young girl appears in the doorway. "¿Eres Janette, sí? From Cusco? What time do you wake up? 6:30, that early, okay. Yes, well, you must come into this room every morning after breakfast and open up all of the doors. Air out the room well, every day. Now we will go into the kitchen." The employer brings Janette into the kitchen, where an older Indigenous woman is seated at the table wearing a blue uniform dress. She rises to her feet when her employer steps into the room, and we immediately see that this woman is the same height as 12-year-old Janette, though plumper. "This is Benita, she's the cook. A very good one. She will help you." To Benita, she says, "You must show her where everything is."

The three of them walk farther into the kitchen, looking very much like a mother with two children from afar. "You must show her where everything is so that she can help you; show her the plates, the pots." Turning to Janette, she says, "Now, Beni cooks very well. Muy riquísimo. You must clean, but when we have guests, you help her here. And when Beni's off duty, you must cook. You know how to cook?" "Un poco," Janette responds, the first audible words she has muttered to her boss. "Cocino estofado de carne, pollo, de cordero." "Ah, Indian dishes. Very well," is her employer's response.

She then points to the cupboards above the stove. "Here is where the plates and things are for guests' use. We don't use these every day." Janette peeks up at them. Benita bends down to open the cabinets lining the floor, and the employer says, "Here, we use *these* every day. The others are a bit high." She pauses, standing nearly two feet taller than Beni. "I like things kept tidy, don't I, Beni? Everything must be put back in its place. As soon as you finish using something, you clean it and put it back." She then takes Janette into the drawing room so that Janette can recite the cleaning ritual again. "And the windows?" "I don't clean them," Janette murmurs on command. "Perfect, you've understood." The employer is seated on a plush sofa surrounded by oil paintings and thick woven carpets while she quizzes Janette on the details of maintaining the room's perfection. Through the curtains draping the floor-to-ceiling windows, two young girls Janette's age play together outside in the yard. Janette is darkened in shadows near the window while the girls shriek with delight and run around the manicured lawn.

Janette is then buttoned into a blue uniform, the same as Beni, in the tiny bedroom they will share. Against the exposed cement wall are two bunk beds, each with a thin pillow and pink blanket. "You sleep above, and Beni is below you." The two can barely turn around at the same time, as there is hardly any space on the floor of the room. "Here is a drawer for your clothes, here is the drawer for Beni. This is your night table, and this is hers. And here is your desk for your homework after school." She leaves to go answer the phone while Janette stands in the room, gazing around the unremarkable space, so different than the carefully curated rest of the house with expensive furniture and spacious accommodations.

Next, Benita and Janette sit at a side table in the kitchen, eating broth with noodles. They speak quietly to each other, out of earshot of the employer. The narrator steps in to say, "Here in Lima, there are over 200,000 girls and women who, just like Janette, work in the households of rich people. You're paid for the work you do, and that's considered enough. Beni, who also started working here when she was a little girl, knows that all too well. At least they will have each other to talk to at mealtimes."

The film ends with a dramatic and pointed scene, as Janette brings a tray of glasses of Coca-Cola out to the employer's daughter and her friends, who are celebrating a birthday party in the backyard. The blond girls crowd around Janette, all with smoothly braided hair with matching ribbons and bright plaid dresses. They grab the glasses, slurp down the soda, and run back to their game, never acknowledging her. Two years older than them, she stands there slumped in her blue, oversized uniform missing a button, staring at the ground with the empty tray in her hands. "Janette does her work, and the children have their party. Young as they are, they've already learned that Janette isn't a part of them. She's the servant girl; the *muchacha*," the narrator reminds us. "Janette now sees what her friends have told her—these children are the same as their parents. Don't expect them to make way for you. Don't expect them to see you standing there, even if they trip over you."

THE DUAL-CENTRALIZATION PROCESS: BECOMING "INSIDERS"

What is striking about this video, a documentary filmed in the early 1980s by the Australian Broadcasting Corporation, is that both Janette's and Benita's stories mirror the lives of women that I interviewed in Lima more than thirty years later. Janette is now long grown up, but other young girls from Cusco and other *provincias* of Peru still flock to the city, seeking work.

Often, like Benita, they work for the same employer for their entire lives, foregoing having their own families and never advancing beyond a few years of elementary education. Indeed, a 2011 survey of household workers across 11 Peruvian cities found that 60% of them were single, and only 35% had children (Bastidas Aliaga 2012:82). Other household workers often have some secondary education but they clean and cook in Lima upon arrival, and the night schools whose classes accommodate their working hours offer low-quality, uninspired education.

The documentary's portrayal illuminates the continued internal migration patterns of Peruvian household workers to Lima as well as the gender and racial hierarchy they encounter inside of the home once they secure work there. Though Peru has experienced several significant political, social, and economic ruptures over the last three decades, including a lengthy internal armed conflict, the continuity of the flow of internal migration and the neocolonial relations that structure the industry of household labor in contemporary Peru is telling. What has stayed the same, then, is part of what I call a *dual-centralization process* that describes both the rural-urban migratory pattern characterized by workers from the provinces flocking to Lima and the spatial concentration of wealth inside the central core of the city that they must traverse from Lima's outskirts. Lima's early architecture was designed to deliberately push Indigenous populations to the outskirts in an effort to isolate and marginalize them, and the capital of now nearly ten million residents similarly spatially ostracizes its new migrant arrivals, just on a larger and more developed scale (Spitta 2007).

I posit this concept of the dual-centralization process as more than just descriptive, however, as it also recognizes the distinctive, Limeño terrain that domestic workers from the provinces must confront, navigate, and endure in order to become an "insider," or part of the sprawling metropolis. Notable about these patterns, then, is the way that the design, development, and architecture of Lima—as a city and as a spatial collection of homes and the private labor practices they contain—mediate continued discriminatory practices.

Susana, a 64-year-old household worker I spoke with in Lima, described a situation akin to that of Benita and Janette when she migrated from the highlands of Tapo, located in the province of Tarma. Currently about a seven-hour drive inland from Lima, traveling from Tapo when Susana did in 1969, before the major highways were constructed, meant a much longer and dangerous journey. Yet she felt she had little choice, as her mother died when Susana was young, her brother was hit by a car, and she needed to help financially support her family. At the age of eight, Susana began working for a neighbor who habitually abused her and paid a wage of only PEN 3.50 (Peruvian soles; USD 1.30) per month.[2]

> While I was in the highlands, I studied only until second grade because then I started working. At her house, I washed the dishes, I swept and everything, and she sent me to do the shopping. So that's how the time passed. I kept working there but she often hit me, and I told my dad and uncle while crying one day, I'm going to quit because she hits me so much. Then she lashed my foot with an electric cord, and it left scars.[3]

On the sunny corner of the district of Jesús María in Lima, where we spoke, Susana gently tilted her right foot toward me and pulled up her navy-blue trousers just enough to display a long mark etched across her ankle, near the edge of her worn leather loafers. She continued without missing a beat, "Then my dad got engaged to some lady and we didn't really get along, so I just kept working. Eventually they told me, "Hey, there's a job in Lima, and they pay well over there." At that time, her Lima-based employers paid a wage of PEN 70 (USD 25.80), which was a substantial improvement from her paltry income back in Tapo. Susana arrived to find decent and caring employers, and yet was living in, without a proper bedroom of her own:

> She was very kind, she treated me well and all of that. However, the bad thing was that I didn't have a bedroom for myself. So, I slept, well . . . there was the dining room and then over there [she gestures to the left] was the bed. I didn't like it like that, because it was uncomfortable, you know? But I was well paid, and I saved a little each month, sent my dad some money each month, and I went to visit him after a year and a half.

Susana addressed the continuing vulnerability of young, new internal migrants when she spoke about changes since the law went into effect.

> Now, however, mostly the ones who have to go through this are those coming from the provinces. Those from here, the *criollos*, they say, I mean from here in Lima, we're more alert. But if you come from the highlands then you're just going to learn—you're the one who gets insulted, you don't know anything, all those kinds of things. Because the customs in the highlands are so different compared to the ones in Lima.

The stories of Susana, Benita, and Janette are the stories of so many other young, internal migrant domestic workers in Lima. This is only one side, however—the side of the workers who silently keep the city gleaming, beautiful, shiny, and new. They cook the hearty dishes of *papas a la huancaína* because many of them are from Huancayo; they know the ingredients to the perfect *ají de gallina*, which is no longer made out of hen because of the high cost. They know to use shredded chicken instead. They wash the sidewalks, scrubbing cement on all fours in the desert heat since it never rains in Lima. They can get the screaming baby to sleep, and they sing songs in Quechua to soothe restless children. They infrequently leave the premises where they sleep because where they live is not actually their home—it is their site of work. They iron the sheets each morning, crisp and cool. Many of them grew up in towns of a few hundred people. They are not an overtly political group, as many of them prefer to find stable employment and reside quietly in their small room of their employers' apartment or house, perhaps visiting their families on Sundays or saving money to go back to the provinces during their annual two weeks of vacation time. And yet for more than twenty years, they have been the newest group of officially recognized workers of Peru. Household workers are legally protected by and guaranteed all eighteen articles of the Household Workers Law 27986, which was passed in 2003 by then-president Alejandro Toledo and his Congress.

To fully understand and contextualize what it means for household workers to access recently granted social and labor protections, we must first understand more about the forces that have historically shaped Lima, and thus how Lima shapes its current residents and their practices today. Who can access the city, and in what ways? And with what consequences? In the rest of this chapter, I demonstrate ways that the development, urbanization, and concentration of wealth in Lima has shaped its previous and contemporary social relations, including the law itself.

PERU AND ITS CITY OF KINGS: A BRIEF HISTORY OF LIMA, THE TERRIBLE

Peru is currently understood as one of the fastest-growing economies in South America, one whose wealth is highly concentrated in the capital, fueling an incredibly centralized and unregulated flow of labor. Peru's history is a storied one, as along with India, China, Mesoamerica, Egypt, and Mesopotamia, Peru is considered a "cradle of civilization," (Museo Larco 2014). Just north of Lima, the city-state of Caral is now understood to have been the site of a highly organized and complex society dating back to 2600 BC, thousands of years prior to the more popularly recognized Incan construction of Machu Picchu, near Cusco. Indeed, Peru is unique in a number of ways: from its rich cultural history through numerous pre-Incan civilizations, creating a highly multi-ethnic population; through its colonial rule under the Spanish Crown; to its more recent political battles, the internal armed conflict during the mobilization of the Shining Path, or *Sendero Luminoso*, from 1980 to 2000 and its corresponding aftermath (Osorio 2008). All of these factors have shaped contemporary Limeño society in the capital, with the last thirty years notably marked by political movements and grassroots struggles for democracy, human rights, labor rights, and women's rights, though with differing measures of success (Blofield 2012; Yashar 2005).

Centuries later, after years of trade relations, geographical fluctuation and fluidity between numerous Indigenous cultures during many epochs, including the *Pre-Cerámica, Inicial de la Cerámica, Formativa, Auge, Fusional*, and *Imperial* periods, the Spanish *Conquista* era began after Francisco Pizarro took Atahualpa, the Incan king, and occupied Tumbes in northwest Peru. Through violence and cooptation, the Spanish colonists extended and enforced their power throughout Peru by concentrating their resources in the capital of Lima, *la Ciudad de los Reyes*, or "City of the Kings." Thus, an entirely new system of colonization took hold, shifting the trajectory of both Peru and other nearby lands occupied throughout the entire continent. Indigenous cultures were systematically exploited and purposefully undermined as a result of European colonialism. Land was stolen and pre-Columbian tribute systems were altered as the members of the Indigenous population were subjected to practices of *repartimiento*, a colonial forced labor system that extracted funds and labor from those subjected to this colonial forced labor system (Johnson and Socolow 2002).

Lacking other economic alternatives, Indigenous women were often forced into providing *servicio personal*, or domestic service in the homes of Spaniards where their bodies were regularly subjected to physical, sexual, and verbal abuse by the colonizers. As Graubart (2007) asserts, domestic service was a "route to the city" early on, a means for many Indigenous women and girls from the provinces to flock to Lima. While most male internal migrants came as young adults seeking waged work, existing employment contracts from the early seventeenth century demonstrate that very young girls migrated as domestic servants for European households (63). These "*indias de servicio*" tended to be young (sometimes only six years old), unmarried, and often positioned in a highly exploitative employment relationship. However, close proximity to wealthy families could hold particular benefits, such as the opportunity to learn Spanish, the potential to learn mastery of skills such as sewing, and "techniques for dealing with colonial life" (Graubart 2007:68).

Though 1824 marked the establishment of an official independence, those dwelling in Peru continued to experience the consequences of these forced cultural, religious, political, social, and economic changes from its colonial period. Due to the effects of geopolitical shifts and rapid, centralized urbanization in the years since, economic opportunities continue to remain sparse in the rural reaches of Peru, and thus, many Indigenous internal migrants continue to relocate to Lima to work in other families' homes; domestic service continues as the "main motor of female migration" (Mick 2016). Pérez and Llanos (2022) found two primary reasons for continued internal migration to Lima in their survey examining social protections and employment practices for Peruvian women—economic mobility and an escape from domestic violence in their home provinces. However, just as during colonial times, once there, they are situated within a vulnerable context since their work is highly gendered, private, and contained within the intimate space of the home, where threats of verbal, emotional, and sexual abuse, isolation, and discrimination based on race, ethnicity, gender, and class loom (Glenn 1992; Parreñas 2001). The rest of this chapter details what happens when they are there, with attention to the construction of Lima, its architecture and space as mediators of discrimination, and the material and discursive struggles for recognition in the industry of household labor, from Susana, Benita, and Janette's journeys through to today.

CONTRADICTIONS IN GROWTH: DEVELOPMENT OF THE CAPITAL

The City of the Kings spent much of its development battling with Cusco as the main urban center of the country. As Osorio (2008) writes in her complicated history of the city, Lima actually enjoyed modern independence before its colonial era, utilizing its positioning as a Roman Catholic city to strengthen both loyalty to the crown and to demonstrate power. Early leaders recognized that a strong Catholic image held significant weight and so they created and utilized local saints as a means of strengthening and promoting this representation in Lima and outside of Peru, even as metaphors themselves, in order for Lima to present itself as a civilized and pious city (Morgan 1998). By utilizing religiosity to strengthen and maintain loyalty within its citizens, Osorio (2008) argues that Lima employed Catholicism as a display of political ritual as well, thus demonstrating power and political legitimacy in the seventeenth century and the years following.

This transition to harness power through religiosity throughout colonialism and into contemporary times also speaks to the divisions and hybridity in Lima's residents, especially with regard to language and other cultural practices. We see this multi-ethnic city living and breathing every day in contemporary Lima, though with rampant inequality instilled since the beginning delineating lines of the city were designed and laid out through the urbanization process. As Silvia Spitta (2007) argues:

> Vital to this process [of urbanization] was the transformation of conquistadors into urban residents. As members of the colonial administrative elite, they were granted central city lots while Indigenous peoples were relegated to the margins. The deeply hierarchical, exploitative caste society that arose was underpinned by the Utopian, absolutely ordered layout of cities in an inflexibly reproducible grid. Lima is a prime example of this arithmetic without imagination. (295)

Between 1940 and 1956, Lima's population doubled, and its resultant growth was expressed along these segregated lines. The numbers in Table 2.1 situate the exponential growth of the city over time (Higgins 2005).

Thus, the city swelled and spilled into the surrounding desert, where its population has expanded significantly since the first recorded census. In 1940, Lima only had one "shantytown," defined as an area occupied by marginalized, impoverished residents, but only twenty years later, the growing population of the poor had been so pushed out of the city that the number of shantytowns soared to fifty-six (Spitta 2007:295). The ostracized location of these areas forced residents to begin a long, arduous daily journey into the city.

TABLE 2.1   Population Growth of Lima, Peru, 1614–2014

YEAR	POPULATION OF LIMA
1614	25,447
1890	114,788
1920	223,807
1940	500,000
1961	2,000,000
1981	3,575,000
2014	10,000,000

Source: Data from Higgins 2005:11, 14

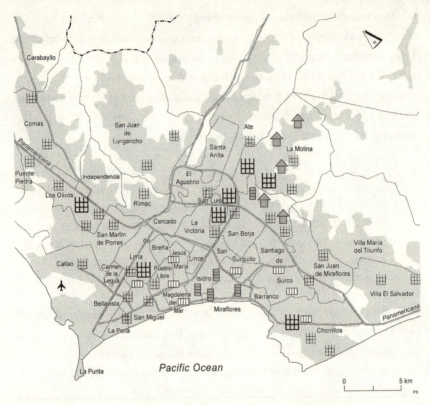

FIGURE 2.1   Map of Lima, Peru, with Concentrated Housing Clusters, 2006. Source: Plöger 2007, CC BY-NC-ND 3.0 EC.

MAPPING INDIGENEITY AND RACE IN PERU

Space thus mediated this process of segregated housing patterns that fully came to fruition in the last sixty years of growth. As James Wallace (1978) explains in his focus on the urban anthropology of Lima, referencing the stigma those who migrate to Lima face:

Nonnative ability in Spanish or the use of what Peruvian sociolinguist Alberto Escobar calls a *castellano andino* dialect stigmatizes the migrant, and native Limeños, whether lower-class *criollos*, middle-class bureaucrats, or upper-class elites, view the high-lands and almost all of Peru outside of Lima as a socially and economically deprived hinterland. For a mid-career Limeño, assignment to a bureaucratic post outside of Lima often is considered to be punishment. (58)

This urban-rural divide ran, and runs, deep into the Peruvian imaginary (León et al. 1998). Marisol de la Cadena (1998) conceptualizes Peru's "silent racisms" as those exclusions made legitimate through biological determinism and superior attitudes (144). Race and space together became a way that Peruvians understood, and disliked, each other, depending upon where they resided—the *centralismo* of the wealthy capital was too much for those in the provinces, while the *regionalismo* was despised by Limeños but openly embraced by *serranos*, or those in the highlands. De la Cadena notes on the mapping on of racial identifiers to geographical location, "[t]he cultural construction of race in Peru hegemonically inscribed it in geography, and considered Coastal inhabitants (particularly Limeños) as 'white,' while deeming serranos '*cholos*,' or close to Indians" (1998:144).

Part of this argument revolves around an assertion that the working definition of race was contested via the site of Peruvian academia, and revolved around three key aspects for each individual: 1) external appearance, phenotype, and physicality (such as Indigenous features, skin color, and "Indian-ness"), 2) "qualities" such as morality, education, and intelligence, and 3) geographical origin, since "Indians were assigned to the highest mountain environments, while residents of the low valleys were deemed 'mestizos.' Thus, the higher the geographical altitude of an individual's origin, the lower his/her relative social standing and the closer he/she would be to Indianness" (de la Cadena 1998:149). The notion of race as a result of social position and geography demonstrates both the contradictory fixed *and* fluid nature of race in Peru, with harsh consequences for even the intelligentsia.

These racisms do not only apply, then, just to those who clean and care in the home; there is a deeply rooted economic class character to them as well. As Peruvian intellectual Emilio Romero, a geographer from Puno, reflecting back on a moment in 1921 at the first university in Latin America, the Universidad de San Marcos (founded in 1551), comments:

> I will never forget my life in Lima at that time, the year of the centennial of national independence [1921]. The mornings in the patio of San Marcos were for us a glorious compensation for our provincial nostalgias, but after

mid-day our Limeño friends disappeared . . . we admired the great writers and teachers from Lima, but they were unreachable constellations for our humble lives. Sometime later, Victor Andres Belaunde, always cordial, democrat to the core, commented on the discrimination against provincial intellectuals, and mentioned that in Lima, the person that could not boast of being Limeño, aspired at least, to be Arequipeño. (de la Cadena 1998:144–45; Romero et al., 1979:11–18)

Here this rampant regionalism tied in with class, and intellect rears its ugly head; if one could not be Limeño, the most desired, elite, and white, then at least one could hope to be an Arequipeño (one who is born in/hails from Arequipa, Peru's second-largest city but containing a mere one million residents, compared to Lima's close to ten million). The coastal inhabitants of the country, Limeños, were interpellated as white, well-educated, and refined intellectuals, while those residing in the "*mancha indio*" (the Indian stain) of the high Andes or the *serranos*, those from the highlands, were Indigenous, less cultured, and devalued. These deeply rooted beliefs were expressed and reified even among the intellectual elites and are accordingly transferred down the economic hierarchy to those performing reproductive labor for the households of Lima.

Of course, Lima is not unique to this process of urban segregation with its centralized, powerful core and marginalized periphery and corresponding consequences. As Carl Nightingale (2012) notes:

For about seventy centuries—arguably since the invention of cities themselves—we have repeatedly committed acts of inequitable and forcible city-splitting. Along the way, we have justified our actions in the name of just about every other concept of human difference imaginable, marking off separate residential territories for different classes, clans, castes, crafts, nations, religions, civilizations, and even sexes. (19)

Indeed, this took place across Peru, which Boesten (2010) describes as a "hierarchical society in which a complex system of sometimes small or imagined and often malleable and exaggerated differences attributed to whole groups results in the placing of one person in a dominant position in relation to another." She continues by describing how these "malleable and exaggerated" differences can lead to great inequality, especially when used to shore up political power and resources in one's own self-interests (2010:22).

Between 1948 and 1980, Peru underwent the violence and repression of three distinct military dictatorships, though these regimes were less devastating than in nearby Argentina and Chile. Toward the concluding years of that widespread repression, the country's population had doubled by 1970 and quadrupled by 2000 (Boesten 2010:22). That same year marked the end of the twenty-year-long internal armed conflict, when Peru's population reached a total of 28 million people, many of whom flocked to the capital to flee rural-based violence (Boesten 2010:22). Boesten notes:

> Economic change led to massive internal migration from rural areas to urban areas, bringing to the cities not only impoverished peasants but Indigenous ones. This was the start of what came to be known as *cholificación*, a process of cultural change that went hand in hand with mixing ethnic identities and increasing urban habits and expectations. (22)

Attributed largely to violence from the internal armed conflict and a persistently unequal distribution of wealth, high numbers of Peruvian women have continued to migrate from the Andean, rural parts of Peru to find employment in the centralized capital of Lima, near the Pacific coast, since the 1960s (Mick 2011). Now over a third of the country's population is concentrated in Lima, with high numbers of internal migrants, creating a division between the capital's "two worlds," of distinct and unequal sets of racial, cultural, and economic privilege. Domestic service's interlocking hierarchy of race, class, gender, and nation is globally tied to geography and workers' intertwined migratory patterns, yet this intersectional hierarchy also adapts a regional character specific to South America and a local one situated in Peru. While some external migration does occur, mainly to Chile and Argentina, the majority of Peruvian household workers are internal migrants, or Indigenous, relocated and displaced women who come to the capital to seek work in the homes of wealthier, often lighter-skinned urban employers of European descent.

Furthermore, household work is ubiquitous in the Peruvian context—nearly all middle-class families and all upper-class families employ at least one *trabajadora del hogar*, who either lives in the employers' home, *cama adentro*, or *cama afuera* (sleeping outside, in a separate location), though household workers who own or rent their own living space is less common. This is not just a feature of the past, however; as Mick (2016) finds in her ethnography with Lima-based household workers, domestic service continues to serve as the "main motor of female migration" in contemporary Peru.

My interviewees reflect these stories, often having left their family and towns behind to migrate to Lima between the ages of twelve and fifteen in search of work. Florentina, thirty-eight years old and the second of eleven children, described what she left behind in her small town near Ayacucho when she migrated to Lima:

> See, where I come from, all the jobs are really about working in the farms, because it's a small settlement and not an actual city. So, you're always helping your mom and dad with sowing the crops, harvesting corn and potatoes, which is what we grow there and what we eat all year, you know? And then, well, there's school. We studied in the morning and the after-noon, we would always help out my parents until I was fifteen. Because at fifteen, I had to come here to Lima for work. For two years, two whole years, it was tough, but that's where I learned the basics, right? Then when I arrived here at my current job, I already knew how to deal with things, I knew about the tasks I had to do and how to deal with . . . everything else.[4]

I did not press Florentina on her use of generalized terms to describe how she learned to deal with "things" and "everything else"; in listening to her life story, it seemed as though her entire history had been dedicated to phys-ically strenuous, but collectivized, labor. "Learning the basics" through an adjustment to living in someone else's home, without one's own family, being immediately racially marked as non-Limeña and situated in a new and over-whelmingly enormous city, though, had clearly been difficult, as Florentina chose her words more carefully when talking about those two years. And yet in her own migration narrative, that she would leave her family at fifteen years of age and come to Lima was woven seamlessly into her biography. It was spoken of as though it was utterly inevitable and naturalized.

Benjamin Orlove (1993) speaks to the historical underpinnings of the nat-uralization of racial difference and geography in the transition to a postcolo-nial Peru:

> Colonial orderings emphasized historicized racial differences among per-sons within a relatively balanced and homogeneous space, while postco-lonial orderings stressed naturalized regional differences among places within a homogeneous, though covertly racialized, population. (301)

Early documents from Spanish colonial rule depict the deeply embedded nature of these particular orderings as imbricated with racial hierarchies

(Poma de Ayala 1613). Other recent work has explored intricacies of racial classification across Latin America, though much of that has focused on Brazil's historical and social context and the development of racial categories (Telles and Paschel 2014; Monk 2016). The term *cholo* has a storied history itself, dating back to colonial Spanish legal categories that classified Peru's Indigenous population within a hierarchical system based on racial characteristics. *Cholos* fit in neither a purely Indian nor purely Spanish category and marriages that brought the two together were more common in Cusco and Peru's provinces, as they were looked down upon in Lima.

However, as Peru's market economy emerged over time and class distinctions began to cut across ethno-racial identification, *cholas* came to constitute what Seligmann (1989) called a "thorny problem for colonial bureaucrats" (696). She noted that *cholas* "represent a crucible between the international-national economy and local-national socioeconomic organization and mores" (695). And after generations of mixed marriages, these distinctions became less and less clear. While still maintaining a strong racialized character, in the capital, *chola* came to be associated with the highly gendered informal economy by working as domestic workers, street cleaners, and nursemaids. This trend continues today, as 73% of Peruvians work in the informal sectors, which is the highest level of informality across all of South America (Silva-Peñaherrera et al. 2022).

Additionally, a higher percentage of women workers, at 76%, hold positions in informal employment as compared to men, at 71%, and those women work mainly as household workers, street vendors, and home-based workers (Ramírez et al. 2023).

Indeed, colonial legacies of geography, gender, and race interweave to construct the industry of household labor in contemporary Peru through the continued rural-urban migration flow to the capital and within the spatial layout of Lima itself. Part of what my study contributes, then, is an examination of one particular occupational category—domestic service—that has crossed regional, national, and global boundaries and yet retained its fundamentally intersectional character. Here, we see some of the entrenched staying power around those categories even when legal reform efforts are made. Said efforts do not specifically address the categorical power of racialized colonial and immigrant patterns; rather they codify those previous inequalities.

Discourses of Divisions and Practices of Difference

Language also functions to further denote or deny accessibility to colonial modes of thought, practices, and cultural understandings in Lima. Indigenous Peruvians—and especially household workers—are demeaned as *campesinas*, *chicas*, and *muchachas*, even when they are well into their fifties and sixties. Yet those women who are called "girls" as a technique of disrespect and infantilization are then required to in turn address their employers with the formal and dignified *Señor*, *Señorita*, or *Señora*. So deeply ingrained is this practice for household workers, however, that they immediately and seemingly automatically address nearly every other person they encounter as a *Señorita* or a *Señor*.

I noted these kinds of normalized discriminatory discourses taking place in my social interactions, as well. Anne, a French-Canadian friend I met while conducting research in Lima, began taking advanced, one-on-one Spanish classes to improve her language skills. I then met Anne's teacher, Karla, a pretty Peruvian woman with strong Andean features in what I guessed to be her early forties, when we were all at a mutual friend's birthday party. I found Karla warm and interesting to speak with, and while I struck up an easy conversation with her that night, she did not cross my mind again until Anne and I met up for lunch a couple of weeks later.

As soon as we sat down at our table in the bustling restaurant in Miraflores, Anne brought up her Spanish teacher.

"Remember Karla?" she asked me.

"Oh yeah, she was great!" I responded brightly. "How's class going? And, actually, what is it like to be back in, you know, "instruction mode" as a student even though you can speak fairly well?" I had several questions in mind but paused when I looked up to see that Anne had a strange look on her face.

"Well, so during my lesson this afternoon, we were practicing the imperative . . .," she started, then trailed off. Then Anne put down the menu that she had not even opened yet.

"And . . .? What happened?" I asked, my curiosity now piqued.

"And . . . so, we were going over the form and when I should use it and all of that. And then Karla told me to practice with an example, like I normally do. But the prompt she gave me said: 'Use as an example how you would talk to your *empleada*. Think of what commands and orders you would give her.' And she read the prompt like, like it was nothing!"

I thought back to when I had met Karla at the party, and how she mentioned that most of the students she teaches are visiting tourists and expatriates living in Lima. Yet as foreigners living in Peru, Anne and I were both taken aback at her coolly delivered suggestion to master the tense that invokes domination by imagining a conversation with a maid, positioned as a subordinate. What Karla proposed was not a typical conversation, as the *empleada* is not brought in as an equal human being and conversation partner. This scene, however, is not akin to what Karla's students most likely remember as early, awkward moments of high school Spanish 1: students sitting in alphabetical pairs and, though no one quite knows what to do with the pronunciation of the letter "j" yet, they have nearly memorized how to too-quickly ask a random stranger about Madrid's weather in October.

Karla's conversation is structurally quite different, as the *empleada* here merely serves as a passive receptacle to absorb and contain whatever linguistic form her employer's domination and control will take—perhaps orders and commands she must then carry out as part of her job, but alternatively, perhaps anger, abuse, or a whole host of possibilities, all delivered through the imperative. Karla's sense that this is culturally acceptable for her tourist and expat students is telling, and perhaps reveals a strategy to signal, or feign, a classed and racialized alignment with her clients. Additionally, it demonstrates the perhaps reluctant, complicated complicity Karla employs as she equips those from outside of Peru with the linguistic tools that perpetuate its internal discriminatory discourses.

Speaking with Marlena, a longtime feminist lawyer in Lima, contextualized some of the various forms through which racism is expressed within Limeño society. We met in the quiet library of the NGO where she works, Flora Tristán, named after the nineteenth-century French-Peruvian theorist whose work early on theorized the intertwined nature of working-class oppression with women's oppression. Marlena, too, drew those intersectional connections, linking race as tied to gendered-and class-based discrimination and as localized specifically in the industry of domestic service:

> To this point about the importance of decolonizing relations of power, then, racism is a heavy part of this relationship. It isn't just class exclusion, but also race and gender. For this reason, the job of household worker demonstrates the intersection of oppressions more than any other. I

believe this is really important, because it speaks to the type of work, the type of employment situation, the type of home and its space, and the type of society we have.[5]

In the same way that Fanon (1952) understands the power imbued in language when he discusses how speaking French presumes the collective consciousness of the French, including all of its overt and covert racism, those who speak Spanish as either a first or second language (with an Indigenous language being primary) point to another layer of colonial distinction. Fanon posits, "To speak means to be in a position to use a certain syntax, to grasp the morphology of this or that language, but it means above all to assume a culture, to support the weight of a civilization" (1952:18). Marlena's statement around household workers' oppression demonstrating a particular kind of society hearkens to Fanon's notion of the collective unconscious (as "the sum of prejudices, myths, and collective attitudes of a given group" [188]) being culturally acquired, rather than genetically, and thus reinscribed through the reproduction of these oppressive relations in the home.

Tropes around Fanon's collective unconscious can be seen as holdovers of colonial-era delineations of social, conversational, and physical space that preserved certain areas for European privilege. Rebecca Earle (2012) argues that much of Spanish colonial legislation sought to accomplish two contradictory goals: the first involved encouraging the Indigenous population's imitation of Spanish culture through clothing, religion, food, and dietary practices, among other customs, while the second set to limit contact between Spaniards and the "Amerindian" population, reflecting the deeply racialized fears around Indian-ness and it being tied to sets of "deviant" practices. Food, or what Earle (2012) calls a "daily necessity and a potent symbol," (183) served as the strongest marker of these contradictory practices. Earle details how Juan de Matienzo penned the tome *Gobierno del Perú* in 1567 in order to catalog the kinds of European customs believed to effectively govern the country.

Part of the imitation of Spanish colonists, then, came through the re-shaping and curtailment of Indigenous practices that retained intrinsic value apart from Spanish involvement or posed a threat to the colonists' understandings of civility. This came down to ways of dress, as Matienzo notes, as well as practices around food (Matienzo 1567, quoted in Earle 2012). Dating back to the sixteenth century, communal eating was a celebrated practice that fortified Andean community. Yet *Gobierno del Perú* legislated otherwise, pre-scribing Indigenous Peruvians to eat each in their own house, "like rational men" (Matienzo 1567, quoted in Earle 2012:53). Akin to the historical section-ing off of formerly shared land through the enclosure of the commons across Europe, widely understood to be a key structural condition of the transition from a feudal into a capitalist economy, the sanctioning of where—and with whom—food could be consumed held significant consequences for the con-tainment of and legal protection over the household as the separate, private sphere (Federici 2004).

Spanish leadership saw "mixing" as part of a civilizing and proselyting mission, and thus encouraged this as part of the creation of a more intelligent citizenry. Yet as Bhabha (1984) and others have pointed out, colonial mimicry poses a danger to the entire colonial project for fear of questioning its legit-imacy through imitation. Much work has been done to examine when and how Indigenous groups contested or adapted particular policies of colonial regimes in various ways. Additionally, the wealth of the colony through its natural resources of silver, gold, copper, and other valuable minerals, then, was early on seen as important to harvest for Spain. This continues to be a profitable sector of the country, yet with significant resistance and mobiliza-tion from the provinces and communities impacted by such extraction (Lust 2014). Important to note here, then, is that Spanish practices early on laid out a contradictory path for Lima's development; they pushed forward a regime of European acclimation while also limiting contact and maintaining strict boundaries between colonizer and colonized.

TROUBLING POLITICS, TROUBLED HISTORIES

We must ask, then, what efforts have been made to organize domestic work-ers themselves and to organize for their right to labor protections. However, first we must look at the overall political climate of Peru for the last forty years to understand more about its complicated political and social past. Among its neighbors of Bolivia and Ecuador, Peru stands out in that it has not experienced a widespread Indigenous movement in recent decades, even though an estimated 40% of its population is Indigenous (Yashar 2005). How-ever, in her thoughtful work on democracy and citizenship struggles in Latin America, Deborah Yashar argues that Peru lacked two key features—political associational space and cross-community networks—which impeded Indigenous organizing. A similar case can be made for the lack of other forms of political organizing, no thanks in part to the stubborn residue of Alberto Fujimori's harmful regime. And more broadly, Peru is recognized as a country where "executive power and domestic turbulence have been far and away the largest obstacles to change" (Ungar 2002:10), which speaks to difficulties also felt broadly across Latin America.

Situating Peru's recent history within a larger context of Latin American labor reform for domestic workers allows for us to recognize the ways that legislative shifts have occurred across different countries. As Blofield (2012) and others (Bunster and Chaney 1985) have noted, the 1980s was a decade of economic crisis across the region of Latin America after numerous internal armed conflicts, which created a structural flow of young Indigenous women migrating from the provinces and the *sierra* to capital cities (Staab and Maher 2006; Blofield 2012:23). Indeed, what followed was a period of remarkable democratization movements across the region, which resulted in efforts to create governments with more stability and opportunities for worker organizing (Luciak 2001). Blofield and Haas (2011) point out, however, that even though these important democratic transitions have taken place across Latin America, the majority of countries throughout the region continue to discriminate legally against household workers (295).

Many recent attempts to organize household workers have been made in Peru. While there has been some success over the last decades, the main household worker union is split into two competing factions. SINTRAHOGARP (Sindicato Nacional de Trabajadoras del Hogar del Perú) and SINTTRAHOL (Sindicato de Trabajadoras y Trabajadores del Hogar de la Región Lima) represent household workers of Lima, where the majority of these workers are concentrated, and yet they are such a divided, isolated population that membership numbers are high and often thought to be inflated. Two other NGOs that I worked with during my fieldwork, La Casa de Panchita and Flora Tristán, have both sought to address the needs of household workers in a grounded and representative way.

Much of this troubled history is due to the effects of Alberto Fujimori's regime and its lingering ability to quell any type of organizing. For the ten years of rule under Fujimori, from 1990 to 2000, activists who assembled together publicly, groups suspected of political activity, and those forming any kind of association were looked at as terrorists and thought to be associated with Sendero Luminoso. Previously under severe persecution for multiple violations of human rights, including his involvement with high-profile death squads and sterilization efforts, Fujimori's presence still remains, even posthumously. Responsible for changing the country's currency and further distancing itself from its pre-Columbian past (the former *inti*, meaning "sun god" in Quechua, the language spoken by the Inca, was replaced with the *nuevo sol*, a highly Spanish-influenced currency meant to reflect the new, modern economy of Peru), Fujimori's drastic economic, social, and political measures across the country have had a lasting impact (Rousseau 2010).

Lead organizers have described the political damper and real threat of danger that his regime instilled. Though Fujimori promised he would refrain from neoliberal reforms during his campaign speeches, the second half of his elected term became known as "Fujishock," with intense cuts to public services and skyrocketing unemployment. He implemented drastic land reforms and passed the Ley de Tierras 26505, which privatized land markets and turned over ownership of long-held community land to the government, challenged local autonomy, and fostered close business ties with some communities while isolating others (Yashar 2005). Due to Fujimori's neoliberal cuts, health facilities stripped of funding could not keep up with implementing international safety recommendations, and thus, a cholera epidemic spread throughout different regions of Peru, even reaching Bolivia and Ecuador. The country found itself in a major economic crisis, which took several subsequent stabilization efforts to improve.

While a democracy in name, Peru was literally under rule by two opposing violent, political military forces during this era—Sendero Luminoso, or the Shining Path, and the Peruvian state military (Schönwälder 2002; Yashar 2005). The Peruvian government responded to Sendero Luminoso's presence, organizing its military to "govern the countryside," by declaring a "State of Emergency" first in Ayacucho and then in other regions where political activity was suspected of taking place (Yashar 2005:247). This led to weakened community ties and increasing peasant skepticism toward the national government, making Peru a difficult and unsafe place to organize.

Yet even in the midst of volatile political times, there are openings and possibilities. After Fujimori's regime, the household workers' law was finally passed under Alejandro Toledo. Blofield (2009) discusses the ways that household worker struggles in Latin America take place today mainly within a neoliberal capitalist context, which has diminished the power of organized labor. This political climate allows for women's, Indigenous populations', and other marginalized groups' voices to be heard, or at least to sound out a call for equality, though those claims may fall on deaf ears.

La Casa de Panchita (LCP), which was located in the working-class district of Jesús María and is now in Magdalena del Mar, has been a site of shelter, advocacy, and community for the household workers of Lima for over thirty years.[6] Based on the comic strip popular in circles around the country, Panchita, a young, Indigenous female household worker, moves from job to job. "But where is her home? Where does she live?" was the commonly asked question as her fans grew and grew, seeing themselves reflected in Panchita's struggles and triumphs (Carstens 2012). In acknowledging Panchita's symbolic power to unite a disparate group of workers, LCP directly addresses the needs of workers on the ground to find community and to learn about their rights. What actually ends up happening, generally, is that girls and women realize some of the treatment they have accepted for years is not, in fact, "normal," or is criminal and yet normalized through repeated practices. Women find a space in which they can speak openly about the painful stories of their working lives, such as the use of their body as fodder for the sons of the household, sons whose first steps they had observed and who they had raised as their own. Thought to be of less worth, deemed "safe" for sexual practice, live-in workers' bodies are treated as available for the boys and men connected to the employer's family. The literature widely recognizes ways that household workers are situated as vulnerable to sexual assault and abuse inside of the home, and the stories of women recounting and recovering from these traumas speak to the deeply entrenched servitude mindset that is only slowly being eradicated in Peru and other countries.

Women's movements were a vibrant part of Peru's struggle for democracy over the last several decades, including mobilizations around involvement in politics, ending violence against women, and eventually, the Household Workers' Law (Jaquette 2009; Mauricio 2012; Vargas 2013). The 1980s were a politically generative decade for women's organizations and social movement building in Lima, as many women voted for the first time in the 1980 elections, and these political practices continued throughout that decade and were institutionalized via state legislation during the following. However, while demonstrative of heightened feminist activism, many women's organizations and NGOs wielded limited influence or ability to introduce legislation on controversial topics, such as abortion and reproductive rights (Alvarez 1999, 2009).[7] Additionally, feminist organizational strongholds, such as Flora Tristán, have played an instrumental role in advocating for and protecting women's rights and resources. Lawyers and advocates from Flora Tristán were kidnapped and disappeared during the internal armed conflict.

Gloria, however, a key organizer of household workers for over thirty years, points not only to the NGOization of feminist groups but to the complicated interests at play when attempting to organize women of different classes, races, and privilege. Below, she discusses some of the challenges facing workers in Lima when even—or perhaps, especially—feminist employers fail to recognize the basic labor rights of their own employees:

> The issues are not the same among all women. So, we already have men who devalue domestic work, and on top of that another woman comes and says: "No! My house is small, you [the worker] don't have much to do. You won't have a lot of work." Therefore, that other woman is devaluing the job this other woman that works for her does because she simplifies everything. She says, "I can't do it because I don't have time, but if I did, I would." But I'm not sure that she'd do it!
>
> So, if women—the other women who value domestic work—they could also include and involve men so that they do that domestic work, let's say that they could cooperate at home, no? It's not solely the woman's responsibility. So, it also has to do with how women overall value domestic work and . . . start acknowledging that it's a job that solves their problems because, thanks to the worker that is there, they are in the places where they are, no?
>
> And women that work at NGOs are not necessarily . . . it'd be interesting to see, for instance, how other women, let's say, so-called feminists, or those who are involved in social work, value their work. Because many of those women, they celebrate March 8, International Women's Day, like it means something to them but meanwhile, her worker is inside the house. She doesn't even know there is a holiday, or that it's also her day.
>
> Many of those women have a worker at home and don't respect the law. So, there's a whole reformation of society pending.[8]

Gloria's recognition of the fact that many even purported progressive women only act in their interest is telling, though not new, of course. It highlights one of the largest historical and contemporary obstacles to organizing domestic workers in Peru, and elsewhere—elite resistance, or reluctance, to structural change that targets the precise arrangement that allows their homes to run so smoothly (Blofield 2009, 2012; Tronto 2002).

CREATION OF THE LAW THROUGH DEMOCRATIC-RIGHTS STRUGGLES

This law was the outcome of a long history of struggle for democratic rights, as broad grassroots mobilizations have swept across Latin America in recent decades. These social movements included struggles for Indigenous rights, land reclamation, women's and reproductive rights, labor protections, and more (Jaquette 1994; Stephen 1997; Yashar 2005; Blofield 2012). However, those reforms in the wake of post-authoritarian rule differently affected groups organizing for state-granted rights, and thus, we see the case of household work as one in which colonial long-standing hierarchies remain etched, even after it has been formally recognized and regulated.

So, while much has been written about the historical dynamics that shaped the trajectory of the colonial period in Peru, its resultant relative period of democracy followed by authoritarian rule, and state-society relations throughout, we know less about the Fujimori period that has characterized recent efforts at reform and rights. While Peru is grappling with neoliberal reforms, lingering coloniality continues to shape class relations, and especially those which comprise the industry of domestic service. What follows is an overview of these movements and their involvement in several stages of household worker legislation, culminating in finally securing the 2003 law.

Just as in other Latin American countries, the Peruvian government recognized low-income women as mothers and institutionalized maternal support while rescinding support from groups that focused on other dimensions of women's strengths, such as developing identities as leaders, workers, and activists, a trend which Alan García continued when creating his democratic government in 1985–1990. While García passed some important labor market reforms, he did not recognize social security for household workers (Blondet 1987:7; Radcliffe 2006; Elias 2010). Furthermore, when women's rights agencies throughout the region have made recent efforts to approach the issue of household work, they generally tend to focus on promoting the professionalization of household workers, rather than the more controversial option of investigating working conditions, systematizing legal enforcement, and considering the home as a site of labor. Furthermore, president Alberto Fujimori's gender politics clashed in important ways with Lima's feminist movement, which was and remains primarily urban and middle-class. Thus, women's movements took on classed strategies during these tumultuous decades, as many female employers involved in feminist organizing failed to recognize the cause of their household workers as women also deserving of equal labor rights.

Overview of Historical Struggles for Legislation and Fujimori's Regime

As I discovered through my fieldwork, the 2003 national law in Peru arose out of a long process of struggle, building upon previous labor law. Minimal labor legislation for household workers existed as early as 1957 in Peru, when Decreto Supremo 23 was passed on April 30, offering the most basic worker protections. Thirteen years later, another Decreto Supremo (002-TR) was passed, which guaranteed overtime pay, eight hours of nightly rest, twenty-four contiguous hours of rest either on Sunday or another day of the week, and fifteen days of vacation per year.[9] This was part of General Juan Velasco Alvarado's (1968–75) "revolution from above," which sought to quell popular unrest. His regime implemented a sweeping agrarian reform that expropriated large estates and turned them into peasant cooperatives, nationalized the mining, oil and fishing industries, and issued several key pieces of legislative reform, including the 1970 decree that recognized household workers (Higgins 2005:13; Cook 2008). While a notable achievement, this decree stipulated that household workers should only receive half of the benefits of workers in the private sector.

Peruvian cultural products reflected the revolutionary politics of this historical moment in important ways with respect to race, gender, and class. Drawing from the influence of New York-based artists Andy Warhol and Roy Lichtenstein and the pop art movement in the United States, Huancavelica-born artist Jesús Ruiz Durand created a series of fifteen works entitled *Agrarian Reform, 1968–1973*. Representing the fresh politics of Velasco's platform, they often directly invoked the iconic revolutionary José Gabriel Condorcanqui—better known by the name of his distant Incan ancestor, Tupac Amaru, which he assumed—and his wife, Micaela Bastidas. Condorcanqui and Bastidas led a significant uprising against Spanish colonial rule in 1780 that spread rebellion throughout the Andes through politics that advocated for a return to aspects of egalitarian Incan governance and did away with taxes imposed specifically on Indigenous Peruvians. The following year, Condorcanqui and Bastidas were captured and killed quite gruesomely in Cusco's Plaza de las Armas. They later became a symbol of popular resistance woven throughout Peruvian literature and poetry, which Charles Walker (2014) points out prompted a much-needed revisit of the traditional historical understanding of Peruvian independence. This narrative had long attributed the struggle to wrest free of Spanish control to the well-known non-Peruvian figures such as Simón Bolivar and José de San Martín, rather than to a Quechua-speaking Indian from Cusco.

Velasco's regime incorporated Tupac Amaru's insurgent spirit and likeness ubiquitously, from the 500-inti banknote to his campaign materials. One poster positions the then-president's image as a virtual extension of Condorcanqui, both men with determined looks on their faces and fists raised in the air. The print's text reaffirms the political lineage of the poster, as Velasco claims to have "fulfilled the promise that Tupac Amaru had set out to accomplish" (Walker 2014).[10] Ruiz Durand's colorful, catchy posters circulated throughout the country and reinvigorated its Indigenous population, reaching those in the provinces who could not read and those without access to radio or television. In addition to advocating for the redistribution of land and social reforms, several of the posters featured Indigenous women delivering powerful messages, as seen in Figure 2.2.

The image presents a militant woman with the Peruvian flag positioned firmly on her shoulder, akin to a soldier marching off to war, rifle clutched tightly. She asserts, "We Northern women support the revolution; you should also take part in building a revolutionary home!" Another features a peasant woman with her thick black braids tucked under a hat and colorful bag slung across the large cow at her side, as she declares, "Now, no one's going to take away your land, sister! This is our revolution!" (Sánchez Flores 2016).

Sánchez Flores (2016) notes that for the first time in Peruvian history, Ruiz Durand's work presented a historical representation of *campesinos* as central figures and as agents of social change, rather than as a caricature. In an interview with the artist in 2016, Ruiz Durand noted that he deliberately drew the central figures as proudly holding their tools for working the land so as to also function as a "softened kind of weapon" (Sánchez Flores 2016).

FIGURE 2.2 *Las Mujeres Norteñas*, c. 1968–73. Jesús Ruiz Durand.
Source: Jesús Ruiz Durand. Reprinted with the permission of the artist.

FIGURE 2.3 *Ya Nadie te Sacará de tu Tierra*, c. 1968–73. Jesús Ruiz Durand.
Source: Jesús Ruiz Durand. Reprinted with the permission of the artist.

While most of Velasco's reforms fell short of their original revolutionary goals, they importantly changed precedent for Peru's peasant and working classes. Additionally, most of them were largely struck down when a weakened Velasco lost power to the authoritarian General Morales Bermúdez in 1975. The Peruvian labor movement was strongly opposed to the repressive measures of Bermúdez's harsh regime and, thus, organized widespread strikes for worker rights as well as for basic democratic freedoms (Collier 1999). Workers in Lima formed the Coordinadora de Sindicatos de Lima Metropolitana, which became a broad-based union effort in conjunction with household workers' organizations in Cusco and other cities of Peru. In 1979, all Peruvian citizens over eighteen years of age won the right to vote, and many women and other formerly marginalized Peruvians voted for the first time in the 1980 elections (Boesten 2010; Collier 1999:119). This set the tone for the politically generative decade of Lima's democratic transition.

This period of failed hopes led into severe economic inflation (7000% at its worst account), however, which eventually led to President Fujimori's neoliberal restructuring of the economy (Higgins 2005). He eroded democratic institutions and declared a "self-coup" in 1992, replaced numerous key governmental figures, changed the entire governmental structure from two chambers to one, and rewrote the country's constitution. He also utilized a maternalist discourse that praised Peruvian mothers for their self-sacrifice for the nation during a time of intense poverty and despair brought about by Fujishock (Boesten 2010). After Fujimori's fraudulent re-election in 2000, he continued to push forward a gender strategy that co-opted feminist causes.

One way in which he accomplished this was by symbolically featured women in key positions, such as his entirely woman-led steering committee, and yet those women merely carried out his agenda. Specifically, these die-hard "*fujimoristas*" pushed forward to implement Fujimori's agenda, including defending sterilization programs of poor Peruvian and mostly Indigenous women (Boesten 2010).

Roselia, a prominent organizer in Centro de Capacitación para Trabajadoras del Hogar (CCTH) and the struggle for household worker rights more broadly in Lima, put Fujimori's impact on the delay of the legislation in context in the 1990s:

At that time, we were organizing together, and we presented a proposal for the law. Yet we were never heard; they always promised us and promised us, and *nothing*. After 1995, Parliament approved a law (without telling us its content) but it never took effect because then Fujimori's government returned to Congress.[11] He didn't want any problems in his return to presidency, and securing the employers' votes and support was very important.

Her comments are underscored by the fact that many employers are involved in Lima's largely urban and middle-class feminist movement, and yet during the organizing back in the 90s, they failed to support the campaign that would consider their own household workers as deserving of state-granted labor rights (Blofield 2012; Boesten 2010).

Indeed, feminist groups and NGOs in Lima were waging their own hard-fought campaigns to end sexual harassment and promote women's empowerment in the labor market and politics (Alvarez 2009; Vargas 1991). However, uneasy tensions continued in these movements around class privilege, political experience (or lack thereof), and ethno-racial oppression, among others. These power struggles took place between the city's *políticas* (women politicians, who were removed from poor women's experiences, mostly Lima-born, and accused of lacking feminist consciousness), *feministas* (feminist activists, who were middle-to-upper class and presumed to be elitist), and *populares* (grassroots women's organizations, mainly composed of poor, migrant, Indigenous women and considered uneducated and politically naïve) (Boesten 2010:27; Vargas 1991).

The organization central in continuing the push for household workers' legislation, however, was the CCTH, which was founded in 1982 by organizers from various Lima-based movements in order to confront the diverse problems facing household workers and move toward stronger legislation (Mauricio 2015). Leddy Mozambite Linares, the secretary general of one of Lima's household worker unions, SINTTRAHOL (Sindicato de Trabajadoras y Trabajadores del Hogar de la Región de Lima), and a longtime organizer for household worker rights, emphasized the slow and steady process of organizing and the proudly non-Limeña ethno-racial composition of Lima's household worker population when discussing the campaign for the law. She described it as a "35-year battle of working to reassert our dignity as household workers and migrants with Andean, Amazonian, and Afro-Peruvian roots."[12]

Similarly, Marcolina de los Milagros Infante Ramírez, from IPROFOTH (Instituto de Promoción y Formación de las Trabajadoras del Hogar) and SINT-TRAHOL, said that the law took "many years of struggle, demonstrations, and traveling around the country to win visibility,"[13] and all the while, many household workers who organized and demanded their rights were fired from their jobs. Yet CCTH continued its efforts until finally in 2003, under the first Indigenous, democratically elected president, Alejandro Toledo, they managed to get the first law of its kind passed through the Peruvian National Congress.[14]

In that historic moment, the Household Workers' Law became the first of its kind to be approved through the Peruvian National Congress. Reflecting back on the mapping of race in Peru, the fact that Toledo was the president who approved the law is significant. Though he earned his undergraduate and doctoral degrees at universities in the United States, as is common practice among Peruvian and other South American politicians, Toledo grew up in severe poverty in Cabana, a small city of approximately three thousand people. Located in the Pallasca province in the Northern region of Ancash, Toledo was the eighth-oldest child of sixteen total, though seven died as infants and young children due to diseases and other health complications. In his biography and life experience he assuredly represents a stark contrast to the white, Polish-descendent and United States citizen (until just before the election, when he renounced his U.S. citizenship in order to run for president of Peru) Pedro Pablo Kuczynski, better known as PPK, who took office after my field revisits. While Toledo's presidency struggled severely at times and he is currently imprisoned in Peru on corruption charges, his name surfaced in my research conversations as a hero of the people of the "real Peru," hearkening to Prada's 1888 distinction around geography and indigeneity of the provinces.

Yet returning to the law itself, I saw through my fieldwork in Lima that as notable as the successful passage of law after a great deal of struggle is, there remains much more work to be done in the post-legislation phase. This is not entirely surprising, of course, as we know better than to expect an instant transformation of social and labor relations immediately following any legislation turned into law. There is also a strong parallel here with the law in New York City, perhaps put best by a Nepali activist who told me, "We have to organize to keep it alive."[15] Yet a number of obstacles have been especially challenging for this law in particular, including the need to continually inform workers of their rights upon their arrival to Lima as well as the myriad difficulties of enforcing a law contained within the private household.

An excerpt from my ethnographic field notes from February 2013 describes the weekly three-hour-long workshop on the household workers' law and contextualizes a number of these key difficulties:

> Scanning the room of nine *trabajadoras del hogar* ranging from age sixteen to sixty-two, her students for the day who are gathered to discuss Ley N° 27986, the Peruvian Household Workers' Law, Roselia asks the group, "So, who does the work of the home?"
>
> Ana Mónica, a thirty-five-year-old from Huancayo, says easily, "Las trabajadoras. Nosotros."[16] "Excellent," replies Roselia, a former *empleada* herself who came from Cajamarca to Lima in search of work at age seven, as she scribbles TRABAJADORA DEL HOGAR on the board. A few women nod in agreement, and she then writes AMA DE CASA directly below. "What about them—housewives? They do work, right? So, what's the difference between the two groups?"
>
> A few seconds pass, and then Blanca, an energetic teenager from Puno, shoots her hand up into the air and waits to be called on. She practically shouts, "We get paid!" Roselia triumphantly taps the board several times with her marker, emphasizing her agreement with the importance of this point. "Exactly; very good, Blanca. You not only get paid, but you have holidays. You have vacations. You have overtime. You have social security. You have retirement. You have . . . *rights*. The law says this. You have rights."
>
> A hush falls over the group as they let this news sink in. Roselia continues: "Now, let's begin to understand them."

During the ten months that I conducted ethnography and in-depth interviews in Lima, I witnessed this scene above play out regularly. Even though there is a long tradition of household labor in Peru as described in this chapter, and even though the law governing and protecting the terms of labor for household workers was passed more than twenty years ago, we see through this glimpse at the law workshop that there is still a general lack of awareness of its existence.

Meanwhile, while we wait for the "reformation of society" that Gloria mentions, young girls like Janette, Beni, and Susana learn how to carefully open the curtains in the drawing rooms of their new workplaces, the elegant, modern high-rise apartments that dot the Lima skyline. They move through the dual-centralization process in Lima and instantly learn that they have a particular sort of limited access to the city, rather than that they have rights as workers. While a partial reason for this can be attributed to the stream of internal migrants arriving to Lima from the provinces, I argue that the more telling and relevant explanatory factor is the labor and the law being contained within the protected, private nature of the household, hidden and separate from public view. What those rights look like in practice inside of Lima's homes, however, is a complicated story, and one that I will let Chapter 3 narrate and explore.

THREE COLONIAL DOMESTICITY

Constructing Insider Vulnerability in Lima's Homes

Women wearing either all dark royal blue, pristine white, or baby blue scrub-like smocks, aprons, and fitted dresses dot the horizon of Lima's *malecón*, the boardwalk that stretches along the Pacific Ocean's coast. Some push strollers and walk dogs, while others line the park benches of wealthy districts, blue and white notes amidst the green, well-manicured gardens.

Their uniforms signify that after the afternoon stroll or time in the park, they will return to someone else's home where they cook, clean, care, or some combination of the three tasks, for pay. Yet uniforms also prevent these women from entering upscale establishments and private beaches due to their status as *empleadas*.[1] The uniform, similarly to the recently passed labor law for household workers, simultaneously signifies and prohibits. It creates a visual distinction of embodied race, class, and gender inequalities, while also conferring a particular set of limited rights on these women as workers, both ubiquitous and overlooked within Limeño society. And yet the law is silent on the most conspicuous marker of the very group it is designed to regulate, the uniform.

Like most former colonial societies, Peru has a long tradition of household labor concentrated in its capital, Lima. Yet only since 2003 has the state legally recognized Peruvian household workers with a specific set of rights, protections, and benefits.[2] However, household workers are regarded differently than most other Peruvian workers in that this separate labor law which governs their working conditions and benefits is distinctively less equal. As such, many of those labor rights are reduced to half of those accorded to other workers or, in the case of a standardized minimum wage, completely absent. Just as in many countries throughout Latin America and in other parts of the world that have recently passed household worker legislation, then, the Peruvian state thus officially recognizes household work and yet also maintains its exceptional and unequal status (Blofield 2012).

While the sociological literature on paid domestic work has acknowledged the difficulties of organizing workers due to their position inside of the isolated, individual home, and has to a lesser degree recognized the challenges of regulating an industry entirely contained there, I argue that the difficulties arise from the historical organization of labor of the home itself—that is, the colonial ordering in the case of Peru, which is fundamentally an ordering of racial subordination. When examined as a place of work, the home is a rich site from which to observe, analyze and theorize historical continuities which persist today, even when there is labor legislation present. As Romero (2011:195) notes, gender, race, class, and citizenship influence working conditions in all labor relations, and yet as Ray and Qayum (2009) demonstrate, the profound inequality of household labor's employment relations takes on a particular cultural character depending upon its embedded historical context. In the case of Peru, we see the colonial fantasies Spitta (2007) references play out through the racialized, gendered relations of labor subordination in the contemporary, recently regulated Peruvian home:

> Like a mirage enveloped in drizzle (*garúa*) and smog, the oligarchy's colonial fantasies disguise the disorder of the modern city. (298)

This chapter thus presents an analysis of social-inclusion legislation in a modernizing state with a persistent, dominant colonial character. Here, I argue that the formal inequality embodied in this new legislation is a *result* of this historical colonial legacy, manifested inside Lima's contemporary homes.

ON INVOKING "COLONIAL"

I understand *colonialism* as the historical process which began racial formation across Latin America that is characterized by changing relations of power
and domination and associated with specific logics of labor exploitation,
slavery, sexual violence, and genocide, among others, which continue to hold
relevance today (Lugones 2008; Quijano 2000; Stoler 2002). Contemporary
Peru reveals vestiges of coloniality which reinforce intersecting categories of
hierarchy and preserve a culturally, racially, and economically dominant elite
(Cotler 1978; Ewig 2010; Qayum 2002). My study positions the household as a
microcosm of that broader set of colonial patterns and practices.

Drawing from that understanding, I invoke the notion of *colonial* purposefully for two reasons. First, the colonial and the feudal are coterminous
in the case of Peruvian history under Spanish rule, and thus the term colonial historicizes and contextualizes the origin of the particular configuration
of Peruvian household work. While the Peruvian economy is organized in a
capitalist fashion, domestic service has been historically unregulated, contained within the private sphere, and originates from the colonial era through
the use of enslaved people and indentured servants under Spanish rule. As
O'Toole (2012) notes in her study of the making of race in colonial Peru,
African and Andean servants and workers occupied specific legal locations
within the colonial context, via shifting exclusions and categorical hierarchies, though as colonial subjects they also contested the meanings of those
legal colonial categories which had been created to contain them (2012:12). In
this way, I echo Stoler and Cooper (1997) in their understanding of colonialism as shaped through struggle. Secondly, following from that point, emphasizing the term colonial also highlights the racial difference involved in that
specific configuration—a European or European-descendant employer with
an Indigenous migrant worker. As Quijano's (2000) concept of the coloniality
of power demonstrates, racial categories and their placement within hierarchical labor arrangements remains as a modern holdover from the colonial
era. Using colonial rather than feudal, then, makes evident a pattern which
still exists in Peru.

In this way, I build upon the concept of *colonial domesticity* as a labor
regime which governs the contemporary Peruvian home. Other scholars have

worked with this concept, developing a rich literature that spans the globe both historically and in our contemporary moment. For example, as Indian women engaged in offering their bodies for international surrogacy services or seek employment as domestic workers in various countries worldwide, Swapna (2010) explores how the concept of domesticity transcends mere cultural boundaries and takes on broader transnational and global significance, encompassing issues related to space, labor, gender, and migration. Fakih (2023)'s work around colonial domesticity looks at the production of urban colonial imaginaries "that were modern and predicated on a fetish of white, European urban spaces" (645), not unlike the colonial dynamics happening in cosmopolitan Lima as opposed to other Andean regions such as the Peruvian jungle, coast, and desert. He notes how Bandung was dependent upon Indonesia's indigenous population for labor and services, though that population was kept apart and invisible, again somewhat similar to the role that household workers play in Lima as they work for elite and upper-middle-class families (Fakih 2023).

I specifically use colonial domesticity in a particular way: referencing the Peruvian context, as a labor regime, and within the institutional regulation of domestic work. Colonial domesticity as a labor regime thus shapes certain limits to democratic labor rights for Indigenous Peruvians while also revealing the pervasive logic of colonialism in modern labor relations. In the contemporary context even beyond Peru, as women engage in offering their bodies for international surrogacy services or seek employment as domestic workers in various countries worldwide, the concept of domesticity transcends mere cultural boundaries and takes on broader transnational and global significance, encompassing issues related to space, labor, gender, and migration (Swapna 2010). This Peruvian labor regime is administered through three elements—*body*, *space*, and *time*—and it is both concentrated inside of the home, where it draws on residual colonial fantasies, and diffused more broadly throughout the city which it envelopes, like the *garúa* (drizzle) and smog Spitta references (2007). I see these meaning-laden practices around body, space, and time as constructing a particular dynamic of labor relations between employer and worker, revealing a fundamental positioning of the household worker as subordinate, lesser than, and distinctly "other."

HISTORICIZING HOUSEHOLD WORK IN
COLONIAL AND CONTEMPORARY PERU

Colonial legacies of geography, gender, and race interweave to construct the industry of household labor in contemporary Peru through the continued rural-urban migration flow to the capital and within the spatial layout of Lima itself. Throughout Latin America, the colonial city was understood as a site of concentrated authority and power, a "planned monument to a particular vision of civilized life" (Restall and Lane 2011:201), and Colonial Lima, *la Ciudad de los Reyes* (the City of Kings), was no exception. As the center of consolidated power in the country and its major commercial and administrative center for the past several centuries, Lima has long been a city of divisions, hybridity, and migration where stigma remains toward those from the outward provinces migrating to Lima, usually in the form of young, Andean internal migrants working for the European-descent core as part of the normalized, holdover practice of racialized labor subordination (Blondet 1987; Boesten 2010; Mick 2011). In contemporary Peru, household labor is still performed primarily by Indigenous women from the provinces with little education and few resources who migrate to the capital in search of employment (Bunster and Chaney 1985; Boesten 2010; *La República* 2015; Mick 2011). As the center of consolidated power in the country and its major commercial and administrative center for the past several centuries, Lima has long been a city of divisions and hybridity, especially with regard to Indigenous language and cultural practices. Dating back to numerous pre-Incan civilizations, later Spanish colonial rule, and waves of immigrant populations from Japan[3] and China[4] in the nineteenth century, the city continues to boast a multi-ethnic, diverse population (Socolow 2000; Osorio 2008; Takenaka 2004).

During the nearly three-hundred-year colonial period of Spanish rule in Peru until 1824, all residents of Lima were dependent upon the lower socio-economic ethnic mixes (or *castas*), who were their Indigenous, African, and European domestic servants (Graubart 2007:18). By the start of the seventeenth century, white (Spanish) women moved out of domestic service as an occupation and Indigenous women, mestizas, Black women, and *mulatas* moved in. However, servants brought from Spain still labored in the homes of the most elite members of Spanish society, such as archbishops and viceroys (Socolow 2000:118). This pattern mirrors later Peruvian labor policy of the twentieth century, which explicitly excluded Indigenous workers from coverage and recognition, implicitly categorizing them as separate and inferior (Drinot 2011:13).

Lima—and its wealth—was therefore constructed by the labor of rural Indigenous populations, Iberian Peninsula immigrants, and African-coast-imported slaves, with colonial authorities using Indigenous and African workers differentially for strategic labor purposes (O'Toole 2012:28). The colonial ordering of Lima's design through its original 117 blocks founded in 1535 displayed a "telltale spatialization of race and power" that was organized via a racialized taxonomy. Salazar Bondy (1964) infamously described Lima's design as embodying "arithmetic without imagination" as central city lots were granted to colonial families and Indigenous Peruvians were relegated to the margins. Lima's *casta* paintings similarly denote place and material status as a result of various combinations of "racial mixing" in the city, where distance from the center of the capital spatially signaled that very marginality (Cahill 1994; Spitta 2007).

The colonial home of the sixteenth and seventeenth century in Lima reflected these divisions along race, space, and gender, as it was maintained and reproduced by the labor of Indigenous servants and slaves serving Spanish and Spanish descendants, who reinforced the family's social status. Socolow (2000) shows how elite colonial women's female servants linked the household with the urban center, while also maintaining the intimate space of the home:

> In urban settings female slaves were overwhelmingly used as domestics. Their labor was considered so essential to the running of a household that one or two female slaves were frequently included in dowries given to wealthy new brides. Slave women were also used to run errands, to carry packages, and to deliver messages. In a very real sense, slave women were used as a point of contact between protected elite women and the public space. (132)

In this sense, domestic servants were liminal as they moved between the boundary separating the two spheres of the public and private, linking the household with the urban center while also maintaining the intimate space of the home. Historically, they fell somewhere in the gray area between servant and worker, part of the family, subject to its exploitative whims, or duty-bound to a master. This "mix of tension and intimacy" (Restall and Lane 2011:164)

pervaded most urban-elite households, and domestic work is similarly ubiquitous in the contemporary Peruvian context—nearly all middle-class and upper-
class, and even those lower-middle-class and lower-class, families employ at
least one worker who either lives in her employer's home (*cama adentro*) or
who sleeps away, in her own living space (*cama afuera*).[5]

Taken together, race and geography became a way that Peruvians understood, and disliked, each other, depending upon where they lived. This
pattern continued throughout Peru's economic changes over the nineteenth
and twentieth centuries and shaped class formation within Limeño society.
In his study of white-collar workers in Lima, Parker (1998) demonstrates
how the middle class went to great lengths to socially distance themselves
from the working class. In this way, though the workers who maintained the
city's banks, schools, shops, and offices were not themselves members of the
elite, through their class boundary practices, they also helped to cement a
fixed labor hierarchy of social distinction that devalued and excluded those
identified with manual labor and household labor. Yet Peru embodies what
Vargas (1991) calls a "simultaneous mixture of historical periods," as household labor is still performed primarily by Indigenous women from the provinces who migrate to the capital in search of employment (*La República* 2015;
Mick 2011).

COLONIAL DOMESTICITY AS A LABOR REGIME

As described in Chapter 2, the first Indigenous, democratically elected president of Peru signed national household worker legislation into effect in 2003,
signifying an important grassroots victory and historical precedent after years
of organizing under political repression (Boesten 2010; Collier 1999). The law
legislates important labor rights, such as paid national holidays off, two weeks
of annual vacation, a cap on hours worked daily (eight) and weekly (forty-
eight), a twice-yearly bonus of two weeks' pay, and retirement and social security benefits. Yet many of those rights are significantly less in comparison
with other workers, who enjoy four weeks of annual vacation and twice-yearly
bonuses of four weeks' pay, for example. Other articles of the law position
workers and employers as obligated to uphold paternalistic, duty-bound tenets
of the law, however, such as the lack of coverage under the national minimum

wage, lack of a written contract, workers' obligation to diligently protect the employer's family life, and employers' responsibility to provide housing, nutrition, and education for workers. The well-known, historical precedent of sexual assault inside of the home, however, remains unaddressed by the law. Just as it was widespread in Peru and across other countries of Latin America, this potent vestige of colonial control still continues in the contemporary Peruvian home (Chaney and Garcia Castro 1989; García 2013).

In this sense, household workers' relationship to their own legal reforms is fraught in two ways: first, regarding the actual rights themselves, as they are categorically subjected to formal discrimination via many of their benefits being only *half* those of other workers; and second, through a lack of clear enforcement methods for those hard-to-come-by legally guaranteed benefits. Despite struggles to regulate the household, then, I show how the law codifies a labor regime of *colonial domesticity* enacted through three elements—*body, space*, and *time*—that heighten the insider vulnerability of Lima's domestic workers. While these categories are lived out fluidly and often overlap, here I analyze them singularly in order to reveal the dynamics of this labor relation of subordination in practice, as residual colonial fantasies limit and shape access to labor rights.

Body

Colonial fantasies are written on the body both discursively and materially through the racial ordering around nutrition, utensils, and uniforms. As Peruvian anthropologist Ernesto Vasquez del Aguila (2014) states, "Limeños not only have the dream to own a house ('*sueño de la casa propia*'), but they also have the dream to own their own *chola* ('*sueño de la chola propia*')" (30).[6] Indeed, this "covertly racialized" (Orlove 1993) colonial desire is deep in the Limeño imaginary, and magnified in blatant terms when workers are called *cholas* on the job. Soledad, who is fifty-one and from Huánuco, links the racialized discourse of her employers as well as their allocation of substandard items that were previously discarded by the family but deemed suitable for her use:

> So, we are *feitos, cholitos*, everything.[7] Because you're a housekeeper you get the torn sheet, the broken plate, the broken cup, the twisted spoon . . . You know, we should also have decent things . . . of course, not on *their*

level or the "best brand" like the employers, but in good condition. But no, *we* get the crooked spoon, a broken plate, chipped cup and bowl; that's what they give you![8]

Yet even when protesting her employer's insults, Soledad is deferential, having internalized that she is somehow less deserving ("*their* level" vs. "*we* get") than her employer's family. Those who must "do the dirty work" of maintaining impeccable order inside of the home are themselves considered "dirty" and "lesser"; they are lower in the home's racial ordering. Indigeneity marks workers as "unclean" in employers' eyes, yet simultaneously preferred to do the cleaning.[9] Speaking to quality but emphasizing quantity, Adelinda described the lack of food in her current position where she lives inside her employer's home:

> Some [employers], well, they don't give you dinner or even a snack. For instance, right now, I only have a breakfast of tea and then lunch until the following day. So you wake up at 5:30 in the morning without having had anything at night, without any fruit, without . . . just lunch, until the next day . . .[10]

Adelinda's voice trailed off as she finished describing the constant hunger she faces, and mentioned how this same employer often hosts parties for her friends, resulting in plenty of leftover food. Her employer, Carla, allows Adelinda to eat only the bread from the extra sandwiches that houseguests leave behind, but not the meat or vegetable contents. Erlinda, fifty-one years old and from Cajamarca, echoed these sentiments of being trapped and left with only substandard sustenance:

> But . . . they don't leave me anything to eat. They don't tell me if there's meat, eggs, or anything in the fridge. And if I touched it, on Sunday they ask: "I left a bit of steak there; have you touched it?" Imagine that.
>
> So, she protested a day where I ate a bit of chicken, the employer. I told her: "Señora, there was nothing to eat for lunch; I ate it." Because I stayed to wash the babies' clothes, the bedroom, the toy room, I was cleaning everything until three o'clock. She complained and said, "What have you done with the chicken?" So, from then on I didn't touch anything. She told me: "There is pasta; you could have done something with butter." What is pasta with butter? Just pasta and fry it with butter, nothing else.[11]

"What is pasta with butter?" speaks to the irony of the fact that Erlinda is expected to cook delicious, nutritious, and satisfying meals for the family, but her employer (who would most likely fire Erlinda if she served the family pasta with butter) demonstrates that she believes Erlinda to be deserving of less—less quality, less food, less nourishment, less dignity as a human being. These comments and experiences point to the deep internalization of racism which views the domestic worker as existing as a corporeal being, having the very basic human needs of food, water and proper health, and yet having no other means of recourse to address these needs while positioned inside the employer's home. Being given only soggy bread, or damaged silverware, or regarded as deserving only the torn sheets that no one else wants, or going completely "without" dinner as a consistent practice thus reveals a fundamental assertion of inferiority and subservience.

Widespread uniform usage in Lima is another form of this embodiment which restricts workers from entering upscale clubs and gyms when wearing the all-blue or all-white antiquated yet conspicuous marker of their category, different from (and less than) everyone else (*La República* 2007). Images of a household worker in a head-to-toe blue uniform or a long white apron taking her employer's son for a walk on a quiet afternoon in the middle of the upscale Miraflores neighborhood is a common sight.

Marlena, the household workers' rights advocate and lawyer from Flora Tristán, described during our conversation the disconnect she sees in Peru between what the law regulates and what it ignores by using uniforms as the visual linkage between regulation and restriction:

> With the case of *trabajadoras del hogar*—their legal rights are cut back. Openly cut back and, in reality, Peruvian society *approves* of that. They actually think that *trabajadoras* should have fewer rights. For example, household workers go with their employer's family to vacation at the beach, and can only use their uniform. Yet because of that uniform and their status, they aren't allowed in the pool area, and some can't even go onto the beach.[12]

Marlena referenced the now infamous event Operativo Empleada Audaz (Operation Brave Domestic Worker) in the wealthy beach resort sixty miles south of Lima, Asia (*La República* 2007; Weitzman 2012). There, in January 2007, over one hundred human rights activists and artists donned maids' uniforms, rushed the beach, and entered the ocean together as a collective protest against the restrictive private regulation of these beaches (Vasquez del Aguila 2014).

Similarly, Roselia relayed a story from one of her household worker law class attendees, Liliana (October 2012):

> See, there's an upscale club near my apartment, a tennis club. Liliana told me once, when she was a nanny, that she used to have to wait outside in the car while the kids were inside because the club would let her in, but inside the club, the household workers and nannies have to eat in a special place and they can't go into the pool. Even when the kids that they're watching are swimming in the pool, they can't go in, which is another issue. But the actual employers didn't want her going into the club with their kids. I don't know why. But they didn't want her going in with their kids! So, she would sit in the car and wait for them. I asked her if she would eat, because it could pass lunchtime, and she said they would leave her *galletas*; I don't know if those were crackers or cookies, but that's all she would eat.[13]

Though Liliana was entrusted with caring for the family's children, the parents were ashamed to have her be seen escorting the children inside amid the high-end clientele of this elite club. So not only can the law not fully address the concerns of workers inside the home or as they wait, hiding themselves out of sight of the exclusive club so as not to be "seen" with the children they are raising, but the law also fails to protect workers' bodies when interacting with the space outside of the home through strategically overlooking the omnipresent uniform usage in Lima.

Restrictive signs—some depicting a woman in a maid's uniform with broom in hand—continue to dot the entryways of elite social clubs throughout the city, while other signs categorize household workers as unfit to "mix" with wealthy clients, such as the Lima Cricket and Football Club reserving bathroom privileges only for guests, and the country club Villa Club Chosica, which relegates a separate service bathroom as appropriate for household workers (Perú21 2011; *La República* 2011).[14] Even when household workers are technically "allowed" to access these elite spaces, they must do so through a separate door and, once inside, they are made to wait in a spatially delineated area, a small pen of sorts in which workers cluster together. In entering this space, they transgress a racialized, gendered hierarchy symbolized by their uniforms. Peru mirrors neighboring Latin American countries in this

FIGURE 3.1 Household Worker in Uniform, Miraflores District, Lima, Peru, 2013. Source: Author.

way, as maid uniforms as a way to demonstrate possession are widespread across the region, and even seen as commonplace within countries with more progressive legislation for household workers (Blofield 2012; Casanova 2013). While uniforms do not in every case have to signify possession, they carry heavy symbolic weight in Lima due to how they are utilized to restrict women's access to certain areas and establishments within the city. In Figure 3.2, a storefront advertises the variations of household worker uniforms for sale in Miraflores.

While the household workers' law eschews any recognition of regulation of uniforms, the Peruvian Ministry of Labor and Employment Promotion (MTPE) declared penalties against employers demanding that their workers wear uniforms *outside* of the home in public space (including parks, beaches, malls, and restaurants) in 2010. "They have been stigmatized enough. Workers wearing uniforms are often subject to sexual harassment in the street. This cannot be," said the current labor minister at the time, Jorge Villasante (*Panamá America* 2009). He declared that warnings would be doled out to employers, and then second-time offenders would be fined between USD 58 and

FIGURE 3.2   Household Uniform Shop, Miraflores District, Lima, Peru, 2014. Source: Author.

USD 2,300, all based upon unannounced visits to districts throughout the city (*Panamá America 2009*). Since then, however, the MTPE has remained notoriously taciturn on the issue of uniforms.

Thus, there is a paternalistic acknowledgment of the harassment and stigmatization connected to uniforms in public space that speaks to a silent recognition of their power inside the privacy of the home. These lingering colonial practices are enshrined and embodied inside the home, yet when entering the public sphere, workers can supposedly freely cast off their markers of inequality. However, many employers still require uniform usage from their workers both in and outside of the home, and uniform shops dot the landscape of wealthy districts such as San Isidro and Miraflores, interspersed with boutiques, upscale resto-bars, spas, and other European-import shops that line the main boulevards just as do workers themselves, marked as a silent, disposable army of crisp white and blue.

This embodiment seen in treatment around food, utensils, and uniforms, hearkens to a deep sense of Limeños' historical ownership and entitlement, as reflected in Vasquez del Aguila's quote regarding the desire to "own one's own *chola*." Household workers eating off a separate plate and spoon of lower quality, set aside from the family's cutlery, signifies deep-rooted hierarchy and racialized fear around mixing and contamination with a "lower" racial group. Juana, a twenty-three-year-old household worker, discussed how her Limeña employer attributed their hierarchical positionalities as being rooted in onto-logical difference, seeing her as something "other" due to Juana's being from Huancayo, Peru. Leaning over the table in a café in San Borja, where we spoke, Juana almost whispered, "She said, 'Don't get used to nice clothes or expensive things. Get used to *how you are. You* are from the countryside." Juana pressed her fingertips to the table as she delivered the last sentence of her employer's admonishing words, "You know how people live there—so get used to that." And if other Peruvians do not know, then the uniform, which remains silently skipped over by the law, is there to visually remind them.

Space
Colonial legacies are enacted spatially inside of the home itself through archi-tectural design that limits workers' privacy, positioning them as vulnerable and sexually accessible to employers. This type of supposed access to vulner-able women within the home traces back to the historical, well-documented colonial practice of ownership and possession, when household workers were expected to sleep with the employer's son (as well as the father and/or other male relatives), often bearing their children (Bunster and Chaney 1985; Diaz Uriarte 1989; Jefferson and Lokken 2011; Rollins 1985). Equally troubling, how-ever, is the fact that the law contains no provision to counter this abuse, let alone acknowledge it.

Peruvian architect Nicolás Kisic reflects upon the moral obligations of his occupation, noting that the Peruvian National Building Regulations stip-ulate that each apartment building's floor plan, for example, should have windows to let in natural light and exterior fresh air.[15] However, many build-ings offer only a window into the laundry room (if one at all) for household workers (*Condiciones generales de diseño* 2012). Most workers' small, win-dowless rooms are a far cry from a decent standard and hearken instead to a colonial past, when the family's servant was to be cared for as a part of the estate. These *habitaciones de servicio* ("maids' rooms," or more literally, "ser-vice rooms"), where workers sleep, are built into older apartment complexes across Lima. But they are also featured in newly designed, modern buildings of the wealthy and upper-middle-class districts, though some people re-purpose these spaces (Ortiz 2012).[16] Figure 3.3, a photo of the 2010 modern, elegant, 258 m² (2,777 sq. ft.) structure, *Casa en La Planicie*, located in the wealthy district of La Molina, demonstrates the minimalist and modernist architectural style of the city's recently constructed elite homes (Ortiz 2012).

Casa en La Planicie was designed by renowned architect Juan Carlos Doblado, who studied at the Universidad de Ricardo Palma in Lima (Ortiz 2012), and in Figures 3.4a and 3.4b below, the blueprints of the second and first floors reveal the spatial layout of the home, including the location and size of the home's four bedrooms.

Finally, in Figure 3.5 below, the meager size of the service room (3.8 m², or 40 square feet), is brought into relief when spatially compared with the other bedrooms' sizes. It is comparable in size to the walk-in closet of the master bedroom, though it is located just off of the kitchen.[17] Thus, architectural practices of Lima's new apartment buildings continue to replicate geographies of inequality as they segregate the family's home from its extension, the household worker.

FIGURE 3.3 *Casa En La Planicie*, La Molina, Lima, Peru, 2010. Source: Daniela Ortiz. Reprinted with permission.

a

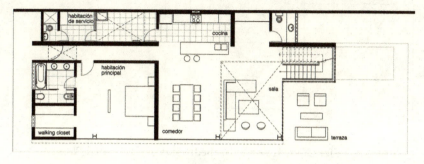

HABITACIÓN DE SERVICIO

3,8 m²

b

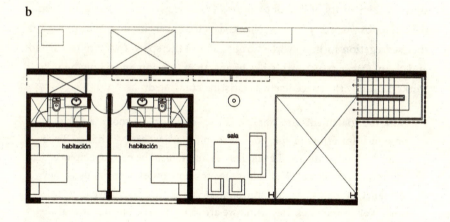

Ubicación **La Molina - Lima**   Area Construida **258 m²**   Año **2010**

FIGURE 3.4   First- and Second-Floor Blueprints of *Casa en La Planicie*.
Source: Daniela Ortiz. Reprinted with permission.

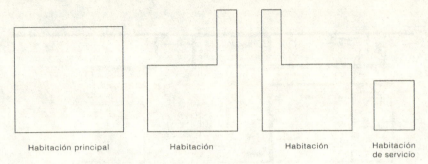

Habitación principal   Habitación   Habitación   Habitación
                                                                       de servicio

FIGURE 3.5 Size Comparison of the bedrooms of *Casa en La Planicie*.
Source: Daniela Ortiz. Reprinted with permission.

Workers who live outside of their employers' homes also face the consequences of this spatial segregation, however, as some employers don't allow live-out workers to use their toilet. A forty-seven-year-old worker from Ayacucho, Cristina, explained how she "felt like she would burst" after a twelve-hour-shift.[18] The majority of live-out workers I interviewed were expected to enter their place of work through a separate elevator or service door, signifying further segregation in how workers must access the space they are to care for and clean. Other structural issues of apartment design affect how household workers occupy the space itself, as Cristina continued:

> Now, the apartments are smaller. If they don't have a room, we change [into our uniforms] in the ironing room, that's where we change. Each time, the houses are getting smaller . . . and to use the private employer's bathroom isn't allowed. Yes, this is the problem now. In many houses, they just don't let maids use the bathroom. Because, well, they have their reasons. Well, sometimes they think we are sick with the plague, or that we are going to steal things.

Suspected theft is prevalent in discourses around trust with employers and how they understand and categorize their workers. Further employer discourses are laden with these racialized stereotypes around cleanliness and character directed at women from the *provincias*, reminiscent of racial segregation and Jim Crow legislation in the U.S. in the mid-twentieth century. This racist legislation designated specific, lesser-quality space and facilities solely to be utilized by African Americans, just as domestic workers are relegated to using certain bathrooms, sitting on certain furniture, and eating off their own plates, lest they potentially "touch" the employers' belongings, save for to clean them.

Workers occupy a contradictory positionality seen through these dual discourses around cleanliness; they are viewed as "unclean" in their employers' eyes, yet are, in fact, those preferred to do the cleaning and to regularly (re) produce cleanliness. As Mary Douglas (1966) asserts, dirt and pollution are symbolic ideas that reflect relationships around superiority, social disorder, and inequalities. These racist discourses are articulated through our understanding and our rejection of that which does not fit into our classification systems and our systematic hierarchies. She argues, "[i]n short, our pollution behavior is the reaction which condemns any object or idea likely to confuse or contradict cherished classifications" (45). These dichotomies around dirt, space, and being "out of place" characterize the contradictory positionality of household workers, then, as they are thought to be "sick with the plague" and unworthy of using the employer's bathroom, which they must bring order to and, thus, rid of dirt.

But Cristina's words also point to the changing design structure of apartments, homes, and condominiums. And as structures change, women are the ones whose bodies must be flexible as they make accommodations, such as changing into their uniforms in the laundry room or foregoing use of the bathroom during the entire day's shift. In this way, workers must map themselves onto the home, know how to take care of all the intrinsic requirements of the physical structure and the emotional well-being of those who dwell within it, and yet remain compliant and without corporeal need at the same time.

Workers also occupy a tense position inside the space of many employers' homes, as they are made aware that they are hired to work nearly all hours of the day nonstop under the watchful eye of their employer. At times this may be mediated by technology, as well. Rocío, a forty-two-year-old from Huaraz, explained to me how her employer, an owner of three casinos in the city, used camera surveillance and individual cell phones to monitor her small army of seven household workers:

> This lady took me to her house, but I couldn't get used to it because her house was full of cameras. There were cameras *everywhere*. I think they were there to keep an eye on us if we talked to each other . . . Each worker had a cell phone that the lady had given to us.

What happened was that when she gave us our cell phones, she had a big TV screen in her room, and from there she supervised any movement in the house. If she saw you stopped for a little bit, she phoned you straight away and said: "What are you doing standing there?"

So no, I couldn't get used to it. I don't know; there was no privacy.[19]

Yet workers are expected to protect the privacy of employers at all costs, as the law prescribes a moralistic sense of duty that workers must maintain privacy regarding matters inside the home.

> Article 4: *Reserva sobre la vida en el hogar*: Workers are obligated to be diligent and private about all that goes on in the employers' home, except if legally required to share that information with law enforcement.

In this way, there is both acknowledgment of the household worker as a captive audience and therefore cognizant of all that happens in the "vida e incidentes en el hogar" (the "life and occurrences of the household") and yet an expectation that she will be diligent, private, and conscientious about protecting (via silence) all that she witnesses, save for legal intervention. Workers being understood as part and parcel of the home (and therefore duty-bound to protect it) hearkens to a colonial notion of the servant as a member of the family estate. Even when they are not, however, workers are still expected to carry with them all that they witnessed while on the job, protecting the sacrosanct employer's home.

Inside employers' homes, however, workers are not protected or safe. Through these segregated living quarters, workers who live in are also spatially demarcated as *sexually other*—a captive, confined prisoner—and therefore "safe practice" with whom to sexually initiate their sons, enshrined in historical precedent (Diaz Uriarte 1989:399). Understood as being part and parcel of the employer's house, many workers are denied control over their own sexuality as they are positioned in a highly dependent and vulnerable situation vis-à-vis the employer and subjected to sexual assault, sometimes lasting for years and occasionally resulting in childbirth. As a founder of the long-standing feminist organization, Flora Tristán told me regarding the tradition of the family "using" the household worker for sex, "'Well, if it's with "*la chola*" then it doesn't matter'; this is the idea here, more or less."[20]

Diana, fifty-one, from Cusco, remembers not even having her own room when she lived in a previous employer's home, where she was expected to sleep on a cold leather Moroccan sofa, rather than a proper bed:

> I slept on the sofa, the leather sofa, with a sheet. So, at midnight I went quietly (so the boss didn't wake up) to sleep on the luxury sofa, because it was warmer. Usually around midnight, or at one a.m., I went over there to sleep on the boss' sofa, the one next to the expensive carpets, and I slept there until five in the morning. Then I got up and quickly went to the Moroccan again, because if the boss came down and saw me there all warm . . . well. Yes, I slept there silently. And I asked her for a bed, a real bed, and she didn't buy one. And so I left.[21]

In this way, Diana was quite literally positioned as exposed and structurally vulnerable inside of the home on a nightly basis, with no other form of recourse. Even listening to her describe the details of each step was exhausting, let alone trying to keep anxiety at bay over waking up late or being caught. If her employer were to discover her sleeping on the higher quality, warmer sofa, Diana knew she would face punishment or termination, and so she hurried back early each morning to the exposed, cold couch. Confronting a continual lack of restful sleep, no privacy whatsoever, and an unresponsive employer who saw her only fit to sleep on a sofa, Diana finally left to look for another job, and therefore another home. Diana's experience of her living quarters stands as a far cry from the provisions that the law, noted in the content of Article 16 below, vaguely describes as "according to the employer's economic comfort." Additionally, it is positioned as nearly last, or the sixteenth out of eighteen legal tenets in total, when for live-in workers, housing and food shape the conditions of their working lives and are of vital importance.

Article 16: *Obligaciones del empleador*: When a worker sleeps in, the employer must provide appropriate housing according to the economic comfort of the employer, as well as food.

It is telling, in fact, that the law must prescribe this responsibility on the part of the employer because if a guest or friend of the family were to be treated this way, it would most likely be an unforgivable social gaffe. Diana, as a worker, occupies a different structural position in terms of her specific role within the home as compared to a visiting family friend or casual guest, of course. Yet the fact that one would be repeatedly relegated to sleep on a cold sofa with only a sheet, forcing her to eventually appeal to her employer's kindness for a "real bed" of her own (and then to be denied said request) is indicative of the way that colonial legacies continue to reinforce the embodiment of subordination inside the space of the home.

Such an extreme lack of privacy also imprisons domestic workers in unsafe situations with other members of the household. While official statistics document that 15% of household workers have been sexually assaulted or abused, numerous interviewees and staff at the worker center report that the number is significantly higher (MTPE 2012). Roselia, the organizer for CCTH, runs a weekly radio program during which household workers from across the country call in to ask questions, learn about their rights, and resolve work issues. "Most of these accounts are not documented," Roselia told me. "Girls and women don't have anywhere else to go; they don't have any other job. It can continue for years before they are able to get out. And because they feel as though they are 'less' since they are from the interior of the country, they are trapped in a kind of nightmare."[22] Yet a noted trend of recent decades is that fewer women become pregnant as a result of rape and sexual assault from male members of the employer's family. "That's something of my parents' generation, really," Aidalinda, thirty-five, explained to me, though like much of Latin America, Peru espouses a strict, traditional sense of Catholicism and abortion remains legally prohibited.

Nataly, eighteen and from Huancabamba, glossed over a negative work experience while we talked. She described how an older boss from her past took advantage of her on the job. Nataly tapped her fingertips quickly on the table between us and tossed her long, dark hair in a low ponytail back over her shoulder as she leaned forward, looked at me squarely, and said:

> It was just a bad work experience. For instance, well, I had a boss who was a bit older and who liked to touch me. But finally, I did tell him "Stop it, that's not happening with me." I spoke up to him and told him what I thought. And the other girls in the house, yes, some allowed it . . . A little later on, the wife found out and fired them.[23]

Household workers do not always find safety in numbers in these situations, either. Ximena, twenty-six, discussed how she survived an abusive situation when she was sleeping in the servants' room with her fellow *empleada* in the bunk above her. The employer's fourteen-year-old son would enter their locked room each night with his key, she explained:

> I mean, the boy, too, got in, because when we went to bed, he had the key and he got in the room at night when we were asleep, around midnight. I slept on the lower bunk bed . . . Um, he tried to touch me, but with that kind of thing if I'm bothered, I get really angry . . . When I get angry, I don't care who he is, I tell him a few things about what he's doing that I don't really like. However, the other girl, she did let him. She let him. I didn't like it. And she said: "But I tell him, but he doesn't . . ." And he got in the room. I pretended I didn't listen. But when he tried to touch me, I said no. Other times he got in, I felt him, because I'm very alert when there are noises nearby. I felt him coming in and I look around, right? The lights are off. It's him. And he climbs up, to the upper bunk bed, the other girl's bed.[24]

Like Ximena, many household workers live in fear of sexual assault while sleeping, since their space and privacy in the home is not truly their own.

Time

Colonial practices persist in the home in salient ways around temporality, as the employer is positioned to have total control over the entire worker. However, even though the law attempts to regulate time, it encounters serious limits inside of the home, where workers are expected to be at their employer's disposal. Alma, thirty-eight, explained to me one afternoon, "When I worked at this house, see, I went to the house to clean—well, talk about people exploiting you. Supposedly, you go to the house to clean, but then they send you to do more things, to do everything. That, I don't like." Workers are simply "there"; they are positioned as the permanently available worker, ready to perform whatever task is at hand when positioned inside the home, much like a servant of colonial days.

The law regulates two elements of temporality for household workers, however—both daily, in terms of the law limiting the working day to hours, and annually, regarding holidays. Discursively, the regulation of working hours signifies an important legal shift, in that the law's language reverses the former 1970 decree's stipulation that rest time should consist of eight hours to instead stipulate eight hours of working time. Marlena, the lawyer, contextualized this important distinction:

> The old decree said that workers should rest for eight hours at least—that meant that in a twenty-four-hour day they could work for sixteen hours. At least that changed. Anyway, there are some important improvements in the decree. The important thing is that *they were recognized as workers.*[25]

Through inverting a required eight-hour night of rest with the implementation of an eight-hour workday, the law in effect deems the other sixteen hours as time belonging to the worker herself rather than at the employer's disposal.

Article 15: *Trabajo para el hogar "cama adentro"*: Workers who live in the home of the employer shall not work longer than eight hours per day and forty-eight hours per week.

While efforts to stipulate working hours for household workers who live in seem like a shift from servant to worker status, the fact that working hours should not exceed eight per day and forty-eight per week demonstrates the exceptionalism of household work, as most of the daily tasks of reproductive labor necessarily require more time since they fall into sync with the day's rhythms. Lydia, twenty-nine and from Cajamarca, explained to me the rationale behind switching from *cama adentro* to *cama afuera* as a means to protect her time as her own:

> Yes, because living in [*cama adentro*] means twenty-four hours with her, with the person you're going to care for, or help. You have no schedule! Sometimes, at night they need you, and you have to be there. Just like with a kid, at ten in the night you have to be there. So, that being said, it's better to sleep outside because then you have your own schedule, you end your workday, and you go to your own place. That's what I think.[26]

She returned to the topic later when talking about past jobs, noting that it is difficult to sleep inside because "[y]ou have no . . . you have no social life. Just weekends. You have no time for anyone. You have no time for anything. You're only dedicated to the house, you're there twenty-four hours a day in the house; you have *no time*." The irony is heavy here, as time is precisely what Lydia is giving of herself on a daily basis, and yet it feels expendable. While at work,

Lydia's time is not her own; she must physically leave her workplace in order to establish her *own* time. Lydia's comments point to the logistical difficulties involved in regulating the working hours of an employment relationship in which the worker is situated as a servant, anticipating potential employer need at any moment.

Yet for Glyceria, twenty-seven, from Ancón, a district north of Lima, choosing to live in offers her *more* time, which she negotiates rather than going through the hassle of a dangerous, costly, and lengthy commute:

> Look, in all my jobs I've stayed *cama adentro* because I'm from so far away, in Ancón. From Ancón to Surco or Angamos, it's a three-and-a-half-hour trip. So, I prefer to stay, yes [laughing lightly].[27]

For Glyceria, living in the central districts of Lima with wealthy employers *saves* her time, as she does not have to commute for seven hours a day. Similarly, Florentina explained her preference of living *cama adentro* with her employers in the upscale district of San Borja:

> Because if you're live-in, you can save money and you aren't. . . When you live outside, see, you have to get up really early and if you don't make it on time, well, the boss is upset with you. Or if you get held up at work, there's traffic and then you get delayed going back home. So, I'd rather work and live-in here. It's quieter, I can sleep, and I save up for my stuff.[28]

Florentina is not alone in wanting to avoid the experience of Lima's traffic, as commuting is not an easy or calm process in the capital. Lima's transit is highly unregulated, and its central avenues are choked with speeding taxis and buses that spew thick clouds of black smoke and a near-constant cacophony of competing horns. They also rack up frequent, serious accidents, to the point where Waze's 2016 Global Driver Satisfaction Index ranked Lima 169 out of 186 metropolitan areas, and an *El Comercio* (2017) article points out a whopping 245 accident-prone locations to be avoided throughout the city (Waze 2016). Yet regardless of the long, loud, and potentially dangerous commute, Lydia and other workers prefer to live outside as they value the freedom to disengage from work and physically leave their employer's home.

Diana, who slept on the expensive sofa secretly in the night, explained to me how she understands the working hours actually required to maintain a household. Justifying the need for compensation when putting in extra time, she likened herself to a worker in a social setting, such as a factory or office, rather than in the individualized, isolated setting of the home as she invoked the language of "shifts."

> It's a lot of exploitation, and frankly, the job's hours never end! The law should stipulate that they pay us 750 soles [USD 277.40] for 8 hours, like for other workers. If I worked 16 hours, my boss should be paying me 1500 soles [USD 554.70]. No? A double shift! Yes, double the time, but sometimes the boss doesn't recognize that.[29]

Similarly, Laura, sixty-four, discussed the impossibility of regulating time due to the long duration and routine of the working day inside of the home. Distancing herself by speaking in the third person, Laura mentioned the generalized employer's near-constant refusal to acknowledge what they are "getting" from their worker, whose time is, by default, structured around their employer's hours. "Well, first of all when they're live-in workers, they are the first to get up, and the last to go to bed," she explained. Shifting to a passive voice when discussing the actual labor of those live- in workers, yet not acknowledging workers themselves as the ones doing the actual work, Laura explained, "*Everything*, the employers get *everything*: everything's clean, the house is clean, the lunch is made."[30] She then included herself in her next statement as the general "you" and made a claim regarding what employers need to change: "More than anything, employers have to be more conscious. There might be only two or three employers out of one hundred who are really conscious. The rest, well, sometimes they shout at you; you do *all* the duties and they have the nerve to shout at you!"

Though the law attempts to put significant limits on the working hours inside of the home, it does so in a way that is practically unfeasible for both parties and can potentially cause extra conflict between them. On the employer's side, their requests and demands align with the daily rhythms and patterns of the life of the household, which naturally extend from the early morning and well into the night. For the live-in worker, however, who is first to get up and last to go to bed, she must continue to perform those tasks required of her that extend beyond a regulated number of hours, or else fear being shouted at, rebuked, and possibly dismissed.

The other element of temporality is seen through struggles around national holidays, vacation time, and twice-yearly bonus pay. Employers are slow and reluctant to come to terms with household workers' legally granted, and paid, time off, especially since the 2003 law extended these benefits significantly from the previous decree's language.

> Article 11: *Trabajo en días feriados*: Household workers have the right to paid holidays off in the private sector. If they do agree to work on those holidays, they will be paid time-and-a-half, or an extra 50% of their salary added to their daily salary.
>
> Article 12: *Vacaciones*: Household workers have the right to 15 days of annual vacation.

While the earlier 1970 decree only granted Christmas Day and July 28, Peruvian Independence Day, as proper holidays for household workers, the 2003 law includes all seven of the national holidays. Household workers' vacation time is fifteen days per year, though other recognized workers' time off is twice as much, at thirty days annually. Workers' legal right to enjoy paid holidays gestures toward a recognition of their labor as "real work," worthy of scheduled relaxation and leisure time, and yet employers do not always abide by this part of the law or understand its extension to workers. Erlinda explained her Italian employer's reaction to her attempt to exercise her right to the Christmas holidays, signifying the deep ontological chasm between employers ("us") and workers ("you"):

> Because, during the holidays, the man said: "Ah really? Those aren't holidays for you. Those are holidays for us," he said. "Not for you. You have to work as per usual."[31]

Mirroring Erlinda's experience, two-thirds of household workers across the country noted that they did not, in fact, receive the extra compensation for working holidays, the time-and-a-half pay that Article 11 specifies (Bastidas Aliaga 2012:97). This sense that holidays are a fundamentally classed benefit, and that household labor is considered so naturalized within the home that workers are therefore undeserving of time off, is telling, as is the unenforceable nature of this newly granted legal right.

Yet Alma, a forty-four-year-old from Iquitos, told me that she noted the change in benefits in a profound way, akin to self-realization:

> The changes that have happened since the law? Yes, there have been a lot. Today, for instance, in regards to health, okay? You have health insurance. Today you get paid holidays and vacation. Now, there is a contract in which they consider you a worker with insurance, working for retirement; they pay you for the years you've worked there; you're given yearly extra payments, vacations . . . *you're not like before*.[32]

Having access to these benefits, such as health care, retirement, and vacation made Alma feel considered *as a real worker*. While her job duties remained the same, she felt different—"not like before"—due to acknowledgment of her labor inside the home. There was, as we see, a real attempt to see domestic workers as *workers* through the law. Their right to enjoy paid holidays gestures toward a recognition of their work as real work in the eyes of the law, and therefore work that should be rewarded with a set of privileges and benefits including scheduled relaxation and leisure time in the form of vacation. However, only a paltry 3% of household workers surveyed confirmed that at least once in their working lives they had received this benefit of paid vacation (Bastidas Aliaga 2012:98). A more recent report by the ILO (2022) estimated that between 15 and 22% of domestic workers were likely to receive paid annual vacations, so there may be a general increase over the last 12 years.[33]

And yet their vacation is 15 days per year, only half of the 30 days granted to all other recognized workers annually. The same discriminatory principle applies to the law's language around *gratificaciones*, or their twice-yearly bonus pay administered in July and December, as noted below in Article 13.

> Article 13: *Gratificaciones*: Household workers have the right to bonus pay twice a year. Bonus pay is 50% of their monthly salary, paid twice yearly—once in July for Peru's Day of Independence, and once in December for Christmas.

While other recognized Peruvian workers receive a full month's salary administered twice annually, domestic workers are entitled to *half* of that amount, or two weeks' salary twice a year. However, 85% of workers surveyed across Peru report not receiving any amount of bonus wage (Bastidas Aliaga 2012:99).[34] We see, then, how domestic workers' benefits are half of those granted to other types of workers to begin with, which amounts to a fundamental assertion of lower status that shapes the dynamic of their employment relationships. Yet even with this provision extending coverage to household workers, the resounding majority still do not actually collect any bonus pay.

Drawing boundaries around time inside of the home, then, whether for rest, leisure, paid holidays, or supposed bonuses, is nearly impossible when workers are positioned at the central core of the household. There, they are privy to the life of the family and responsible for supporting all of its moving parts, which in practice often do not easily align with the law's attempts to regulate and organize it. The resultant consequences for workers often obligate them to work longer and more erratic hours. To this point, a 2014 study of Lima's household workers found that 41% of those who live in worked for more than eighty hours per week, demonstrating the continuity of servitude status from the past and the new challenges present in efforts to regulate the temporal aspect of household labor (*El Comercio* 2014).

NEGLECTED BY THE LAW

The more blatantly discriminatory features of the Peruvian Household Workers' Law also pertain to what it does *not* say, such as its failure to require a written contract or extend coverage of the national minimum wage to household workers.

Article 3: *Celebración del contrato de trabajo*: The work contract may either be in verbal or written format.

Article 5: *Monto de la remuneración*: The wage rate is to be decided by mutual agreement. The employer is obligated to pay for food and/or housing for the worker, according to the economic level of the employer. Housing and food should not be considered part of the salary.

A verbal contract clearly reinforces the internal power relations of the home as it benefits the employer, who may change the terms of employment at will. And the law stipulates that a wage is only required to be "of mutual accord," which favors the employer and whatever amount they think they can pay or deem appropriate to offer. This language thus frequently creates a situation such that young migrant girls from the provinces work for extremely low (and sometimes no) wages in the capital, similarly to when they worked as colonial servants in the past (Socolow 2000). Young domestic workers discussing this experience of exploitation was remarkably common during my interviews, as Camila, twenty-six and from Chimbote, elaborated:

> And when you come to Lima from the province, people here basically abuse you. They pay you whatever they like, and because you didn't make that much money in another city, this amount of money you get paid seems like a lot. But if you're observant, the prices are higher, and they go up. Everything goes up, everything's expensive, and that money isn't enough. It just isn't enough.[35]

A comprehensive study with household workers living in 11 of the largest cities across Peru found that 92% of household workers surveyed reported earning less than the then national minimum wage of PEN 750 per month (in 2012), the equivalent of approximately USD 260.[36] Broken down more specifically, 40% of workers earned between PEN 401 and PEN 675 (USD 148.30 and USD 249.60), 35% earned between PEN 251 and PEN 400 (USD 92.80 and USD 147.90), and 16% earned less than PEN 250 (USD 92.50). A study across Lima from 2014 also attests to the prevalence of low wages as it found that 85% of the country's household workers earn less than the minimum wage, with their average salary at roughly PEN 457, or approximately USD 180 (*El Comercio* 2014).[37]

Because the language neglects any mention of a defined salary or minimum wage, then, it thus easily avoids the awkward position of having foisted too much economic pressure upon employers. It also deftly steps aside from the weight of substantive conversations about the social and economic value of work performed in the home. Thus, without a minimum wage setting the base foundation upon which to build upward, domestic workers are regarded as less than deserving of what other workers are entitled to. The law slips into an understanding of domestic work as not real work and of the domestic worker herself as merely an extension of the household, whose basic needs of nutrition and shelter must be sustained via the paternalism, and benevolence, of the employer. In this way, then, the law grants certain rights to household workers, yet codifies a labor regime of *colonial domesticity* when lived inside of the home, as those rights encounter the resistance of residual colonial practices that shape the home to perpetuate the past by perpetuating the present.

The 2003 law regulates household labor relations, and yet symbolically, it also creates an understanding of how the home itself should be organized and structured, much like the colonial home of the past. Colonial domesticity, in practice, is a labor regime through which employment relations inside of the home construct a subordinate worker. In Lima, within this "profoundly antidemocratic sociality" (Spitta 2007:298), the space of the home is rife with lingering colonial fantasies that hearken to a distinct historical moment characterized by gendered and racialized subordination through labor relations. The law confers and limits labor rights for household workers; they are rebuked, like Juana by her employer, to "get used to how you are."

We see, then, how household workers and their employers' labor relations, connected through the "link" of the employment relationship by law, are fraught in relationship to that very law. I find this both through the nature of the legal rights themselves—such as what the law avoids acknowledging or regulating, including employer's privatized and unregulated behavior around sexual assault and uniform usage, or when granting discriminatory rights that are half those of other workers—and though challenges of enforcement inside of the protected space of the home. Many of those labor rights are reduced to half of those accorded to other workers or, in the case of a standardized minimum wage, completely absent.

The decision to even mention contracts signals recognition of their legal heft within the employment relationship itself. However, the law's quick willingness to remain ambivalent regarding the precise form said contract takes, either verbal or written, is highly contradictory and in practice serves to codify an already unequal set of labor relations. While 64% of workers confirm that they have a work contract, 87% of those contracts are, unsurprisingly, verbal (Bastidas Aliaga 2012:94). This chapter has drawn out examples of this separate, and significantly less equal, labor law in practice through workers' own responses and reactions, revealing the way it governs practices of the home through what it legislates and through what it neglects. In its particular set of contradictions, limits, and failures, then, we see how household workers are regarded differently than most other Peruvian workers, and how the law heightens the specific kind of insider vulnerability that workers experience there. In this way, the law grants certain rights to household workers, yet codifies a labor regime of *colonial domesticity* when lived inside of the home, as those rights encounter the resistance of residual colonial practices that shape the home to perpetuate the past by perpetuating the present.

This chapter has shown how colonial domesticity continues to marginalize Indigenous women household workers, and efforts to regulate domestic work through law reveal problems with the inequitable treatment of household workers. Hearkening to Simone de Beauvoir's (2015) critique, then, this chapter shows that in fact, colonial domesticity's labor practices around body, space, and time also serve to perpetuate the past, one that is etched with colonial fantasies which continue to limit legal reforms and labor rights for those who work inside of the home.

Furthermore, the unenforceable nature of these newly won labor rights reflects a continuous logic and practice of coloniality in the private sphere, allowing us to contextualize the importance of household-labor protections and also understand the devaluation of other occupational sectors, as well. This focus on historicizing the organizational structure of labor within the home holds profound comparative implications for other contexts, such as how the following chapters explore the racialized legacies that shape immigration law and labor rights in New York's homes.

This analysis contributes to a growing recognition of contradictions inherent to the practice of paid domestic work stemming from modernity, colonialism, servitude, legal change, and worker rights in Latin America and elsewhere (Ray and Qayum 2009; Carrillo 2014; Feliu 2014). In this way, the Peruvian case makes clear that while efforts to regulate labor rights attempt to democratize the space of the home, colonial domesticity continues to sanction the private sphere through practices around body, space, and time, ultimately demonstrating both the political possibilities and the very real challenges of carving democratic legislation out of a complex colonial past. Emphasizing the colonial ordering of the racialized subordination in the home and its lingering effects upon democratic labor legislation for this distinctive kind of devalued labor reveals both the continuity from the colonial era and a new analytical lens through which to understand the law's lack of purchase.

FOUR FROM SLAVERY TO SERVICE

Continuing Struggles to Regulate Domestic Worker Rights in the United States

Domestic workers have been more prominently featured in the American popular imaginary recently than in years past, thanks in part to films such as 2011's *The Help*. It certainly brought attention to the stories of African American domestic workers' exploitation and some everyday resistance efforts in the South during the civil rights era, though many have argued that this kind of media attention is flawed in a number of respects. First, it continues to propagate a narrative that too heavily highlights white women as purely benevolent rather than as actors benefitting from their own participation in racial subjugation, as did Childress' work (1956).

Additionally, it leaves out the voices of African American domestic workers telling their own stories since they are filtered through the young white journalist's book, as Nadasen's (2015) important historical account of previously unacknowledged African American domestic workers attempts to correct. Finally, some critiques have found an embedded nostalgia for the antebellum past expressed through films like *The Help* which paint those struggles in an optimistic light and concentrate racist attitudes in one or two key characters, while the white majority shrugs its shoulders. While entertaining and well-acted, this mainstream media portrayal did little to challenge the continuing racial anxieties and issues alive and well in the United States, and least of all those that continue to shape domestic worker employment relations today.

I introduce this film as a frame for what this and the following chapter attempt to move away from—the telling of a simplistic, saccharine story of a huge win for domestic workers who previously had nothing. There is a much stronger narrative of decades of domestic workers' on-the-job resistance practices, maintaining personal dignity, and organizing for labor rights that I will only briefly delve into here.[1] Yet I also mention *The Help* to historically situate the practice of domestic work in the U.S. context as drawing a continuing parallel with slavery, following others (Nadasen 2015; Tizon 2017). This connection stems from my main argument that focuses on the historical organization of labor inside of the home, and it also relates to the continuity of the unquestioned, supposed privacy of the household that remains to this day. Years after slavery's official end, then, seeing the patterns continue through racialized exclusions of domestic workers by law helps to draw attention to the nuances that films such as *The Help* glossed over.

African American household workers organizing in the 1960s also referred to slavery-related stories, anecdotes, and themes as organizing narratives (Nadasen 2015). In my interview with Onika that I discuss in Chapter 5, she did the same when describing domestic workers waiting on the auction block in Harlem, which also draws a visual parallel to Diouana being chosen by her French employers in the opening scene of *La Noir de* . . . Furthermore, prominent leaders within the global domestic worker movement currently invoke the direct language of slavery and situate legislative wins as a powerful way to distance domestic workers from those previous labor confines. Celebrating in Geneva at the International Labour Organization's passing of Convention 189, the first international set of labor standards for the industry of domestic work, South African former domestic worker and longtime staunch activist and leader Myrtle Witbooi (1947–2023) reflected, "Our dream became a reality, and we are free—slaves no more, but workers" (Boris and Fish 2014).

Yet stepping back allows us to grasp the magnitude of this parallel between slavery and domestic service enduring over the last century and a half. From

1870 to 1940, after controlling for changes in census categories and definitions, domestic service was the leading occupation for women workers in the United States (Van Raaphorst 1988:4).[2] For those seventy years, however, white U.S.-born and foreign-born domestic workers fared much better even in the face of occupational sexism than their fellow Black U.S.-born and foreign-born domestic workers. In the early decades of the twentieth century, Black workers migrated to New York from the Southern U.S. as well as from Caribbean countries, Mexico, Cuba, and Central America (Gray 1993:6).

Van Raaphorst found that by 1930, 75% of all Black workers who migrated to New York from the South remained concentrated in New York City, with 80% of those workers living in Harlem around the time that the Harlem Renaissance began. In the twenties and thirties, Black women faced little competition with Black male counterparts in New York's industry of domestic work, as men found jobs as chauffeurs, valets, butlers, and cooks, while women were hired into homes that employed one servant who performed various labor duties (Gray 1993:20).

However, this soon shifted with the rise of "slave markets," or street corners where U.S.-born Black and immigrant Caribbean and African domestic workers were forced to seek work. As Gray (1993) explains:

> Unlike native and foreign-born white domestics, black women, in response to their situation, had to resort to standing on street corners in white neighborhoods and waiting for employers to come by and hire them directly off the street. These "slave markets" as they came to be called, were the most overt manifestation of the mistreatment of black females. (15)

In this way, Black domestic workers were subject to continued labor patterns that have also shaped the slavery economy of the South. As mentioned earlier, in Glymph's (2008) focus on the plantation household and its gendered and racialized social relations, she argues that there was nothing private about the employer's home for the slaves and servants who labored there (43). She also extends that analysis from the plantation to the contemporary "domestic arena" as she points to the fact that labor is carried out in the home as its defining characteristic. For Glymph (2008), when the "work of the household is carried out by non-family members" is what matters, regardless of if those workers are wage laborers or enslaved people, and that continues to hold meaning for the home as a site of labor well beyond the historical period when slavery was widespread in the U.S. (43).

Popular white labor leaders of New York City at the time, largely immigrants themselves, contributed to Black women being channeled into domestic service. Feminist socialist Rose Schneiderman, famous for her years of organizing and insisting that women workers "want bread, and roses, too" in one of her rallying speeches, contributed to the occupational racism already structuring Black women's labor market experiences. Schneiderman, then-president of the Women's Trade Union League, restricted Black women's entry into the garment trades, stating that "factory work requires too much grind for the colored girl who was not willing to endure hard work" (Grey 1993:21). Black domestic workers had to combat heavy stigmas and limited job scope, though as discussed in Chapter 1, World War II brought about new opportunities for white women to leave domestic service and therefore created somewhat more bargaining power in the hands of Black domestic workers. Numbers declined from one-third of all U.S. women working in domestic service in 1930 to only one-fifth by 1940, and agitation from newspapers, social critics, worker associations, and even the *New York Times* brought down the street-corner bargaining zones, though in the following decades they resurfaced sporadically.

RACIALIZED LEGAL HISTORIES: NEW DEAL CONVERSATIONS CONTINUE

Historically unregulated or under-regulated by federal and state labor laws, domestic work as an industry has never really fit the typical categorical distinctions of American employment regulation. As early as 1900, the New York City Legal Aid Society documented that 2,000 domestic workers sought legal assistance in claiming wages from employers (Van Raaphorst 1988:70). And in 1906, New York, Massachusetts, Indiana, and Nebraska prohibited women from working at night in a paternalistic grand gesture, but this limit on working hours excluded domestic workers (Van Raaphorst 1988:68–69). New Deal legislation continued to purposefully restrict the rights of domestic workers, as under Section 2(3) of the National Labor Relations Act (NLRA) of 1935, domestic workers, day laborers, and agricultural workers (among other categories) are excluded from the guarantee of the right to collectively organize (29 U.S.C. § 152(3); Feldacker 1999:59).[3]

May's (2011) historical work on New York State labor reform points to the need to revise the commonsense understanding of parts of this story, however.

She shows how the domestic workers' legislative exclusion in the U.S. stemming from racist Southern democrats' decision to block domestic workers' inclusion in the Fair Labor Standards Act of 1938 is true, and yet there is more to the story. While New York in the 1930s was what May calls the "vanguard of labor reform," she also notes, however, that labor reformers had advocated for distinct, occupational-based reform agendas for domestic workers dating back to the nineteenth century that finally came to a head in the late 1920s and early 1930s (4). After a final two-year legislative battle, these earlier efforts to pass a state-level law for household workers were denied in the 1930s in New York State (4). So even in a Northern, non-Jim Crow legislative state, domestic workers were legally excluded.

Looking at the details of these legislative decisions more in depth, legal scholars (Campbell 2014; Perea 2011) have shown how New Deal labor legislation drafted in the early 1930s featured a statutory exclusion of agricultural workers and domestic workers, which was racially motivated to restrict the labor rights of Black workers. This strategic and intentional move, including the categorical exclusion of agricultural and domestic employees, was well understood as a race-neutral proxy for excluding Black people from basic labor protections and state compliance. Just as Campbell (2014) argues that more recent race-based exclusionary law in Arizona is not, in fact, a contemporary phenomenon but rather an extension of a historical practice, the 2010 law for domestic workers is the product of exclusionary practices over the last century. Its weak final iteration only follows that pattern.

In fact, New York Democratic Senator Robert Wagner's definition of *employee* in the 1935 Wagner Act was initially quite expansive. He stated the law should extend the right to organize and collectively bargain to:

> "Any person employed by an employer under any contract of hire, oral or written, express or implied, including all contracts entered into by helpers and assistants of employees, whether paid by employer or employee, if employed with the knowledge, actual or constructive, of the employer." (Perea 2011:119)

Yet during Legislative hearings on the bill, other senators raised concerns about how the language would affect farmers and individual housewives. As then drafted, the bill would potentially apply to a farmer or a housewife who employed two persons on the farm or in the home, respectively, so argued the opposition (Perea 2011:119). The bill was thus referred back to the Senate Committee on Education and Labor, which narrowed the definition of employee:

> "The term 'employee' shall include any employee . . . but shall not include any individual employed as an agricultural laborer, or in the domestic service of any family or person at his home." (Perea 2011:120)

The bill was also amended to apply only to employers with ten or more employees. Thus, while no explicit mention of race occurred during these particular discussions of this section of New Deal legislation, through these debates, Congress carefully legislated *around* the two largest occupational sectors comprised of Black workers, agricultural (those in the field) and domestic (those in the home) employees. Wagner's attempt to appeal to his constituency of working-class New Yorkers and the resistance that met that effort, then, effectually continued a pattern of historical exclusion for both domestic and agricultural workers that continues eighty years later for domestic workers.

Domestic workers thus utilized alternative organizing strategies to maintain standards and dignity in the work itself, especially against the racial and class power wielded by employers in New York (Nadasen 2015). In 1938, Dora Jones, President of New York's Domestic Workers Union, listened to a distraught Corrine Washington, a former tobacco factory worker who had recently been recruited from the South to migrate to New York as a live-in domestic worker (May 2011:146). Fired suddenly for asking her employer for a quarter to go to the movies, Washington found herself alone in a new city without resources or a place to sleep, as her employer had even deducted recruitment agency fees from her already meager pay. She turned to the union for assistance, and Jones began noticing a pattern emerging throughout the city's population of domestic workers.

Armed with a representative from the National Association for the Advancement of Colored People (NAACP) and Washington's testimony, Jones voiced these concerns to Mayor Fiorello LaGuardia, appealing to the New Deal-era regulatory politics of LaGuardia to help defend Black domestic workers' wages, working conditions, and industry share. She touched on a number of issues—the false promises of lucrative employment in New York made to trafficked Southern migrants, new migrants' wages depressing those of the unionized domestic workers, and employers' temperamental terminations stranding new migrants without homes, which positioned these young women as the "charge of the City of New York" (May 2011:147). The following year, LaGuardia wrote letters to Southern government officials and federal law enforcement officers, notifying them of unlicensed agents trafficking young women into domestic work in New York. The tensions in Jones' plea—both defending her union members' employment standards while also pointing to the uniquely vulnerable position of Southern migrants and the undercutting of wages—shaped a public debate about rights that continues to ring true in contemporary New York City. Workers unify across ethno-racial groups to speak out against the human trafficking of their fellow workers, and yet they also defend and strengthen their particular ethnic community boundaries in so doing.

Nadasen (2015) finds that Black domestic workers in New York were deeply rooted in activism throughout the decades that followed, including the civil rights movements and social protest of the 1950s and 1960s, though traditional accounts have skirted over their organized work as social actors and agents of social change. Legislative efforts came to fruition when Harlem Democrat assemblyman Mark T. Southall sponsored a 1964 bill intended to cover the 126,000 domestic workers at the minimum wage rate of USD 1.25 per hour (Martin and Segrave 1985:128). However, then-Governor Nelson Rockefeller vetoed the bill while on vacation in Venezuela that July, stating that it would "place a hardship on housewives if they had to keep detailed wage and hour records for a six-year period" (1985:129). He also purportedly feared that housewives would be arrested for violating the terms of the bill by failing to keep those detailed records, an ironic concern considering the United States' infamously weak labor law and enforcement process.

Similarly to the Wagner Act, the Social Security Act (1935) and the Fair Labor Standards Act (1938) also initially excluded domestic workers, though both have (albeit gradually) sought to address this racialized exclusion. The process of extending coverage at the national level to domestic workers was a slow and reluctant one (1951 and 1974, respectively), though currently, the National Labor Relations Act still maintains its exclusionary language (Perea 2011). The Occupational Safety and Health Act (OSHA) of 1970 also stubbornly clings to its 1975 decision to omit domestic workers from its protections "as a matter of policy," (29 C.F.R. § 1975.6; Castro 2008).[4] Domestic workers in New York State won minimum wage inclusion in 1972, however, when Bronx State assemblyman Seymour Posner used survey data from the Department of Labor to demonstrate that the state's domestic workers earned an annual salary of USD 1,108, or roughly USD 0.50 per hour. This wage was significantly less than New York's USD 1.85 minimum wage at the time, and with this final push, New York's domestic workers gained coverage under minimum wage laws (Bapat 2014:58; Martin and Segrave 1985:128). Several other landmark legislative shifts have occurred since then, including the 2013 inclusion of home health-care workers in protections of the Fair Labor Standards Act and several state domestic worker laws.

However, I find a racialized exclusion still continues through the Domestic Worker Bill of Rights. Just as previously, the origins of the law-making itself revealed its deliberate intentions to legislate around and away from the population who formerly comprised the majority of domestic workers—Black women; I argue that the exclusion has shifted to neglect regulations and protections for the overwhelming majority of those who do the work today—immigrant women. Chapter 5 will address this point directly and show why it matters that a long-sought historic law, when finally attempting to regulate the work on a statewide level, continues this pattern of racialized exclusion. While the law initially avoided including domestic workers because of the specificity of the industry and those who do the work, when it finally attempted to regulate their work, it failed to recognize and account for the specificity of those who do the work—immigrant women workers—inside of the home, which results in the production of outsider vulnerability.

THE WORK OF THE LAW: OVERCOMING PERSONALISM AND ACHIEVING RIGHTS

Yet, what work do we, and should we, expect from the law? In her study of South African domestic workers transitioning into democracy, Ally (2009) calls apartheid-era labor relations in South Africa's domestic worker sector a "toxic cocktail of informality, personalized dependence on employers, and the failure of recourse to state institutions" (94). She provides rich insights into the complexities of domestic worker legislation in practice, demonstrating how in the South African case, workers were highly mobilized in national unions and yet, in what Boris calls a "paradox of independence" in the aftermath of the passage of labor law, they become demobilized and weakened.

Thus, Ally (2009) argues that modernizing and formalizing rights for domestic workers *as workers* firmly tied them to social positions of little respect in the political economy of reproductive labor (190). More importantly, however, she emphasizes that domestic workers' lives are not greatly improved under this legislation not only due to a lack of enforcement or compliance, but also due to the "simultaneously embodied logics" of state power at play:

> In South Africa, the embedding of paid domestic work so deeply in racialized ideologies of servitude shaped a historical organization of paid domestic work that severely restricted workers' capacities to develop more formalized and contractual relations of work. (101)

At its best, the New York Bill of Rights attempts to formalize and recognize an industry which for too long has been susceptible to the misgivings of strategic personalism, as workers have been left in a highly unequal, vulnerable employment relationship to negotiate and navigate for themselves. However, workers themselves have consistently advanced collective efforts to secure rights, benefits, and protections, resulting in a series of key victories and challenges throughout the last century. In line with recent literature that revisits the history of New York City's industry of domestic work, then, current organizing is very much part of a tradition of struggle, as domestic workers have long organized to publicize, organize, and improve the industry (May 2011; Nadasen 2015).

Implicit in the theorizing around paid domestic work in the home is the argument that replacing affectively based employment relations with bureaucratized, contractual ones will improve the conditions of domestic work. Some of this scholarship has explored what this labor arrangement looks like when including the addition of home-service agencies, which shift the dynamic to a third party to orchestrate cleaning a number of houses, minimizing the interpersonal dynamics of that relationship. Mendez (1998) finds that household-service agencies do not, in fact, greatly shift the dynamics of inequality inherent in the work itself, and actually serve to reinforce the gendered, ethno-racialized hierarchy that characterizes the industry. In this way, working women of color are still subjected to the discriminatory elements more often associated with personalized domestic work, as agency managers utilize gendered and racialized ideologies in their relationships with workers to profit off of their labor.

Moreover, Mendez (1998) notes that drawing upon the personal relationship with their employers may offer domestic workers the opportunity to negotiate higher wages, benefits, and working conditions. However, this *strategic personalism* (Hondagneu-Sotelo 2001) is highly individualized rather than collective, and in enacting personalism in their relationships with agency managers, workers may even invoke particular stereotypes around race and gender identity. In this way, while workers socialize and talk collectively through the organizational structure of service agencies, elements that characterize structural vulnerability persist.

So, while Ally (2009) and others have shown the efforts to standardize and formalize domestic work can ideally lead to a desirable outcome in some political contexts, historically, we know that these attempts do not necessarily translate into more equitable working conditions. For example, white housewives in El Paso, Texas, organized into the Association for Legalized Domestics (ALD) in 1953, laying out a twelve-point set of provisions regarding wages, working conditions, length of employment, and other regulations in order to bring domestic workers from Juárez across the border as "non-immigrants" in order to serve a so-called labor shortage. The ALD reached out to the Immigration Naturalization Service (INS) for assistance in instituting this plan, called the "bracero maid" contract, which met great resistance from domestic workers in both Juárez and El Paso, who pointed out housewives' desire to underpay "*Mexicana*" workers (Chang 2001; Ruiz 1987).

The bracero maid program never reached fruition, however, as the U.S. Department of Justice failed to recognize it. Yet the ALD sheds light on the contemporary industry of domestic work in New York City in two important ways. The first is that it visibly demonstrates the long-standing interconnectedness of immigration restriction and control with the industry of domestic work, and its tension with regulation. Secondly, the highly specific nature of the ALD's twelve provisions, while blatantly racist and discriminatory, when taken together, paint a much more dynamic portrayal of the labor process of domestic work than the Domestic Workers' Bill of Rights. Thus, while the bracero maid program clearly served the self-interest of middle-class white Texan employers at the expense of *Mexicana* (and Texan) maids, and shows how these employers made exploitative use of Mexican domestic workers, including requiring only immigrant workers to present a reference attesting to their moral character and abide by other paternalistic rules, its detailed attention to benefits such as standardizing and regulating time off, living accommodations, and hiring and firing procedures are notable. Similarly to Romero's (1992) finding, then, more structured and formal labor relationships around domestic work do not necessarily raise industry standards, and these efforts do not fully diminish the intrinsic inequalities present within the relations of domestic work (1992). This speaks to the embedded contradiction of the work itself, as the move toward modernizing domestic work often results in placing the burden of negotiating terms, intimacy, standards, and power upon the worker herself.

Women of color and immigrant women have historically waged struggles for reform, dignity, and labor protections for domestic workers, though victories have not come easily due to the difficulties of organizing and overcoming industry-specific obstacles (Coble 2006; May 2011; Nadasen 2009, 2015; Van Raaphorst 1988). Early comparative work between New York and Los Angeles pointed to the class and racial inequalities that affected the privatized relationship between employer and worker, showing how parents chose "difference" or "similarity" when selecting workers to care for their children (Wrigley 1995). And while other recent scholarship has focused on organizing efforts for domestic worker law and resultant successes (Boris and Nadasen 2008; Boris and Klein 2012; Goldberg 2014), little of this work has examined how domestic worker law succeeds or fails in addressing the specificity of the industry itself, such as the diverse backgrounds of the workers, the location of work in the home, and the personal relationships found there.

However, the first successful attempt to regulate the highly diverse and segmented industry of domestic work in New York has fallen into the same trap as the literature Glenn (1992) critiques when it universalizes the women—largely female and immigrant—who do this kind of labor. In Glenn's formative analysis of the racialized hierarchy of service work, she analyzes the bulk of Marxist feminist contributions to the study of domestic work, arguing that by positing gender as the basis of assignment for reproductive labor tasks, that work is thus assumed to be universally experienced by women. Yet, Glenn and others (Chang 2001; Colen 1995; Hondagneu-Sotelo 2001; Rollins 1985; Romero 1992) show that this is far from the case. Hence, though the law attempts to extend labor rights to domestic workers in New York City, it presupposes them to share a common social position by creating a universal domestic worker, thereby leaving ethno-racial, citizenship, and other divisions between domestic workers unspoken. This outcome holds significant consequences especially for immigrant domestic workers, a structurally vulnerable population.

Thus, despite the law's existence, today's domestic workers in New York employ similar strategies to what Bonnie Thornton Dill (1988) found in her research decades ago as they navigate the life of the home. What is important to note here is that the key difference from Dill's study of nearly forty years ago is that the industry is now regulated. Yet relevant consistencies specific to the nature of the work and its relationships in the household remain.

Dill's foundational study showed how U.S.-born Black domestic workers in New York and Philadelphia constructed buffers between themselves and their employers, relied upon the strength of their Black community ties, and managed the employer-employee relationship in such a way so as to maintain self-worth. To improve one's status as a domestic worker, it was about "making the job good yourself," Dill found (1988:33). This chapter points to the need for the domestic worker law to move beyond a universal understanding of the industry by reconsidering both the specificity of the home as a site of labor and the divergences of the domestic worker population along ethno-racial, citizenship-based, and other lines of distinction.

NEW YORK CITY AS PALIMPSEST: LAWS REWRITTEN ON THE SPACE OF THE CITY

As Glenn (1992) points out, an ethno-racialized hierarchy has structured the industry of domestic work and other low-wage reproductive labor positions across the United States throughout several immigrant waves. Many immigrant women working as nannies and domestic workers in New York City maintain cultural ties to their ethno-racial immigrant enclaves which dot boroughs across the city (Logan et al. 2002). These cultural ties to their particular ethno-racial immigrant enclave matter in how workers understand the terms of their work, how they move through the city itself and navigate between the private and public sphere, and in setting up opportunities for community-building and worker organizing around law and labor reform. This is true not only historically, as Mose Brown's (2011) work demonstrates. Through time spent conducting ethnography with West Indian babysitters and nannies before the Domestic Workers' Bill of Rights was passed, she shows how they simultaneously negotiate their identities as workers while also shape a broader sense of cultural community through their use of Brooklyn's social spaces such as parks and playgrounds.

What these historic cycles moving into the contemporary in New York show, however, is how the city can at one level be a leader of progressive politics and a place where sustained labor organizing can result in policy change and thus broader recognition and rights of workers, while at the same time, remain locked into highly contradictory politics, steeped in rampant inequality and discriminatory practices of labor exploitation of particular groups of marginalized workers, just as before. The commonly held notion of New York as bastion of progressive politics and avant-garde moves for the rest of the U.S. remains but written over with a revision by domestic workers themselves through current and former law.

The city has been historically structured and then re-structured anew, lived out with new existence and potential futures, yet all set upon a storied past that continues to shape those who keep its bustling economy alive. I conceptualize New York City as a *palimpsest* due to its storied relationship with the law and the various limits, contradictions, and failures for its domestic workers. The term traces its roots back to Greek for "rubbed smooth, again" and describes the very lived-out, lived-upon, steady, breathing, rushing mass of echoes and new sounds happening at the same time. Tensions still remain, which reveal themselves at each turn, and at the same moment the palimpsest metaphor also signifies exposure, and the vulnerability involved in disclosing or encountering parts of oneself still buried deep. A study of these laws and their layers in the city reveal a history fully embedded. How do we understand and analyze, then, a *new* law that replaces that which went before—not only a city's previous decrees, declarations, and ordinances, but also the former sets of social relations and conditions in practice? Is what came before completely wiped away as simply as deleting an ad to hire domestic workers on "the boards," the private employer networks in New York City? To this point, Boaventura de Sousa Santos (1987) remarks:

> Since law and society are mutually constitutive, the previous labour laws, once revoked, nevertheless leave their imprint on the labour relations they used to regulate. Though revoked, they remain present in the memories of things and people. (282)

A memory is relived in a completely new moment; a law is passed that carries with it all of the efforts and struggles that came before it.

Spatial Relations in the City

The domestic workers of New York City are tireless, as their struggles and their work only continue. They are also everywhere—commuting from Brooklyn and Queens to Manhattan, coming down from the Bronx, and crossing Central Park between the Upper East and West Sides. They are in parks and libraries, pushing double strollers, waking up early, putting others' babies down to sleep, and then getting to bed late. As Mose Brown (2011) notes, through their daily childcare work they are "raising Brooklyn," and are the primary users of the majority of parks throughout the city on weekdays. Literature on domestic work recognizes that among other factors, such as a lack of respect, low wages, and few labor protections, isolation—or being situated inside a private home unrecognized from the outside as a place of work—is cited as one of the most difficult facets of domestic work. As Mose Brown (2011) points out in her research and as I also found in my interviews, the density of New York does not completely alleviate the isolation embedded in domestic work, however.

Centralized parks spread throughout clusters of neighborhoods allow for easy access and a sense of community among nannies which are fostered along immigrant lines, as West Indians meet others from their home countries and the Eastern Europeans generally talk to those who share their language skills and cultural understandings. The same thing can be seen with U.S.-born, recent college graduate nannies, whom other domestic workers tend to characterize as being "paid more, but doing less" at their jobs, as they are said to often spend time texting at the playground while ignoring the cries of their charges. However, unlike the women in Pierrette Hondagneu-Sotelo's study in Los Angeles or those in Mary Romero's focus on the Southwest, where residential neighborhoods are sequestered away and only accessed by private cars, New York City's urban, densely packed environment allows for ease of access to public space, housing units, and metro-accessibility that connects people, places, and parts of the boroughs together.[5] Indeed, few global cities match the density of people and the concentration of wealth.

Images of household workers in a full, formal uniform on the periphery of Central Park are not nearly as commonplace as in Lima. During my fieldwork, I observed domestic workers wearing official maid uniforms only a handful of times, and each occurrence took place in the old-money landscape of either the Upper East or the Upper West Side neighborhoods. Central Park bridges those two sections of the city and is visibly bordered by homes of the elite on its East and West sides. There, even in census tracts just blocks from each other, severe wealth disparities persist. Geographic Information System (GIS) mapping visibly shows, for instance, how the median household income on a segment of Fifth Avenue in the Upper East Side is more than USD 200,000, while only a few blocks away in East Harlem, it is USD 16,000 (ESRI 2016). Charlene, whose first position was in one of these wealthy homes, reflected upon how those employers required her to wear a uniform. During our conversation at the children's story hour at the New York Public Library, Charlene described the servant-like expectations of the position, including daily breakfast in bed for the family:

> So, in that first job, I had to prepare dinner and serve it as though I was in a restaurant. I had to wear a uniform, and I decided that was it. You can't be paying me $275 to wear a uniform! Cleaning your house from top to bottom, cleaning your silvers, cleaning your chandeliers, do this, do that. So, looking back, I tell people I've come a long way.[6]

However, uniforms are far from the norm in the city's public spaces. Domestic workers caring for children and pushing strollers while wearing their own, casual clothes is a much more frequent occurrence even in those wealthier neighborhoods.

All of the women I spoke with in New York—regardless of immigration status, ethnicity and race, and class background—agreed that living out was preferable to living inside their employer's home for a number of reasons, including pay, independence, and issues of well-being. Jacinda discussed what it was like to do otherwise, when she first sought work in the city as a young undocumented immigrant from Trinidad and Tobago, "with her daughter on her hip." Once she finally secured a job, Jacinda soon realized that her new job would require her to sleep with her daughter in a dank basement of the employer's home. This setup is a far cry from what Frances Perkins, the first female Secretary of Labor, had laid out in 1939 as the established description of working and living conditions for New York City's domestic workers. These guidelines mentioned that "[t]he homes in which this job exists *usually* have modern conveniences and pleasant surroundings," perhaps forgetting to mention that the description *usually* applies only to the living conditions of the employer, which only reaffirms this exclusionary pattern keeping domestic workers from accessing basic labor protections (Perkins and Stead 1939:49).

However, the unified response of every single interviewee preferring to live out is a notable finding, echoing what Pierrette Hondagneu-Sotelo (2001) encountered in her interviews with domestic workers in Los Angeles. While conducting my own comparative interviews in Peru as well as in other conversations with domestic workers in several countries throughout Latin America, workers expressed preferences for both living in and living out. While domestic labor occurs within the private realm of the home, the worker's ability to disassociate from the employer's family life and return to her own dwelling place remains a key differentiating factor for New York City's domestic workers in the structuring of their own work.

These individual, private homes or apartments are not easy to come by in such an expensive city, however, where affordable housing is being pushed farther and farther to the outskirts of the boroughs. New York City's "poor door" controversy of ten years ago calls to mind the similar markers of distinction and *puertas de servicio* that household workers must use to enter their employers' apartments found in Lima (Navarro 2014, 2015). It also demonstrates the complexity of class relations in New York City, which are not nearly as straightforward as employer vs. worker and demonstrate how large-scale housing projects and design are reflective of and also shape dominant social norms of the time (Collins Cromley 1990; Munro and Madigan 1999). In the "poor door" example, a large, new, glassy complex on the Upper West Side was built with two separate entrances with distinct addresses meant to denote prestige—one specified for condominium owners, and the other for apartment renters. Thus, those who cannot buy—and therefore lack stability, necessarily succumb to surges in the market, and actively maintain a fluid, fluctuating sense of home—are relegated to an entirely different address altogether than those whose bank accounts can handle the more than USD 25 million purchase price: 50 Riverside Boulevard for the condominiums, and 470 West 62nd Street for the rentals (Navarro 2015). The desperately high demand to rent in this development (at least 88,200 applications for only 55 units) also speaks to the severe affordable-housing crisis plaguing New York and other cities, pushing low-income workers farther and farther to the periphery of the city, increasing commute time and access to the centralized core of employment possibilities and city life.

Architectural historian Dolores Hayden's (1981) work from decades ago sheds some refreshing insight here, as she draws connections between the rapid development of cities, changing politics, and women's positioning in the domestic sphere. In her meticulous study, Hayden evaluates what she calls "feminist designs" that were dreamt up and then actualized over the three-generation period between the end of the Civil War and the beginning of the Great Depression. In evaluating each of these projects, she notes how they either attempted to spatially reorganize the individual domestic workplace through *technological* innovation, or socialize the individual domestic workplace through *collective* innovation. In her linking of spatiality, the individual (woman) worker, and domestic labor, Hayden's work stands out as a creative example of what has been done and what kind of thinking could open up new types of possibilities. In this way, Hayden's array of feminist designs and her comprehensive evaluation of said projects addresses the continuing issue around separate spheres—by connecting them—and addresses many of the plaguing issues of domestic work itself—by proposing alternative arrangements that speak to the core difficulties of such unending and undervalued work.

IMMIGRANT DOMESTIC WORKERS SHAPING NEW YORK CITY, THEN AND NOW

Domestic work has proven itself to be an invaluable and long-lasting part of New York City life, and a practice that continues to be shaped by generations of immigrant women and women of color. Historically, groups immigrating to New York in the early twentieth century were European, while over the past thirty years, immigration flows draw mainly from countries throughout Latin America, the Caribbean, and Asia (Waldinger 1999). All European countries' migration to New York City has declined since the 1980s to become a numerical minority, and Russia, the only European nation that was in the top 10 migrating countries in 2000, fell to 15th place in 2015 (Waldinger 1999:41; NYCP 2017). Immigrants born in European countries compromise only 15% of the total population of immigrants, while those from Latin America make up 32% and those from Asia are a close second, at 29% (NYCP 2017). Until 2007, more Hispanics than Asian immigrants arrived in the U.S. each year, though that reversed from 2009 to 2018 and then reversed again from

2019, with more Hispanic immigrants than Asians arriving each year (Moslimani and Passel 2024).

The Hart-Celler Immigration Act of 1965 ended the Asia-Pacific Triangle immigration exclusions, abolished the quotas based on national origins, and also lowered European quotas (Coble 2006), thus changing the landscape of the industry. The current makeup of New York's immigrant population reflects that diversity, as it is far more heterogeneous than in other U.S. metropolitan areas (Milkman 2006). While the overall foreign-born population of the U.S. is 13%, New York's is three times that percentage, at 36.3% (Office of the New York State Comptroller 2024). Additionally, immigrant workers make up nearly half of the city's labor force at 44% of all employed residents, and they are a highly dispersed population that is found working in all major industries of New York City (Office of the New York State Comptroller 2024).[7]

The percentage of immigrants as part of the total population of New York City in 2011 was 37.2, nearly identical to the 37% it comprised in 1900 (Lobo and Salvo 2013). While the percentage fluctuated from as high as 40.8 in 1910 to as low as 18.2 in 1970, it has steadily increased since 1970. Immigrants furthermore are geographically dispersed, as they make up nearly half of Queen's population, at 47.8%, and over a third of Brooklyn's and the Bronx's populations, at 37.5% and 34.4%, respectively (NYCP 2017). According to the Pew Research Center, the U.S. foreign-born population reached a record 47.8 million in 2023, an increase of 1.6 million from the previous year, which is the most significant annual increase since 2000 (Moslimani and Passel 2024).[8]

There is currently an estimated population of anywhere between 200,000 and 600,000 women employed as domestic workers in New York, though due to issues of documentation and the location of the work itself, precise numbers are difficult to collect (Burnham and Theodore 2012, NDWA 2024). Of that population, the majority of domestic workers are immigrants and women of color. Based on U.S. Census Bureau data and the American Community Survey (2019), 94% of New York City domestic workers are women, 78% were born outside the U.S., 38% are Hispanic/Latinx, 27% Black (non-Hispanic), and 18% Asian. At the time of my fieldwork, Carolyn, a 31-year-old community organizer in New York City, described the demographics of those who are paid to do the city's cleaning, cooking, and caring, which are akin to the current numbers of today:

Here in the city, 92% of workers are women, 80% are women of color, 50%+ are foreign-born, and that's in the formal sector of care workers. The NDWA [National Domestic Workers Alliance] estimates that over 70% could be undocumented. [9]

She went on to observe that:

This is care work generally—women's work, women of color's work, immigrants' work, underpaid and undervalued, and in my own analysis of it, *this country has an unhealthy addiction to not paying for work, particularly work that happens in the home.* So we have this unhealthy addiction and long-standing legacy of not wanting to pay people for what they do in the house.

Survey results presented in Table 4.1 align with Carolyn's assessment of the industry. Here, the data shows the significant impact of "not paying for work, particularly work that happens in the home," as the majority of domestic workers struggle with injury, lack of sustainable pay, no sick leave and, thus, they often work when ill or injured, sometimes at multiple jobs.

TABLE 4.1   Impact of Immigration Status Upon Working Conditions and Earnings

	U.S. BORN	DOCUMENTED	UNDOCUMENTED	ALL WORKERS
Spends More Than Half of Income on Rent or Mortgage	50%	61%	62%	60%
Hard Time Paying Essential Bills	33%	35%	51%	40%
Assigned Work Outside of Job Description	19%	23%	31%	24%
Required to Do Heavy Strenuous Work	40%	33%	46%	39%
Injured on the Job	54%	61%	74%	64%
Worked While Sick, Injured, or in Pain	56%	60%	77%	66%

Source: Burnham and Theodore 2012. (National Domestic Workers Alliance, 2011–12 National Domestic Workers Survey, in Burnham, Linda, and Nik Theodore. 2012. *Home Economics: The Invisible and Unregulated World of Domestic Work*. New York, NY: National Domestic Workers Alliance.)

The table demonstrates the greater cost of such employment facing un-documented domestic workers as members of an already underpaid indus-try. The U.S.-born population fares substantially better in all categories, and the documented population considerably so when compared to those without papers. Undocumented workers earn significantly less than their documented and U.S.-born counterparts (Hall et al. 2010), and thus most domestic work-ers enter the U.S. labor market at a disadvantage, encountering the racialized and citizenship differentials embedded within it (Burnham and Theodore 2012). Additionally, this same survey of over 2,000 domestic workers in major metropolitan areas found that 85% of undocumented immigrants who en-countered problems with their working conditions in 2012 did not complain because they feared their immigration status would be used against them.

Immigration Law and Worker Vulnerability
Recent changes in immigration law have further positioned immigrant work-ers in precarity as many reside in mixed-status households, which are de-fined as those that include some combination of undocumented immigrants, temporary visa holders, legal permanent residents, naturalized citizens, and birthright citizens (Kasinitz et al. 2013:279). While this combination of legal statuses did not present a problem in past decades, when more possibilities to obtain citizenship were available, a mid-1990s shift to restrict opportunities for gaining legal status (along with a spike in deportations) severely limited economic options for this population. This more restrictive regime increases fear of deportation and constructs an underclass of long-standing semi-per-manent undocumented workers (279). They find themselves very much a part of the city, and yet for all of their cultural, economic, and social participation, these workers remain on the political and legal outskirts.

Furthermore, U.S. immigration law is constructed so as to create and maintain docility among immigrant workers, legally binding those who ac-company their employers to the country. Some domestic workers travel to the U.S. on employer-sponsored visas with diplomats, and yet these workers cannot leave their position of employment, even in cases of serious abuse, without also relinquishing legal visa status (May 2011:179).[10] Other visa re-quirements restrict and impede immigrant domestic workers' ability to secure work legally, and position them in potentially long-term situations of waiting. This is especially true of Filipina migrant domestic workers in New York City, as a 2010 survey found that 73% had migrated on a tourist visa and then were made to pay a hefty sum to apply to change their immigration status, and work-permit application fees, upon arriving to the United States (Caballes et al. 2010).[11] However, there is a growing body of research connecting international migration to environmental changes and civil violence, suggesting a dynamic interplay between these factors as part of a broader push-pull system (Massey 2020). This is trend that we see reflected well beyond New York, however—while the global number of international migrants rose by 46% from 2000 to 2017, the number of refugees increased by 64%, and the number of all forced migrants rose by 221% (Massey 2020).

These numbers shed light on the limitations domestic workers face, as few other visa options exist for domestic workers. They cannot access temporary visas due to their category of work, and the limited number of employment-based permanent visas that do exist for "low-skill" workers are few and far between, which creates a backlog of applications and years of delays (Covert 2013). Thus, we see how immigration law shapes domestic workers' employment opportunities as it interacts with the Bill of Rights' efficacy, situating workers in a structurally vulnerable and dependent position.

In this way, then, while the Bill of Rights technically extends its protections to all workers regardless of documentation status, that so many domestic workers are immigrants matters structurally in three important ways. First, being undocumented affects how workers navigate subjection to exploitation and poor working conditions, as documented workers enjoy much more freedom to shift employers and leave an abusive situation. Second, it affects workers' ability to advance in the profession, as they quickly reach limits to their ability to earn certifications and medical training and thus improve their professional status and experience social mobility. Finally, it matters in relation to the state's rational self-interest in heeding workers' labor rights claims. Similarly to Goldberg's (2014) research with domestic workers in New York City, I found a great deal of fear when talk of papers, documentation, and legal status surfaced in the conversations I had with workers, as nearly all either were, or had been, undocumented and therefore understood the accompanying myriad difficulties. Documentation status thus not only affects workers' ability to advocate for their newly won rights, but it also inevitably sets limits on the state's interest in responding to and enforcing these claims (Goldberg 2014:271).

MOVING TOWARD STATEWIDE LEGISLATION

Building upon that previous history of mobilizing and organizing for broader political inclusion, the 2010 Domestic Workers' Bill of Rights resulted from years of coordinated organizing in New York City and regular three-hour-long bus journeys to the state capital, Albany, where domestic workers sacrificed pay and risked termination to campaign at the state house. Here, I lay out an overview of the organizing involved in getting the bill passed and an analysis of the contents of its final version, which ultimately lost its most crucial, intended provisions.

Organizing for the Bill of Rights

Household workers had been gathering in the parks and other communal spaces of Manhattan, Brooklyn, and Queens for years, reaching out to fellow nannies and babysitters to support each other and build relationships through conversations. Julia, thirty-nine, from Barbados, described how organically she began organizing:

> Well, for me it was easy, because within the neighborhoods that I worked, I would always find myself in a cluster with other nannies talking about the issues of the job, and we would all have the same issues, all of us, regardless to which neighborhood I was in, Midtown, Upper East Side, Upper West Side, wherever. Same conditions, long hours, lack of respect, you know. It just goes on and we were so identical that it was ridiculous.
>
> And when I heard about DWU [Domestic Workers United], I was working in the UWS [Upper West Side] at the time, taking care of a little girl, and I immediately knew without a question that I needed to be a part of the work they were doing. I was super excited about it and I knew I had to jump in, because I was already doing the work in my own world. You know? Just talking to workers, understanding what the conditions are within the industry, and I knew my voice would lend to the conversations to organize something.[12]

Through building relationships with fellow domestic workers, Julia had quite naturally started "doing the work in her own world"; joining DWU merely gave her a structure. At that time, in the early 2000s, the organization was fighting for citywide legislation which became the precursor to the statewide Bill of Rights. Julia continued to discuss the forward momentum that propelled workers in organizing toward larger goals:

When I got involved, they were fighting for the city bill and they were at the end of actually passing legislation at the city level, so it was like a really interesting time. And we took on the state campaign shortly thereafter— we knew we couldn't stay there. We knew that was just city level—we have the whole state to take over. Because there are workers all over! We couldn't just benefit the workers from the city, so it was like literally right after. It was the spring that we had passed the city legislation, and by the fall of that same year we were already thinking about statewide legislation. We knew we had work to do!

Rather than resting on their laurels, workers immediately began strategizing for the statewide legislation in 2003. The statewide campaign formally began when Southeast Asian, Filipino, and Malay workers organized through the Women Workers Project (WWP) of the Committee Against Anti-Asian Violence (CAAAV) to develop a standard employment contract for all domestic workers (Fine 2007; Poo 2010). They modeled this idea off of the standard contract used in Hong Kong, as DWU organizer Barbara Young explains:

There were a number of Filipino domestic workers who had been in Hong Kong and then came here as secondary migration. In Hong Kong, all domestic workers, no matter the ethnicity, no matter when they arrive, they all have a standard contract that women work under. So a lot of the women who were part of the WWP were really emphasizing the need for us to try to unite the industry as a whole and establish some kinds of standards. (Fine 2007:222)

After drafting a standard contract and a survey about working conditions, the groups soon joined forces with the Caribbean and West Indian domestic workers of DWU, and "news of the contract spread like wildfire," according to now-director of the National Domestic Workers Alliance, Ai-jen Poo (Fine 2007:222). Onika, who was central to DWU's organizing, described the process:

In 2004, we took to Albany. Let's hear it for People's Power, now! Our allies, JFREJ [Jews for Racial and Economic Justice], a coalition of churches, SEIU [Service Employees International Union]—we didn't do this alone, I wouldn't take kudos for this, we got together, we had a dynamic director, Ai-jen Poo, she directed while we women worked, and somebody had to see the movement move. And we went together collectively in 2004, knocking on the lawmaker's door, going back home to revise laws, break it down some more, break it down some more; chisel it in! Chisel it down! And come back.[13]

The concerted organizing by domestic workers all across the city with coalition support from progressive, labor, and faith-based organizations, including significant employer presence from JFREJ and organized labor support from SEIU 32BJ (a Service Employees International Union local of organized building trades), continued for more than six years. Local city-based organizing was also paired with countless trips to lobby state legislators in Albany until the Domestic Workers' Bill of Rights was signed into law on August 31, 2010, by then-Governor David Patterson, the first African American governor of the state. It went into effect on November 29, 2010, becoming the first labor law of its kind in the entire country.

What the Proposed Law Was, and What the Actual Law Is

The law extends a number of material benefits, including that it 1) extends coverage to babysitters (except for those who work on a casual basis) and *companions*, as well as domestic workers; 2) guarantees overtime pay at a rate of 1.5 times the base pay over 40 hours a week for live-out nannies and over 44 hours a week for live-in nannies; and 3) guarantees one day off per week and three vacation days annually (after one year of work for the same employer).[14] Early studies suggest many workers are not enjoying these benefits, however, as a 2011 survey conducted with over 1,000 employers in Brooklyn's Prospect Park neighborhood revealed that only 15% of nannies who work more than 40 hours a week receive overtime pay (Burnham and Theodore 2012).

However, of more importance is what the law does *not* include in its final iteration, as it was severely weakened from its original state. The right to collectively bargain, present in standardized contracts, and the creation of a livable, elevated minimum wage were the most significant provisions missing in the final iteration. As Onika described the process quite literally above, the coalition had to continually "break it down some more; chisel it down," in order to hammer out the Bill's strongest pro-worker provisions and then trek back up to Albany until it was so stripped of any worker power that it was rendered less threatening and, thus, finally approved.

Matilda, fifty-one, was visibly discouraged in the aftermath of the law. She told me one cold November afternoon in Harlem about how she felt, looking back on the process of organizing:

> If I could do it all over again, I wouldn't want to do this. Not because of the children, but because of the way we're being treated . . . and I'm one of the ones who fought! I remember when I was in Albany until so late at night, when a guy who was there with us said, "Matilda, you're gonna bring home the bacon." It was the final push! I remember it was like seven o'clock in the night; we were in the legislative office, waiting and waiting. It was a very hard road, but thank God, we persisted, because it took a *lot* of persistence. 'Cause, I mean, sometimes when we went to Albany and came back we were so disappointed when we met with them [the legislators], with what they said. "Oh, you can't do this, you can't do that. Nobody else is getting fifteen dollars an hour. This would be like getting preferential treatment . . ."[15]

The wage issue thus remained untouched, as the final law only extends minimum wage coverage to domestic workers, rather than offering "preferential treatment" to domestic workers. Because of this very low standard, salaries remain a divisive topic among workers. Issues around secrecy of wage rates showcase the problems of having nonstandard rates, as Matilda and others I spoke with voiced what the literature on paid domestic work already documents—employers fear that their domestic worker will, through conversations with other nannies, learn of their higher wages and better working conditions and so they forbid her from making social contact in the neighborhood or the park (Wrigley 1995:23; Zelizer 2005:178).

For many involved in the organizing, the final law—what wasn't chiseled down—left much to be desired. While the initial organizing was formed around the standard contract from Hong Kong, the actual law looks quite distinct, resulting in the production of outsider vulnerability for workers in New York City. What the Bill of Rights does, in effect, is extend and introduce selected coverage of preexisting law to this long-excluded population. However, the law's benefits are available to workers differentially; differences arise both between workers born in the United States, documented workers, those without documents, and within ethno-racial hierarchies within the category of undocumented workers. In this way, though regulated, domestic work in New York City mirrors much of the broader industry in that there is no standard employment contract since this industry constantly skirts the line of intimate and formal, of private and professional. Due to that specificity of the industry itself, difficulties remain in that most domestic workers and employers bristle at the thought of discussing contract terms, since the employment relationship involves negotiation over the economic components and their social meanings (NYDOL 2010; Zelizer 2005:179).

Paid domestic work has long been made invisible and excluded from collective labor reforms enjoyed by other occupations, yet domestic workers have long been organizing for rights. As a result, numerous countries have made recent strides in implementing national domestic worker legislation, including the twenty-two countries that have ratified the International Labour Organization Convention 189, which establishes decent working conditions and standards for domestic workers. However, the United States lags severely behind with respect to both national legislation and international ratification. Statewide labor protections for domestic workers are a recent phenomenon in the United States, and New York sets an important precedent as the first example.

New York City as a case study thus holds importance for shaping future policy that attempts to recognize the home as a site of labor and formalize the relationships of those who live, and work, there. While key provisions of the law were lost in negotiating its final iteration, such as collective bargaining and an elevated minimum wage, this law has set an important precedent and kicked off a series of other states also passing similar legislation. Those important material gains notwithstanding, however, the law's origin story reveals language and practices of racialized exclusion that have shifted to target the women who do this work. In the early to mid-twentieth century, this meant legislating around and away from Black women domestic workers, while more recently and especially seen in the (lack of) language in the Bill of Rights, this has meant doing the same to immigrant women domestic workers.

These findings hold relevance for the reconceptualization of how domestic work as an occupation is regulated and the need to recognize the structural vulnerabilities of domestic workers in various contexts. In light of statewide movements to pass bills similar to New York's happening across the U.S., and global efforts to ratify domestic worker legislation more broadly, that personal employment relationships still elude compliance emphasizes the need to sculpt out creative ways of bringing labor rights into the home.

FIVE IMMIGRANT DOMESTICITY

Producing Outsider Vulnerability in New York City

Onika sits next to me on a bench in Fort Greene, Brooklyn, her long braids piled atop her head and wrapped up in a colorful silk scarf. Her painted wooden earrings swing back and forth as she emphasizes "hi-hi-hi-hi," said quickly in a row, whenever she wants an important point to stick. A trained performer and longtime activist, Onika commands an audience when she speaks, seamlessly jumping from story to reflection from her twenty-four years of care work in New York City after leaving Trinidad. She leans forward to tell me of the highly individualized and racialized way that employers select their workers, as well as her own reaction to that selection process.

> The industry has a lot of racism. And it's so underneath. It's so subtle. But it's there. What you look like—you understand? The heavier and darker the person, "She can lift my grandfather; we would hire her." You know? Depending on what she looks like. If you look young and spunky, "Yes, you can run behind my child." Ageism, too. You look a certain way—they may not hire you because you don't have that *je ne sais quoi*, so to speak. You know what I'm saying? It's a little, a little sass, it's a little kink; however they don't

want the overconfidence, either! Because you know *too much*. Somebody like me could intimidate. *May* intimidate. But they wouldn't want someone like me. How could they not, though? And I pride myself in that, too—that was always my trade-off. Musician, writer, actress, and so on. Come on, what would you want for your child? Somebody *dowdy*? [She laughs].[1]

All in the same breath Onika recognizes what is desired by employer preference, knows she can only adapt to those tropes within established limits, and yet chooses to embrace the aspects of her personality in question, such as her "overconfident" attitude or her being thought to "know too much." Thus, she described her strategy of doing her work with integrity and reframing her skill and ability by recognizing them as only part of who she is, alongside her identity as a musician, writer, and actress. She continued:

> But you know what? I did my job with integrity. So that lasted 5 years, $350 a week. It still wasn't much looking back, working from 8 a.m. to 10:30 p.m. But because of cultural nuance, you get a US dollar, you think that is boss, that is *money*! And we are afraid to speak up, because we are afraid we will be fired, because it's a lowly job, and we're replaceable; there's a line of women behind me waiting to get this job; there are women who are working right now, and while they think their job is secure, their employer is online interviewing somebody (it happened to my sister). So here it is, it's from a place of truth. She—my employer—couldn't dismiss me. *She knew that I come with all that I am. Not all that I can do.*

While she brings her full self to the work, Onika does not let herself be fully defined by the job, similar to Toni Morrison's reflections in a poignant short story (2017). While cleaning a white woman's house at a young age, Morrison initially felt proud to earn her own money and help out her family. Yet as the tasks began to mount and as she began to see the way her employer thought of her, Morrison grew uncomfortable at the way she was being treated and at how the work made her feel, both physically and psychologically. Her father plainly told her, "You are not the work you do; you are the person you are," words that are akin to Dill's (1988) research on African American domestic workers practicing the maintenance of dignity while on the job (Morrison 2017).

As discussed in Chapter 4, in the United States, domestic work's exclusionary past changed with the historic passage of the New York Domestic

Workers' Bill of Rights in 2010. Yet as significant as the first law dedicated specifically to legalizing the rights of domestic workers is, the resultant tenets of the law are notably weaker than its original, intended provisions. Based on ten months of fieldwork in New York City, this chapter speaks to the broader comparative argument of the book by demonstrating that when the law finally regulates domestic workers, it heightens their most structurally vulnerable characteristic—their immigrant status. This is part of a labor regime that I theorize here as *immigrant domesticity*, as the law institutionalizes employee dependency by shouldering employers with the onus of immigration status. In this way, I show that the Bill of Rights is hindered by its interaction with immigration law, as it neglects the specificity of the industry of domestic work, and as it fails to recognize the divergences of the domestic worker population along ethno-racial, citizenship-based, and other lines of distinction. And yet since the law has failed to live up to its promises, workers have consequently responded by utilizing reframing strategies about the law and about themselves to create their own narratives of dignity and self-worth on the job as they combat employers' racialized preferences and cultural tropes.

This chapter then examines two distinct immigrant communities that are represented by domestic worker organizations—Afro-Caribbean workers organized through DWU and Filipina workers organized through Damayan. These two groups played a central role in the Bill of Rights campaign and continue to shape New York's domestic worker movement. Filipina workers choose to recognize the law as a broader moral victory that achieved something positive for the overall movement, while at the same time highlighting the fact that many of the law's benefits were already won through individual negotiation. Many Afro-Caribbean workers, however, consistently deal with a different kind of racism than what Filipino workers are exposed to, in that Caribbean workers are racialized as American-born Blacks by employers and others in the city, often with explicit references around slavery (Waters 2005). Onika's words echo this self-affirmation when she states, "I come with all that I am. Not all that I can do." In this way, Onika knows better than to wait for permission to access the law that will most likely never truly materialize, and she knows that it will not be accessible to everyone. Onika puts the law to work for herself. Put differently, I suggest that domestic workers reframe themselves through the law, understanding it as part of a broader cultural change as well as a means through which workers find and assert their political voices.

IMMIGRANT DOMESTICITY

In addition to workers reframing strategies around cultural changes and locating their political voices, they also spoke to three distinct ways that the law establishes a labor regime of *immigrant domesticity* in New York City. The law in practice reminds workers of their outsider (i.e., "foreign") status instead of improving working conditions. I find that the law circumscribes the rights of domestic workers in three ways: it *institutionalizes* dependency by shouldering employers with the onus of immigration-status enforcement, it is *inconsistent* because it subjects workers to their employers' whims by failing to create a standardized contract, and it engenders *informality* by permitting private employer networks to shape labor market access and thus skirt formal regulations concerning hiring and firing. I argue that this produces a particular kind of vulnerability for the city's majority immigrant domestic workers—outsider vulnerability—as a result of the law granting negligible protections and deliberately eschewing language around immigration.

Institutionalizing Employee Dependency

As previously discussed, due to shifting immigrant restrictions and a number of legal exclusions pertaining to citizenship, domestic workers in the United States have remained a sizeable yet vulnerable population that lacks formal recognition and resources. Deeply entrenched racism and discriminatory labor practices shape access to jobs for these groups, combined with lack of legal status that positions workers as susceptible to employee threats and deportation. Restrictions around guest-worker status and family reunification are reflective of limited political incorporation in ways that reinforce workers' vulnerability to the peculiar exploitations of paid domestic work (Stasiulis and Bakan 1997). Outsider vulnerability, then, is heightened for workers through the precise way that the law deals with immigration by the decision to place responsibility into the hands of the employer.

Analyzing the discourse around immigration on the New York State Senate floor illuminates the uneasy tensions around regulating the industry of domestic work and especially its interaction with immigration regulations. During the legislative session regarding the law's content and consequences in 2009, immigration was the first question brought to the table. Senator Frank

Padavan asked, "Would an illegal immigrant be covered by the provisions of your bill?" (NYSS 2010). Senator Diane Savino, sponsor of the bill, answered:

> It is against the law currently for an employer to hire someone who is not here legally in this country or does not have the right to work legally in this country. That is the employer's responsibility to verify the immigration status of their employees. If they do not, though, that does not absolve that employer of abiding by the labor laws of either the State of New York or the United States. [A]n undocumented worker isn't supposed to be in someone's employ, but the burden of that lies on the employer. (NYSS 2010)

Through her emphasis on employers' power to decide the relevance of workers' immigration status, Savino reinforced the unequal power dynamic inherent in the domestic service employment relationship. Workers frequently spoke about the law's presence making it more difficult for undocumented workers, as well. As Linda, fifty-seven, from Saint Vincent, explained:

> The problem is that those who are undocumented, they find it harder to get something to do now. Because now employers don't want to take chances to hire someone. They think, oh I could be penalized, or I could be this or that. And you still have women (especially in the Filipino community) at the mercies and the hands of their employers, at the bottom of the ladder. They're struggling because one, some don't speak English, two, they are undocumented. It's just like what I went through when I first came here.[2]

The irony of protection and refuge tied up within the idea of home rings heavy as, now, workers are subject to a different kind of gaze and surveillance since employers must watch their practices and, thus, that affects the industry even further. Outsider vulnerability is created since the industry is now "regulated" and "protected," and yet the onus to check workers' papers now falls on the employer and shifts this vulnerable dynamic to remain ever present in the home between domestic workers and their employers.

Lack of Standardized Contract Language

While remaining consistent with the understanding that domestic work is analytically distinct from jobs in a factory, service setting, or office, the fact remains that there is no standardized, measured way in which to deal out job duties, hours worked, pay schedule, and other specific working conditions. Workers are more frequently confronted with "to-do lists" from their employers, which simply spell out tasks that must be completed, rather than articulate job duties balanced with job protections, as is the role of a contract.

Many workers take umbrage at the fact that the law lacks language around specifics of the terms of employment. They navigated the uncertainty of that terrain by selectively employing their right to leave a job if they felt that they were no longer being respected. Matilda, fifty-two, had been previously responsible for one son in the family for years. However, she soon discovered the way her pregnant employers would deal with the arrival of a new baby:

> My pay was $215 per week. And then, when the second child came . . . that week I was going home and I had $230. So, when I went back and told her, "I think you overpaid me." She said, "Oh no, that was for you!" So, she gave me a raise, didn't even tell me it was a raise, and how much was the raise? Fifteen dollars! $215 to $230; that was for having an entire second baby. A second life! Only fifteen dollars.[3]

For Matilda, this was problematic in two ways—the actual low amount of pay that was sorely insufficient considering the work of caring for a newborn baby, but, more importantly, the manner in which she was (not) told or consulted about the pay increase corresponding to new duties. There was simply no conversation about job duties shifting, and no contract that spelled out the time allotted to caring for each of the family's charges, in addition to cleaning the house and cooking meals. What this lack of language around specifics of the terms of employment does, in fact, is reinforce the view that it is appropriate for employers to treat their domestic worker as familiar and almost akin to "part of the family," while obscuring the unequal employment dynamic at its core. It is reminiscent of what domestic worker and organizer Carolyn Reed clearly pointed out back in the 1960s, when she said, "I don't need another family. I just want a job" (Nadasen 2015). Instead, Matilda's employers decided that slipping in fifteen extra dollars to her weekly pay, "giving her a raise," would do. Matilda continued:

> Oh, yeah, after that I was ready to go, oh yeah. I was staying with my stepmom, and when I told her, she was so mad. She said: "Don't go back." She was so mad! So, I left.

By leaving, Matilda retained a sense of dignity and strength about the value of her labor and the importance she places on the children for whom she cares.

However, the original Bill of Rights *included* a termination notice clause, and this came up directly in discussions and debates on the Senate floor prior to the bill's passing, in 2010. In response to Senator Padavan's question regarding revisions made to the Bill of Rights since its initial introduction to the Senate, Senator Savino explained:

> There have been several changes in the bill. One of the things that we included in the original bill which was the subject of a lot of debate here in this chamber was the 14-day notice of termination. That has been removed from the bill, as we could not get that reconciled with the Assembly or the Governor. (NYSS 2010)

What the Bill of Rights does then, in effect, is extend and introduce selected coverage of preexisting U.S. labor law to this long-excluded population, rather than address any of the specificity of the industry itself. As it stands, it is more an extension of watered-down rights already granted to other recognized workers rather than a separate law in and of itself. Jacinda, fifty-eight years old, noted that low pay and sudden job termination were the most difficult aspects of a job that she otherwise described as loving, as she rattled off the names, ages, and grades of all of her seven previous charges to me proudly. Describing the sudden job loss in detail, Jacinda explained:

> Well, being underpaid and them dismissing you without a proper reason. You know, even though if you've given them, like maybe four years, and okay, yes, you get a weekly salary. But after four or five years, [when] they just dismiss you like that without an actual good severance pay or something? After the years you've put in!? 'Cause, I've seen it . . .
>
> On Monday, there was a young lady in the building where I work and, you know, she was told right before the holidays that they don't need her anymore. And the mama is expecting another baby and the grandparents are coming in to help, so all of a sudden, they say, "We don't need you."[4]

When I inquired as to what happens after being dismissed in such a way, Jacinda just shook her head and looked at the floor.

What are you gonna do? You can't do anything! You just take it or leave it. "We don't need you, we don't need you. That's it; I'm not looking for you Monday morning."

Part of the reason this is so difficult for domestic workers in New York City is structural, as losing a job suddenly sets off a series of connected and overwhelming obstacles around paying one's bills, personal safety, reference letters, and their reputation, and if workers had previously lived in, the need to seek new and affordable housing. This is an especially precarious period if workers are immigrants, however. Losing one's job is broadly understood as a potentially devastating event that can lead to a series of financial struggles, self-esteem issues, and other traumatic consequences, depending upon the social context (Juravich and Bronfenbrenner 1999; Weinbaum 2004). Yet the severing of emotional ties following a sudden termination is especially difficult due to the close connections and relationships that embody domestic work. For Jacinda, those intimate, caring relationships clearly recognize the racial distinctions between worker and family, and yet still profess a deep bond of care. She continued:

It *is* personal, because there's like a connection between you, regardless; working for a white family, there's a connection. It's like every morning you get up, you're looking forward to go to work. This is a part of your home; this is, so to speak, your other family. That's where you eat, you drink. You spend like nine, ten hours a day there. You go home sometimes and straight to bed; you go back to work. So, it's like you build a chemistry, you know, for five days, sometimes six days a week.

Jacinda's plaintive line—"it *is* personal . . . working for a white family" (emphasis hers)—shows how racial cleavages continue to manifest themselves in employment relationships inside the private space of the home. Her use of the word *other* here and her understanding her work as it being a *part* of her home is a refreshing perspective that offers an excellent corrective to Mrs. C's comments about Mildred (Childress 1956). Here, Jacinda embraces the real connections and emotions of the work itself, even when caring for white families, and yet she affirms her right to live her own, distinct life.

Ethel, sixty-three, shared a story of an impetuous employer who fired her close friend over an issue involving chicken fingers. Her friend cooked the chicken fingers for the employer's children for lunch, and after they finished eating and were no longer hungry, Ethel's friend ate the rest of the chicken fingers instead of throwing them into the garbage. Ethel leaned over to finish the rest of the story in a near whisper:

> But then, when the employer came home, she said she didn't know how the woman knew, but she knew right away! Maybe she had a camera on in the house? Anyway, she marched in and asked my friend, "Where's the chicken?! What did you do with it; where is it?" And just like that, she fired her.[5]

Ethel raised her eyebrows and shook her head slowly after she finished speaking, clearly thinking about her friend's situation.

Perhaps the domestic worker-employer relationship here between Ethel's friend and her boss was fraught in some serious way in order to have such a seemingly minor issue result in her termination. However, and more to the point, perhaps it was not fraught in the least—regardless, the employer retains the right to fire her worker suddenly and without notice. Perhaps the employer simply had a bad day, was in a foul mood, and reacted harshly when frustrated by her domestic worker eating the chicken fingers, for whatever reason. Or, alternatively, this action continued a pattern of underlying issues around trust and privacy inside of the home, prompting her to act as she did. Yet, for Ethel's friend, this seemingly capricious reaction underscores the law's inattention to the structurally vulnerable positioning of household workers. In this way, the law glosses over setting any contract language standards around working conditions or just cause for dismissal, and yet sudden termination stokes anxiety and fear for domestic workers as they are often dependent upon the employer's home as a place to live, and certainly dependent upon their income to survive. In what the law neglects to legislate, then, it reveals the characteristics of marginality that are inherent and specific to domestic work, including the private, isolated home as the site of labor, the dependency of that relationship's location, and the ever-present uncertainty of termination.

Informality Around Hiring and Firing

This kind of informality also structures hiring and firing practices, as workers are hired by and through "the boards," or personal-networks-based online platforms through which employers can rate, review, and select their workers from a pool of options. One of these popular networks, the "Hudson River Park Mamas," describes its classified message board as:

> An incredible resource for local parents. It's also a great way to reduce, re-use, and recycle. Frequent listings on our classifieds include, but are not limited to the following:
>   * **Buying/selling/trading new and used items** as well as donating free items.
>   * **Looking for/referring household services**: household help, child-care, in search of nannies, recommendations for nannies, sitters, etc. (HRPM 2025)

Hidden from public view, it indeed becomes a site for where domestic workers are sold and exchanged as "used items" themselves, as their livelihoods are commodified through an elite-access-only glorified Yelp. These password-protected, membership-only selection networks concentrate and obfuscate employer preference, leaving domestic workers anxious and powerless. As Sharon, an older nanny originally from Barbados, noted:

> If she [the employer] decides not to put your name down there on the boards, well then, that's just too bad for you! Even after twenty-eight years of walking down the street with their children, I still feel helpless . . . there should be some kind of compensation when you're fired. Obviously, they can't keep you in their house, but I would like to see us treated like every other worker, because this is a job. That we would be protected, with severance, for that hard work.[6]

We briefly discussed the idea of severance, and then returned to the private networks.

> So now I've been on the website for the past couple of months and it's like *I'm* choosing. A lot of people have called me; some of the hours I think maybe it's too much, because maybe from eight to three and then I come here from three until eight, three until perhaps ten; it is a lot. So, I get to choose my hours. Right now, I'm on HRP Mamas, so to speak. And each week you get to, you know, you may have a list of nannies seeking jobs, so each week you can go and bring your nanny up to the top, so each week you have to update it.

Listening to Sharon, I immediately responded by asking if the nanny herself could do the repetitive weekly work to "bring herself up to the top," to which Sharon firmly shook her head no.

> No, you can't even go in to see the website. It's just the parents who sign up on that website. And some of them can have communication with your employer, so you don't know what they discuss. They put up the ad . . . Sometimes you may wonder, "Why am I not getting any calls?" I don't know what exactly they'll tell 'em about you, but maybe that could prevent them from getting in touch with you.

Sharon at one point grew so frustrated with the boards that she posted her own job advertisement fliers around the city in the hope of getting a call-back more quickly.

Esther also reflected on the powerlessness she experienced after being fired and not immediately posted to the boards.[7] Much like sitting on a hasty seesaw that soars up and then plummets down just as quickly, Esther described the day she was asked to leave the family she had lived and worked with for the past seven years. Still in shock, she gathered her belongings that evening, and in the morning, as she prepared to leave, her employers handed her a Coach bag and a photo album. It took Esther almost a full year to find decent work again that didn't require her to drive, which was the reason for her previous dismissal. Esther's farewell present was hardly practical, and it speaks to her employers' lack of awareness about her structural vulnerability without work, since Esther herself cannot join "the boards."

Rather than sending her off with a recommendation and some funds to tide her over, Esther's employers gave her a lavish yet impractical gift, treatment reminiscent of employers of previous decades. Referencing these historical continuities, Brenda Clegg Gray (1993) notes regarding Black domestic workers during the Great Depression in New York City, "Nor were domestics often compensated for these overtime hours, except occasionally with a cast-off article of clothing" (1993:70). The law engenders informality as it allows for private employer networks to shape labor market access and offers no language around formal regulations concerning hiring and firing.

The resultant outsider vulnerability constantly reminds New York City's workers that at any moment they may be asked to leave the household in which they live and, at worst, be deported outside of the country. Elements of this vulnerability are also seen in the law's elision of any standard contract for terms of employment, and its perpetuation of informality by granting employers the right to hire and, more importantly, fire at will. In what the law neglects, then, it reveals the characteristics of marginality that are inherent and specific to domestic work: the private, isolated home as the site of labor, the intimacy and dependency imbued inside that location, and the ever-present uncertainty of termination.

WORKERS' SUCCESS AT REFRAMING THEMSELVES VIA THE LAW

Just like those generations of women who have come before them, domestic workers "speak back," by utilizing reframing strategies about the law and themselves to create their own narratives of dignity that re-value themselves in the midst of disrespectful treatment (Levenstein 2009). Thus, two important symbolic understandings have emerged from the Bill of Rights, and here I show how workers identify a *cultural change* as a broader collective win rather than an individual benefit, as well as a newly sharpened *political language*, rejecting racist claims and asserting power and pride on the job.

Cultural Change Within the Movement

Filipina workers choose their words carefully regarding the law. They position it as a broader moral victory that achieved something positive for the overall movement, while at the same time highlighting the fact that many of the law's benefits were already won—for them—through individual negotiation. They emphasize the cultural shift that has occurred, rather than substantive improvements through specific provisions of the law. As Nilda, a second-generation Filipina, noted:

> We think it's, you know, more like a moral victory, right? But the Domestic Workers' Bill of Rights itself is . . . you know, most of what's written there has already been achieved by the workers, by struggling with their own employers. And actually, you know, some of them have negotiated for their pay, for their hours, for their vacation days—they have negotiated for more than what's stated on the Domestic Workers' Bill of Rights. So if you actually refer to the employer about the Bill, that won't be good for the worker, right?[8]

In this way, she argues that it would actually be *detrimental* for workers to even refer to the Bill itself. She continued:

> So, it's a moral victory; it's good to have it in paper, but I think the original Bill is a lot better compared to what got passed. The original Bill was really a collaboration between the different domestic worker organizations, right? But the final Bill was what we have now. So, I think the moral of the story there, for us, is that a Bill is good, but it shouldn't be used against the worker. You know, it should complement the organizing that's happening, but if it's gonna be used to pacify the workers, then we should really think about it.

For Nilda, the law quickly turned from a tool to improve working conditions to one which would lower conditions and which could, finally, be used against the workers to "pacify" them.

Similarly, Annabel, who was formerly jailed for her political activism in the Philippines and then exiled from the country, emphasized Damayan's take on the Bill itself:

> I would say that the biggest impact of the Bill of Rights is in the culture. There's a cultural shift, because before the workforce in the industry weren't in the mainstream consciousness of the New Yorkers, and the workers had internalized their invisibility. They don't talk about it, they're scared, they're ashamed, they know there are main problems but they don't know what to do. So, I think the Bill of Rights was a great opportunity to address all those issues. It was very powerful in creating consciousness and public education on the value of domestic work and the many problems facing domestic workers. Also, it created a movement and coalition.[9]

Annabel spoke of how Filipina workers, as a community, can garner higher wages, longer vacation time, sick days and holidays, and overall, more privileged treatment:

> It was a great opportunity to work together, to make a vision, planning, implementing the campaign. But in terms of real impact, I've been asked at different places about it and I always say it's symbolic. The Bill of Rights has remained symbolic for many workers. I think, first, because what's in the box is not compatible with what the market provides. For the Filipino community, we're able to get one week of paid vacation every six months.

So, when you work for one employer over the year, you get two weeks of paid vacation. And then we get a number of sick days. And then we get a number of holidays.

Though the Filipino community has many of its own challenges, she clearly positions them as advantaged within the labor market. Annabel noted one material gain from the Bill regarding overtime and its calculation, however:

One big win in the Bill is the adjustment of the overtime. Do the computation—overtime hours are still the same, but the way your overtime is computed differs before the Bill. Before when you're a live out, your overtime is computed based on the federal floor wage. If you're making $15 an hour, you get less, then.

Workers organized through Damayan note that they would prefer to improve the law by adding several protections, including a living wage, better and longer paid vacation, holidays and personal days, notice of termination, severance pay, and health insurance (Caballes et al. 2010). Members of other domestic worker organizations recognized this sentiment expressed by Damayan members, as they reflected upon it in our interviews. As Carla, thirty-two years old and from Barbados, told me:

For a lot of workers, this is where I feel there's a level of contention within the industry, where workers are feeling that the Bill may have done a disservice to them, because they don't understand that the Bill was just a platform for the industry as a whole. And this is why a lot of the workers in the other organizations are continuing to have these conversations, to stress that it was a platform, especially for workers who were not able to access those benefits, vacation days, anything of that sort.[10]

The notion of a law that is intending to provide reforms but then in practice is understood as a "disservice," especially after years of cross-cultural worker mobilization, is indeed heavy. Carla sought to universalize the idea of the law as a stepping stone of progress, then, along a path that would lead to more recognition and provisions overall, and yet in so doing she recognizes the variations in the access to benefits experienced by domestic workers within New York City. Yet, as it stands, since Filipina domestic workers tend to enjoy individual bargaining power paired with strong employer preference, they de-emphasize the material benefits of the law while framing its success as enacting broader cultural change within the industry itself. So for Filipina workers, employer preference and a racialized notion of docility shape their more favorable position in the labor market. For other workers, the law is a "platform" to stand upon, as it allows them to access more basic kinds of rights that they previously could not.

Vocalizing Politics and Self-Pride

Workers see being involved in the Bill of Rights campaign and the resultant law as a means for vocalizing politics to resist deeply racist encounters on the job and to speak of liberation and freedom. Onika described her sense of the continuing historical trend of (generally) white employers assessing and denigrating the available pool of Black workers by their racialized, physical features:

> The nature of the job for me? Well, I woke up with an epiphany—that white women and Black women could bond. There were many areas to this because we came in mistrustful of each other. Race plays into it. What we look like determines the job we still get, believe it or not. Like the women they had on the auction block in Harlem, post-slavery. When they were still coming up to see what they looked like on the auction block. It still happens today—in a sense today.[11]

Her words and experience hearken to domestic worker testimonies from earlier decades in New York, with more than twenty-five "slave markets" spread across the Bronx, Brooklyn, Staten Island and Queens by 1940 (Gray 1993:58). As a Black worker explained in 1937, "You would go to the Bronx, and there was certain corners that you would sit on. So some people had a box they would sit on, some would lean up against a store or wall . . . And they would come and just pick out a nice clean girl they thought they could trust" (Dill 1988:101). However, Onika quickly acknowledges that link and, yet, also sheds her feeling of utter objectification by focusing on the changing meanings of domestic work from "*slave work*" to *liberation*.

> See, it's so much liberation now. I'm not pent up; it's not slave work, as the fellows say; the fellows look at me over the park on 84th Street and 5th Avenue; they call that the Egyptian park. A guy who had known me, he said, "I never knew you used to do slave work," because of the stigma, the

Black nannies, the Mammies, the wet nurses, the stigma the job has, the connotation over the job; in the meantime the demography has changed, it has become more "ethnic." However, what I found out is it's not the job that is difficult, it's the parents sometimes, it's dealing with different emotions, mixed up attitudes, complexes, and little things that still steep in where colored women are supposed to take care; that's our place, that's our duty.

She recalls her reaction to a particularly traumatic presumption of "duty" when Onika was expected to read aloud a racist nursery rhyme to her employer's son, one which held cultural significance from her childhood spent on the colonized islands of Trinidad and Tobago:

She [the employer] had in her cupboard the 1956 edition of the "Mother Goose" nursery rhyme. What comes to mind? Think about it. Hi, hi, hi, hi. You hear what I'm telling you? That is what I talk about, "Ten little N-boys"— that's where that came from! It came from a place of truth. Her name was on the book, too, and they taught the children from that book. Now it came to mind, that we in the Caribbean—we also recite it, because we're colonized by the English! Those nursery rhymes change hands over a time, but their contents are racist in nature, and she *still* had it in her bookshelf.

Well, *I got stone cold*. I called her immediately into the room. I said, "What do you want me to do with this book? Look at this book. I know you grew up with this book." She said, "What should I do with it?" I said, "I'm not telling you what to do with it. But if there will be somebody who will come and take an enlightened read of this, I can't tell you to get rid of your heirloom, I can't, but the poems are racist." I didn't know what to think or what to feel.

Onika went on to describe the discomfort she continues to feel due to that encounter, though it was never addressed again by her employer.

Charlene, from Trinidad and Tobago, kept both hands out to catch the newly toddling charge of hers, Kevin, while we talked at a Brooklyn library's story hour. Charlene wove seamlessly in between our conversation in which she reflected upon her previous experiences of domestic work and the child in front of her, always attentive to Kevin and his curly locks of brown hair:

What do you want, Kevin? Here's the baby Elmo; okay now, he'll do. Well, I worked in Long Island—that's a nightmare—crazy women . . . and not only the isolation, the attitude of the people. It's as though you're a slave. I got that feeling from them. From out there. So I did not like it, but again, I found favor. Because the woman I worked with out there, the first day on my job she flipped the top on me, and I flipped the top back on her. I had . . . And we hit it off right there—because she realized, I think, "I've reached where I want to be with this one." And you know, the workmen would come in and they would say, "Oh, you're still with her." And I'd say, "Because she understands me, and I understand her, and we have a wonderful relationship."

Long Island's relative geographic distance further exacerbates the isolation already characteristic of the industry, and yet Charlene "found favor" with her employer by "flipping the top back on her," as she harnessed her own power within the domestic worker-employer dynamic and rejected being treated like a slave. Rather than feel powerless, Charlene asserted herself and her limits early on with her employers as a means of exerting control of the situation. She discussed leaving a job after only one week because of the servant-like expectations of the employers:

I made $275. I did it for one week, and I walked away. Let me tell you, I had a folder with what I was supposed to do. I don't know who was their previous employee, but they used to have me take them their breakfast in bed! No, thank you. I've seen so much. Been through it. Maybe I'm a hard-nosed bitch. But because of my personality, I make it what I'm taking, what I'm not taking, and what I'm doing and what I'm not doing.[12]

Through this delineation of asserting personality to control the terms of her employment, she preserved self-respect and dignity. Onika, similarly, learned resilience from standing up to her employers, while the law dignified and elevated how she saw her work, and herself:

Us, domestic workers, we say that loosely—what don't kill you makes you stronger. *It's not always true.* I think it taught me resilience; as I said before, it's not something that you would do. But! In order to get through the system, sometimes you have to go low. It's a pride thing. I felt shame. I never used to tell people "Listen, I'm a babysitter"—now I can say that boldly. I'm a caregiver. Because the Bill gave it some teeth, some support.

Onika moved from a place of shame to one of unabashed pride, thanks to the Bill itself legitimizing her experience and providing her a place from which to stand up for herself. By relying on the teeth of the Bill, Onika remembered that she comes to her work with all that she is, not all that she does, shaking off shame and finding her political voice.

This chapter has pointed out how the law universalizes the experience of domestic workers in New York, negating the industry's specificity of domestic vulnerability and condensing a divergent domestic worker population into one common social position. This case also highlights domestic workers' agency in organizing, negotiating, contesting, and unpacking the law on their own terms to reflect cultural significance or embrace their self-worth. In analyzing the law, I attempted to provide a historical context for how racialized immigration policies and practices shape women's work in order to recognize the complexities of intersectionality at play within the industry and within the way the law resulted. However, in its disavowal of language on immigration and corresponding failure to address the precarious immigrant status of domestic workers in New York City, the law further perpetuates social relations of inequality. Many cleaners, nannies, and caregivers spend their entire lives as "citizens on the edge" due to their ethno-racial, gender, and class positioning in the informal economy, and currently, the Bill of Rights does little to respond to the intersectional inequalities intrinsic to the industry.

What began as an effort to create a standard contract of employment has done little to standardize, let alone improve, the working experience of most domestic workers in New York City. Based upon their social positioning, particular ethno-racial groups experience the industry of domestic work and the law's regulation of that industry in highly divergent ways based upon an unequal ethno-racial hierarchy in an already feminized, racialized, and low-status occupation. This case study shows how regulation of a highly stratified industry under the 2010 Bill of Rights functions as workers utilize strategic frames in order to maintain independence and autonomy within an occupation that by virtue of its definition strips those attributes away.

Equally important, as I have highlighted, is how the law created a cultural change and gave domestic workers a political language through which to understand themselves, as they utilize reframing strategies to create their own narratives of dignity and self-worth on the job in order to combat employers' poor treatment.

They must do this because, of course, the law does not. The story that Ethel recounts regarding her friend and fellow domestic worker being suddenly terminated for a seemingly trivial occurrence demonstrates just this point, as the law offers no protections or standards whatsoever around the firing of workers. And while a superficial read of this story in connection with the law might assume that it would simply be too difficult to stipulate and regulate conditions around termination in the home, my comparative analysis shows otherwise. Turning away from the United States and briefly revisiting Peru, we see that Lima's labor legislation describes and regulates the necessary conditions for the termination of a domestic worker, even going so far as to stipulate that a fourteen-day advance notice must be given on the part of the employer or the worker (whoever initiated the transition). It can, and has, been done. In this way, a comparative lens allows us to draw from examples when imagining the creative alternative possibilities to bringing labor rights into each site, as these two cities and their findings inform each other.

Additionally, the New York City case demonstrates the increasing importance of this attention to structural vulnerability around immigration status, especially in our contemporary political moment of heightened fear and threats of deportation. Widespread concern is being normalized at a rapid pace, as detainment and immigration raids, the defunding of sanctuary cities and an end to their already limited sovereignty, and the termination of 2012's Deferred Action for Childhood Arrivals (DACA) either in the short- or long-term become real. The discourse around these various actions often invokes a false moral dichotomy of "bad" immigrants—those who are deserving of state punishment and deportation as compared to "good" immigrants. These moral discourses shape the way we more broadly understand, accept, or at least tolerate how immigrants are treated, especially with respect to their ability to work and earn incomes. Outsider vulnerability as an organizing frame can be adapted and extended to apply to other categories of workers and other immigrants, as well, who are consistently reminded of their increasing precarity.

Furthermore, this case has assessed the important consequences of immigration law's interaction with the Bill of Rights, as I demonstrate how nearly all New York's domestic workers being immigrant workers matters with respect to ways that workers navigate exploitation, advance in the profession, and make labor rights claims on the state. This insight is relevant as we try to understand the limits to achieving social inclusion and equality for a marginal population through legal avenues, as well as the challenges of governance over the employment relations inside the home. Looking beyond enforcement, then, the social organization of labor in the home reveals some of the limits to law as an effective instrument in regulating relations of labor inside households. And yet the insights from the comparative case of Peru remind us that this can be done, allowing us to see in practice distinct other alternatives to bringing labor rights and law home.

SIX TOWARD NEW SITES OF LABOR, TOWARD NEW LABOR RIGHTS

On a recent trip to Lima, I met up with a wealthy Peruvian friend, Manuela, who lives in one of the most elite districts of the city, La Molina. "Lima is small," she said to me as we drank *chicha morada* at a waterfront restaurant on Lima's coast.[1] With the ocean waves crashing underneath us and the cliffs of the city's edge above, I thought for a second about Manuela's Lima, how differently she experiences the city, and how by virtue of being her friend, I had also observed and experienced just a glimpse of that lifestyle. Manuela's Lima is the Lima of the wealthy employer class, one in which she is welcomed through the VIP special entry into private clubs, in which she vacations on the pristine beaches, and which grants her access to an easy, convenient way of life supported by a type of underclass. I shook my head. "No—Lima is huge. Its circles are small," I responded. Manuela paused briefly, and then quickly nodded in agreement. "That's it; that's it exactly," she said. Lima is a city where a powerful elite has firmly maintained its grasp, even throughout recent democratic reforms that allow for some subtle changes and obstinately block others.

My mind then drifted to the working lives of my other middle-class Peruvian friends, including those I interviewed, worked alongside, and learned from while living in Lima. Manuela's Lima is distinct even from their experiences, and in important ways. For instance, Peruvians wearing the most on-trend, expensive clothing who show up to exclusive clubs with an attractive ensemble of friends with Indigenous features are either socially discouraged from entering or, quite literally, denied entry.

A young, light-skinned Limeño friend confessed to me how he covered up a friend being denied entry to a club by pretending that they were both too drunk to be allowed in, while in actuality this was a protective gesture designed to shield his friend from feeling the normalization of discriminatory social policies that perpetuate this system. Upon hearing this story, I empathized with the way he responded by quickly trying to protect his friend from this harsh treatment; who would do otherwise in that situation? Yet the very fact that he imagined he could, in fact, offer protection speaks to how deeply internalized his privileged experience is as a light-skinned Limeño.

On this return to Lima, several years after formally concluding my fieldwork and follow-up visits, nothing felt new to me. The city's patterns were instantly so familiar—the salty ocean breeze kicking up the cliffs to mix with the daily morning fog, the crowded buses spewing exhaust and racing each other down the central avenues, older women selling warm quail eggs and tiny bags of popcorn under leafy shade, wherever they could find it. I embraced these moving pieces of the city, as I had missed them. But in fact, other parts of Lima felt a bit too familiar—the uniform shops selling head-to-toe white household worker dresses and aprons, the service elevator entrance to another friend's apartment, and the assumption that I wouldn't dream of doing my own cleaning which prompted the owner of the Airbnb apartment I rented to automatically schedule a "cleaning lady" to visit three times during my brief stay. In returning, then, I took on that heaviness in the desert air that never rains, where hazy clouds are seemingly forever pregnant with ripe humidity. My once-smooth index cards containing jotted-down lists and notes revealed their curled edges after less than a full day back in Lima, a rapidly expanding city with cultural practices just as immovable as the heavy humidity.

Through conducting a comparative ethnography over the span of several years, I became accustomed to remembering where I was and what types of social cues and practices were accepted, and when. In moving back and forth between these two cities that share so much, upon returning to one of them, I instantly remembered what sets Lima apart from New York City for me as a researcher. I immediately recalled the feeling of being an outsider myself—a sense of which I experienced not as a type of vulnerability, but rather as something advantageous I could harness as a sociologist, enabling me to navigate conducting interviews and ethnography on the ground.

Stepping back from both cities and returning to Berkeley after I concluded my fieldwork enabled me to gain new perspectives on each city individually, which then enabled me to better position the domestic worker laws of Lima and New York City in conversation first with each other and later with other international sites of household worker organizing and legislation.

REVISITING KEY QUESTIONS AND
THE COMPARATIVE CASES

In reflecting upon how these laws and their consequences in each city can inform the other comparative site, we must revisit earlier questions that remain: What does it look like to embrace a model of legal regulation and rights for such a historically informal occupation, perpetually looked down upon as not "real" work? And in a more straightforward manner, we must ask: Can we legislate vulnerability away? Bringing law home in each site was indeed not without its complications, and legal scholarship reminds us of the sometimes-contradictory ways that the law can play out. Yet, as we think through the interviews, lived experiences of domestic workers, and sociological observations noted here in my findings, Sally Engle Merry's (1991) words remind us that law can engender a "new consciousness, a new set of understandings of persons and relationships" (892). Taken together then, I follow Merry's (1991) understanding and hooks' (1990) theorizing of the home as a site of political agency and new consciousness, and a space of resistance for women workers. There, law lived out in practice as we see through the production of insider and outsider vulnerability shapes women's working conditions and their possibilities for both individual resistance and collective activism.

Analyzing the laws together rather than in relation to their respective sites of governance, it is evident that they share similar aims and are the result of many years of worker organizing. Yet in their essence, they are different both with respect to the *quantity* of articles and provisions and their *contents*. While much of this book's focus has been devoted to interrogating the problematics of both laws as they stand and as illustrated through the lives of the very workers the laws were designed to govern, protect, and regulate, the Peruvian law imparts a serious recognition of the specificity of household work itself. This stands in sharp contrast to New York's Bill of Rights, and thus, the value of the comparison shines forth here as both a contrapuntal reading of the law, hearkening to Said (1994), and a straightforward one displaying the stark distinctions in the scope, terms, and details of the laws themselves.

The Peruvian law is, in fact, much more straightforward and candid in its attention to household work as a distinct form of labor and thus one that demands a different kind of legislation. Additionally, the Peruvian law brings forth obligations on both sides of the employment relationship—both the *worker* and the *employer* hold legal responsibilities in the law's tenets. My fieldwork stressed this point, as the Peruvian Household Workers' Law workshop would often involve conversations around workers learning both their "rights *and* responsibilities" expressed by the law. While my research also demonstrated the difficulties in putting both of those worker obligations and protections into practice, it also reveals the significant amount of thoughtfulness embedded in the intentions of the Peruvian law's tenets.

Interestingly enough, however, employers played a significant role in supporting the 2010 New York State Bill of Rights, and yet they are virtually absent from the tenets of the New York law save for their vague presence as the party who will pay the minimum wage and overtime, and who will grant the three days of vacation per year. Except for the New York law bringing domestic workers into state minimum-wage coverage, then, the Peruvian law is stronger, more specific, and bolder with respect to every single other claim it makes regarding regulatory efforts to govern the working lives of household workers.

Yet in returning to a contrapuntal reading, the New York State Senate transcripts reveal discussions regarding a fourteen-day termination clause that was, at one point, considered part of the law in draft form and would have been nearly identical to the Peruvian law. What was left out of New York's legislation has been a part of the law for now more than twenty years in Lima. As previously discussed in Chapter 4, Senator Savino explained that the termination notice was removed from the bill, as it could not be "reconciled with the Assembly or with the Governor," (NYSS 2010). And as I mentioned at the end of Chapter 5 regarding the termination clauses as they stand in both laws—one included in the final version and one cast away to remain on the cutting room floor—looking at what was left out of each specific law and examining them in conversation together allows us to "dream big" and see what has, and can, be done. Additionally, we know that the laws do not end with their specific tenets written on the books, and in this way the varied content of these laws themselves, then, lends itself to particular kinds of ways that workers can (and must) utilize it when on the job. As Carla, a thirty-two-year-old domestic worker and organizer from Barbados, told me:

> Like I said, for me it [the law] benefited me, because when I started a new job, I was able to say, "this is what the law says" to all the employers I interviewed with. A lot of 'em looked at me like I was crazy!! [laughter]. "Is there a law?" they'd say. "Can you demand this?" And I was like, "Yeah, I'm serious—this is what I can demand."[2]

While the flaws of the final Bill of Rights itself remain very real, then, Carla arms herself with the law when mapping out her future in a new employer's home. Rather than pointing to one specific right or benefit, she instead employs the law in its entirely as a tool through which to negotiate the power dynamic with her potential employers and establish herself from the start as aware, informed, and in control.

Through conducting this comparative fieldwork and seeing the way that the law took shape in both cities, then, both in what it says and in how workers experience, challenge, and respond to the law, I soon began to realize that Sarat (1990) was right—the law *is* all over. This research has sought to map out the places where the law ought to be but is not, as well as the places where it is, though we do not recognize it as such. The dissection of day-to-day intricacies and implicit meanings, then, answers Javier Auyero's (2012) question aimed at ethnographers who enter into the familiar, "How are we to see?" Seeing again what had once been new to my perspective, especially as someone born and raised in the U.S. and poised at the ready with a critique of the plentiful discourses around meritocracy-as-justificatory-of-inequality and accompanying discriminatory treatment, was powerful.

As I scanned the city again, my eyes landed on what had previously shocked me—plentiful dots of blue-and-white-uniform-clad women in the lush green parks of a city built atop a desert. The chance to re-experience my initial reactions to those scenes from 2012, however, was a powerful reminder of the value of comparative empirical research as well as what it both requires from us and pushes us to understand about ourselves, and a further reminder of how a contrapuntal reading of law can make visible particular kinds of social interactions and social relations. Domestic workers' struggles for labor rights—both historically and currently—necessarily draw attention to the private sphere of the home as an unregulated site of gendered and racialized labor. And yet their work has consistently and universally been overlooked across historical moments and economic configurations, though this book tries to bring visibility to these important struggles.

In his advocating for the importance of political ethnography, Auyero (2012) states that as a method, it is "uniquely equipped to look microscopically at the foundations of political institutions and their attendant practices, just as it is ideally suited to dissect politics' day-to-day intricacies" (13). Taking this concept of political ethnography to a study of domestic work, then, enabled me to conduct an analysis that took as its central focus the texture of lived experiences in a place normally considered private, separate, and hidden—the home.

Re-Theorizing the Home as a Site of Law

In this book perhaps I, like many others before me, am guilty of having woven together a narrative of domestic workers as vulnerable in the way that I have depicted them. Yet, regardless of how one interprets my portrayals of domestic workers throughout these chapters beginning with Diouana, an important difference remains in that the vulnerability I speak of and describe is *structural*. It is both a part of the work itself and an outcome of the very legislation that was purportedly designed to address it, and it takes two different shapes in the two cities I studied. In this way, speaking of the vulnerability that characterizes the industry, the labor, and workers' experience inside of the home *especially* after passing such hard-fought legislation is one of the primary ways in which we begin to change the naturalized understanding of these dynamics by crafting instead a participatory and collective narrative. The structural vulnerability domestic workers experience continues to play out globally through high-profile coverage of recent, extreme cases of abuse and even death of domestic workers, and especially migrants. Recent cases in Beirut (Su 2017), Hong Kong (Ives 2016), Saudi Arabia (Kelly and Thompson 2015), and Singapore (Lum 2021) only continue to demonstrate this trend.

Yet revisiting Beauvoir (2015), how do we move away from perpetuating the past and instead perpetuate a different kind of present? There is a heavy resistance to doing so, both historically and in the contemporary moment. As Casanova (2019) points out, the most difficult thing to change about domestic employment in Latin America is the "predetermined set of assumptions about class and culture" (128), speaking to the weight of concepts like servitude that domestic work continues to carry with it. Even amidst the existence of law, we see this reflected in the daily discrimination that domestic workers face in Lima, where colonial legacies are written on domestic workers' bodies both discursively and materially as they fall into a deep racial ordering that structures class and status in the city. We have seen the nature of the industry, which has strong parallels between Lima and New York City, and yet it is organized very differently in each city due to a particular colonial past that codifies colonial domesticity in Peru and a specific racialized past that codifies immigrant domesticity in New York City.

In examining the effects of the law in these two major global cities, I find, despite their strikingly different social contexts, the law in practice produces outcomes that are actually quite similar. We have seen the limits, contradictions, and failures of law in practice, and that the deep origins in colonial and racialized relations of this occupation shape its legal regulation, thus reproducing those inequalities in practice and shaping both constraints and possibilities for resistance.

My findings demonstrate how regulation of the home fails to fully account for its specificity as a site of labor, thus preserving social hierarchy and, consequently, creating further structural vulnerability for domestic workers. I show how progressive labor laws for domestic workers are stifled by historically entrenched patterns of racialization and labor informality, finding that the Peruvian law extends to household workers only half of the labor protections afforded to other occupations, codifying preexisting inequalities and shaping a labor regime of *colonial domesticity* around body, space, and time inside Lima's contemporary homes. In New York City, the law grants negligible protections and deliberately eschews language around immigration, thus establishing a labor regime of *immigrant domesticity* instead of improving working conditions. That workers experience insider vulnerability in Lima and outsider vulnerability in New York pushes us to consider the interplay of power and the personal bound up within this highly specific site of labor with its storied history of gendered, racialized, and classed hierarchies, and there remains much political and intellectual work to be done.

Domestic Workers Organizing for the Future

Back on a chilly December evening in 2013 near the Barclays Center in Brooklyn, Carla, a nanny who had discussed how she brought the law to her employers' attention when seeking a new job, leaned across the table where we sat eating frozen yogurt and said, "Let's be real—care work is here to stay." She was—and continues to be—right, of course, as is Paul Osterman (2017) when he points out that many of us will need help when we get older, and simply asks, "Who will help us?" (3). Those needing care workers and those working in the care industry have both been steadily growing (Krutsch and Colato 2023). To this point, Burnham and Theodore (2012) found that the number of workers classified as nannies, housecleaners, and caregivers by the Bureau of Labor Statistics rose nearly 10% between 2004 and 2010. The profession totaled 3,636,900 workers by 2021, and this occupational group is projected to grow even more rapidly at 25.4% between the years 2021 and 2031 (Riles and Rolen 2023). Anne-Marie Slaughter's (2016) predictions around growth skyrocketing in "care-sector jobs" became true, then, as home health and personal care aides edged out retail sales and fast-food workers to become the largest individual occupation in the U.S. as of May 2023.

Not only will the work continue, then, along with the growing numbers of those who do it, but if the historical lessons unearthed by May (2011) and Nadasen (2015) continue to bear out, so too will the organizing and mobilizing taking place both nationally and globally. Yet we know that even in places where political struggle has brought about laws to recognize and regulate this specific employment relationship in the home, implementation tends to be inconsistent partially due to its highly personal, intimate nature and dependency on those individual relationships.

However, domestic workers have assuredly become more visible and acknowledged due to their strong networks and global scale in recent years, rocking the boat with their systematic, strategic, and inclusive mobilizations taking place globally.[3] The first global union of domestic workers that connects domestic worker associations and organizations from more than forty-eight countries, the International Domestic Workers Federation (IDWF), was founded in 2013 in Montevideo, Uruguay. When I began this research in 2012, the International Labour Organization (ILO) had only passed Convention 189, the Domestic Workers Convention, one year earlier. Now, more than thirty countries have ratified C189, and many of these countries have also passed their own national household worker legislation (Seiffarth, Bonnet, and Hobden 2023). The IDWF has organized extensively and grown to more than 88 affiliates from 68 countries across 7 regions, representing over 670,000 individual domestic workers. And in the United States, New York State's 2010 Domestic Worker Bill of Rights sparked organizing across the country, of which now eleven states and three cities presently have some form of domestic worker labor protections, while the National Domestic Worker Alliance has organized over 250,000 domestic workers through more than seventy affiliate organizations in its years of existence. The global domestic workers' movement is the definition of a living, breathing social movement, inspired by each other's work and constantly striving for C189 ratifications and implementation, as well as stronger legal protections, solidarity, sisterhood, and collective resistance.

What does the collective project look like, then, to "bring law home"? As domestic workers and their employers have experienced firsthand over the last century, and as I have shown with this book's two case studies, the act of bringing labor rights home is not a straightforward or simple task, regardless of where it takes place. Moving from my comparative research, then, paves a way forward to consider other approaches to bringing labor rights home and to valuing the work performed there, whether paid or unpaid. As this book recognizes, a redefinition of work relations more generally and of domestic worker relations specifically must address the varying ways that race, class, gender, and immigration status *together* shape and constrain particular opportunities for resistance. This approach leads us to bring this research and theorizing to the space of the home as well as to other sites of the informal economy in order to develop a broader framework through which to advance labor rights. Here, I briefly point to a few ideas that recognize and build upon scholarship of the past and yet signal promising new research directions, ultimately embracing the need to push forward a more grounded understanding of the challenges inherent to labor informality and precarity.

Forging Connections and New Directions

In an important advancement, after more years of organizing and advocating for change, a new Peruvian household workers' law was enacted in April 2021, Ley 31047. Several important tenets that were previously never legally included have now been inscribed in law, including the requirement of a written rather than verbal contract, the guarantee of two full months' bonus pay per year each July and December, when this was previously only a half-month's bonus salary twice a year, and thirty days of vacation per year rather than the fifteen guaranteed previously (Pérez and Gandolfi 2024). However, a study performed in conjunction with the International Labour Organization found that, like my interviewees, very few household workers were aware of the law—this new law, or any previous version prior—and only 6% of household workers had a written contract (Pérez and Gandolfi 2024). Yet this is still a remarkable step forward, especially when recognized in conjunction with the fact that Peru ratified ILO C189 in 2018. Indeed, it is a drastically different legal and social terrain than when I conducted my research, one which is ripe for equitable and consistent labor rights.

One of the goals of this book has been to think comparatively about workers' struggles and to bring history to bear upon our changing understanding(s) of the home as a site of work and law. However, as Anderson (2017) argued and as we see through the language on workplace discrimination cases (Berrey, Nelson, and Nielson 2017), the home is far from the only site of labor in struggle to bring about labor rights and law. Debates and challenges around problematizing informality and informal labor continue, as Rosaldo (2021) shows, and the "informal sector" is far from a perfect descriptor. It is more of an "overburdened concept" as noted by Rosaldo (2021), and yet the work that the term does is needed in order to include the majority of the world's workers and bring them and their working conditions into broader conversations about employment and workplace rights. Indeed, in light of growing informality shaping so much of how work is categorized, practiced, and understood, I hope that this book will add to growing efforts to bring the political into all kinds of informal workspaces that remain hidden, devalued, and made invisible.

Being situated in this particular historical moment that is rife with growing, global informality points to challenges but also the creative possibilities for household workers' movements as well as for the broader informal economy. For example, at the IDWF Congress in Belgium in October 2023, there was a featured panel discussion on "Workers Overcoming Informalities" which brought together representatives from waste pickers' associations and street vendor organizations in conversation with household workers. These connections between domestic workers and workers in other informal sectors prove hopeful for genuine policy solutions and other potential collaborative alternatives that are inclusive and worker centered. Furthermore, opening up discussions about paid and unpaid household work in spaces that are themselves distinct from the private household helps to trouble the boundary that protects, and thus obscures, its work.

As widespread efforts to regulate the growing informal economy continue, my contribution enables us to better understand the ways that long-standing patterns of legal exclusion can shift the political landscape, helping us to more accurately predict ways that legislation positively or negatively affects marginalized populations in their struggles for labor rights. Future research should emphasize the critical importance of defined, contractual benefits for the legal concept of the "employment relationship" within domestic work and other sectors of the informal economy. In light of both national and global movements to create and pass legislation that regulates the personal dynamics of employment relationships in the home, the fact that these relationships elude compliance and remain firmly grounded within the realm of interpersonal negotiation holds relevance for sculpting out ways to creatively bring labor rights into the home. Furthermore, these findings also remind us of the continual need to re-theorize its very space, rather than taking its limits and boundaries for granted.

Because domestic work is a job that often involves duties which transcend beyond the realm of typical and into that of the intimate, it also often seems to remain just out of reach of regulation (Parreñas 2015; Poo 2010). Yet we know this is not true, as workers are not defined by the law; that is not "all that they can do"; in fact, "all that they are" is a much deeper and profound story. In this way, we also know that household workers, their labor, and their site of work are not limited to exclusionary categories. Workers have organized for rights through various political and social forms, and we can turn to some of these historical examples for a reminder of the creativity that existed previously in various sectors. In 1878, members of the Working Women's Union (WWU) in Chicago, including Lucy Parsons, Alzina Stevens, Lizzie Swank, and Elizabeth Rogers, tied together two pressing concerns of its membership—the right to vote and the 8-hour working day. The next year, members of the WWU led more than 300 seamstresses in a protest across the city to demand a shorter working day, walking from shop to shop to gather more workers along the way (Roediger and Foner 1989:166). These women later organized the Ladies'

Federal Labor Union No. 2703, which brought together women workers of all stripes, including candy makers, music teachers, bookbinders, clerks, dressmakers, typists, gum makers, and housewives (166).

This kind of "adventurous" diversity of bringing together various worker categories, as well as their ability to connect various political demands together across occupations, serves as a reminder of workers' potential to creatively connect with others across seemingly disparate experiences of work. I turn to these examples as a reminder of the innovative possibilities that seemed out of reach at the time, as inspiration for ways to fully take on the question of labor rights at home. This is a means of perpetuating a particular kind of past, one that has learned from its exclusionary practices and is ready to shape history anew through a fresh narrative that explores power and the personal embedded in the home as a site of work and law.

METHODOLOGICAL APPENDIX

I visited Lima for the first time in August 2011 to conduct preliminary exploratory research for a month. Thanks to support from the Tinker Foundation and the Center for Latin American Studies, I spent that time exploring the capital, staying in the El Centro district, and writing in the afternoons at the Peruvian National Library. El Centro is located far from the ocean coast and houses the main central plazas of the city, Plaza de Armas and Plaza Bolívar, as well as the presidential palace and other important government buildings. I assumed that this was the right location to choose, as it would literally be in "the center" of everything, and so I flew there with two suitcases—one full of far too many books, and the other packed with clothes that were not nearly warm enough for the chilly winter month of August. I rented a small room in what turned out to be a drafty hostel with no hot water, and I fell for the city over those four weeks that passed by quickly.

Yet I soon realized that living in El Centro, where shops close early, the streets are empty, there are hardly any residential zones, and only a few scattered nightclubs continue on past dark, did not expose me to the inner workings of class in Lima. Only by wandering to Miraflores and then eventually San Isidro did I begin to see not only the tourist hubs, but also the wealthier homes wherein the practices of domestic service were reproduced. August 2011 was incredibly useful, then, in helping me to situate where I should position myself when returning to conduct fieldwork. For that reason, I rented a studio apartment in Miraflores where I was not only centrally located—much more so than in El Centro where I began—but also very close to parks and the *malecón* where household workers spend much of their time. Not including August 2011, then, I conducted ten months of ethnography and seventy-two in-depth interviews of household workers between 2012 and 2014, plus several revisits later on for shorter periods of time.

In Lima, the weekly three-hour workshop on the 2003 Household Workers' Law held at La Casa de Panchita was a central focus of my fieldwork, and I eventually came to co-teach the course before transitioning to teach it on my own. We did the exact same thing every single week: individual introductions, an overview of the law, collectively reading through its eighteen verbose articles, and then discussing them in connection with workers' lived experiences, bringing together a particular group of individual workers with their specific questions and experiences. In those three hours, workers learned about their unique and complex set of legal rights and protections, which was usually a very new concept for them as the vignette alluded to at the end of Chapter 2.

Depending on the group of household workers in attendance each Sunday, the workshop often grew emotional as women discovered that they could, often for the first time, share some of their challenging and painful experiences as household workers. Others listened and chimed in at different times as the group collectively processed the various scenarios they had experienced in their working lives inside of employers' homes. The workshop thus served as an important point of departure for labor-rights consciousness for the household workers of Lima, and it additionally fostered a sense of solidarity and feminist community as women listened to and learned from each other.

REFLECTIONS ON HOUSEHOLD WORKERS AND PERUVIAN CUISINE: EL TALLER DE COCINAR

In addition to the fieldwork described in Chapter 1 and discussed throughout Chapters 2 and 3, I also taught reproductive rights classes to teenage domestic workers at a total of five junior-high night schools throughout the city, and I participated in a weekly cooking workshop with household workers. Both of these activities soon became a routine feature of my fieldwork, and they correspondingly offered key insights in contextualizing the world of domestic workers in Lima as well as the limits to the household workers' law.

The cooking class, taught by the knowledgeable and serious Josefina Medina, demonstrated the laborious intricacies of Peruvian cuisine. It was held at the household workers' center from nine until twelve or ten until one on Sundays, right before the Law Workshop, and it importantly provided a collective lunch for those at the center on its busiest day of the week. As part of the requirements for seeking employment through the center, which guarantees a written contract, a secure third-party advocate, and at least the national minimum wage, workers had to attend the cooking class three times. However, Josefina's stern yet supportive instruction brought back many of the same workers even after they had secured employment, week after week.

Alongside the domestic workers in the class, each Sunday we learned how to prepare a number of classic Peruvian dishes and desserts that showcased the cuisine's fascinating blend of a number of international and regional flavors and adapted traditions. This fusion is very much a historical one, as it reflects the waves of immigration patterns to Peru and includes influences from Japanese, Chinese, West African, Spanish, and Italian cultures, and Indigenous populations dating back to the Inca. Additionally, it celebrates Lima's coastal location with incredibly fresh and unique preparations of *ceviche* but also draws from preparations and ingredients more familiar in the jungle and highland regions of the country.

Potatoes, peppers, corn, and quinoa are key staples of Peruvian cuisine, but besides a basic understanding of the flavor combinations, what I took away from these classes was an overwhelming sense of the sheer amount of work that preparing each of these traditional dishes requires. Josefina, a skilled expert at visualizing the specific division of labor necessary given the spatial constraints of the tiny kitchen inside La Casa de Panchita, patiently assigned the twelve or thirteen of us in the class each Sunday a set of tasks. Over the next two to three hours, we prepared that day's combination of meat, vegetables, fruits, grains, and seafood according to Josefina's verbal instructions and printed handouts that often involved fifteen to twenty steps. A former household worker herself, Josefina drew from her experience and peppered the three hours with tips and practical advice for those preparing for a new job. We discussed when each meal would be appropriate to prepare in an employer's home, considering specific holiday gatherings, religious practices, seasonal customs, and employer preferences while we learned the recipes to-gether. Finally, we set the large makeshift table with plates, silverware, and paper napkins, plated the correct number of dishes, and sat down to eat the meal together, by that point usually very hungry and somewhat exhausted from the process.

Joining in this workshop and cooking together with domestic workers each Sunday illuminated three important and related points. First, as in most cultures, food is central to the (re)production of the Limeño household and is celebrated as such. Employers place a premium on workers who are skilled cooks and can prepare *comida típica*, or the classic dishes of the country. In another central activity of my fieldwork, the workshop on the law, workers practiced reciting with confidence the various dishes they enjoy cooking in preparation for upcoming interviews with potential employers. In the open-ing vignette of Chapter 2, the first question Janette's employer asks her is if she can cook, even though that is the specific duty of the other worker, Beni, while Janette has been hired to clean. However, and leading to the second point, Limeño homes' designs reflect the importance of those who *eat* the food, but not those who *prepare* it with respect to the size of the dining area as compared to the actual kitchen. An employer I talked with who is originally from South Africa, Sabina, spoke to this point precisely. She described the house-hunting search process when she, her husband, and their young daugh-ter first arrived to Lima:

> Lima has the most gorgeous homes . . . but such small kitchens! When we were looking for homes, we were shown thirty beautiful places around several districts. But all of them had such small kitchens, I couldn't get over it! And now, after being here for a while, I *do* get it. It's because all of the maids here . . . *they* are the ones doing the cooking.

Finally, conducting an ethnography of household labor in Peru allowed me to see, smell, taste, and respect the cultural importance placed on these traditional and labor-intensive Peruvian dishes. I grew to love most every-thing I ate and drank there, from fruits I had not previously known to exist (including *lúcuma*, *aguaymanto* and *camu camu*) to Inca Kola, a bright-yellow, lemon-verbena-flavored soda owned by Coca-Cola everywhere save for Peru, to the standard, classic recipes (*ají de gallina*) which I tried to replicate back home to varying degrees of success. I am clearly not alone in being enamored with Peruvian food, as Latin America's largest food festival, Mistura, held annually on Lima's Costa Verde, in Magdalena del Mar, is only garnering more international attention with its mix of Peruvian chefs, international cuisines, a "Hall of Pisco," and more than three hundred farmers from various regions demonstrating their harvest in the capital through the Gran Mercado (Moseley-Williams, 2014).

Yet those innovative chefs positioned with the resources and legitimacy sufficient to depart from Peru's *comida típica* in their restaurants, including Gastón Acurio, Pedro Miguel Schiaffino (the "jungle chef"), and Virgilio Martínez, among others, have made international names for themselves and earned global acclaim for the unique ways they refashion these "authentic" dishes and ingredients. In March 2013, I was fortunate enough to dine at Martínez's upscale restaurant, Central, when it was clearly recognized as an emerging star of Lima's culinary scene but did not yet demand a reservation three months in advance. That experience alone remains one of the most fascinating and memorable meals of my life.

And yet as my research progressed, I came to find this seemingly exciting global recognition bittersweet, if not sour. The more that I spoke with household workers and learned about *their* culinary experiences, or lack thereof, while working and living in their employers' homes, the more I was struck with a fundamentally troubling realization of the deep contradiction my interviews were revealing at each turn. I mentioned only a few of those worker testimonies in this book, but they represent a significant swath of the daily treatment that workers endure—Adelinda, only allowed tea for breakfast, a light lunch, and nothing else until the following morning, and Erlinda, scolded for eating chicken and ordered to settle for "pasta with butter," rather than eat a more satisfying and filling protein. Household workers are, thus, the only category of Peruvian worker guaranteed employer-provided nutrition, and yet in a deeply ironic fashion, even though they are tasked with the creation of those meals and prized for their cooking skills, they are frequently denied regular, sufficient meals and nourishment. We see the law fall away once the employer's table has been set, then, and this disconnect certainly tempered and troubled my understanding of the previously purely exciting and long-overdue global recognition of the Peruvian culinary scene.

POSITIONALITY, ACCESS, AND NAVIGATING THE CITIES

When establishing contact with domestic workers in Lima, I positioned myself as a researcher and sociologist "interested in studying domestic workers' experiences." I purposefully offered a vague motivation to begin an open dialogue, as many workers were surprised to encounter someone intrigued by their lives, and many were altogether unaware of the 2003 legislation. My educational capital, social class, and racial privilege situated me in Lima as a highly educated, upper-middle-class (since I rented my own studio in an affluent central district of the city), white, non-native Spanish-speaking woman from a U.S. university. I exercised reflexivity by employing my outsider status thoughtfully by using a semi-structured interview agenda with space for workers' responses and questions, when selecting neutral, secure locations for our conversations, and by valuing their time with a piece of fresh fruit and a small box of tea (Anzaldúa 2000; Collins 1990; Naples 2003). The final translations of my interviews and conversations are my own.

At my side during many of my initial interviews was Victoria Maraví, a linguistics student at Pontificia Universidad Católica del Perú, or "La Católica," with a penchant for social theory and literature who became my trusted research assistant in Lima. Interestingly enough, through hiring Victoria, I became for the first time someone else's employer, and while the dynamic was quite distinct from the domestic worker-employer relationship at the heart of my study, it still structured our relationship. Beyond her simply providing translation for local references and Limeño pop culture, we talked through several key interviews together and processed where the research was going as I began seeing patterns arising in my findings. Having lived and worked in the United Kingdom and the United States previously, Victoria shed important light on my cultural understandings of the Peruvian context yet could also harness her own sense of outsider-ness, as she, too, had started to see Lima's practices around domestic work in a new light.

In Lima, I conducted two interviews with both employer and worker present for the conversation, and thus, I adjusted my questions and analyzed what was and, more importantly, what was *not* said in my presence in a manner different than all of my other interviews, with respect to the power dynamics at play as well as the potentially precarious position of the household worker in her employer's presence. I later interviewed one of these workers separately and she discussed her frustrations when her employer "spoke for her." This is further indicative of the specific nature of household labor, as well as the complications of the positionality of household workers, since they labor (and often live) inside their employer's private home and are thus subject to the schedules, plans, agendas, and—especially in the case of this particular employer—entitlement of their employers.

New York was a different story completely, both in terms of how I accessed workers and how workers understood me. I draw from nine months of ethnography and fifty-two in-depth interviews in New York City conducted in 2013 and 2014, as well as the analysis of policy documents from the New York Department of Labor and organizational materials and research reports from Damayan Migrant Workers Association, Domestic Workers United (DWU), and the National Domestic Workers Alliance (NDWA). I spent the bulk of my time reaching out to Afro-Caribbean workers organized through DWU and Filipina workers organized through Damayan, as these two groups played a central role in the Bill of Rights campaign and continue to shape New York's domestic worker movement. Additionally, I spent each Sunday with Adhikaar, a community and workers' center for the Nepali-speaking community that advocates for its many domestic worker members. While there was understandable trepidation about allowing an academic into the safe spaces of these organizations, I am grateful to KC Wagner from Cornell's Worker Institute for vouching for me. Over time, these organizations seemed to recognize my commitment to support their efforts for labor rights and protections, and eventually came to trust me enough to allow me to attend events and talk with workers. Thanks to the generosity of those four organizations, I joined many of their meetings, workshops, classes, and protests.

I am especially grateful to five members of DWU for their extraordinary compassion upon having just met me on a warm July afternoon in 2013. DWU was good enough to organize a gathering with me and these five activists in their headquarters in Manhattan. We were talking and sharing in what seemed like a low-key and informative conversation together, but then while talking about our families, I suddenly broke down and began to cry at the table in front of all of them. My family and I had just buried my grandmother the previous week after losing her very quickly to pancreatic cancer, and I had returned from Lima just in time to spend a few nights with her in the hospital. Before this July afternoon, however, I am not certain I had ever truly experienced *compassion* before. Their hands were gently patting my arm in a soothing manner, the entire tone of the room changed, and I instantly felt even more welcomed by these incredible women. The whole encounter only lasted a few minutes, but I will never forget it, and I felt that connection for the duration of my fieldwork, whenever I would run into them at NDWA events or related meetings.

Innovative and exciting conversations about the cost of care and the future of care work in the city were happening during my fieldwork, and so thanks to information from various contacts in domestic worker organizations and JFREJ, Jews for Racial and Economic Justice, I joined meetings of the Eldercare Dialogues, Hand in Hand, and the Employer Codes of Conduct campaign. The Eldercare Dialogues were an interfaith forum between the progressive Jewish community of employers, home health-care workers, and household worker organizations to facilitate discussions of the impending problem of how to care for the city's elderly population and think through policy. These gatherings brought together the majority of domestic worker organizations, activist groups, and immigration advocacy associations, providing me with a broader understanding of organizational responses to the recent legislation in action as well as a sense of the main partners and strategic alliances.

My interviews took place in all of New York's boroughs except for Staten Island, and my interviewees ranged in age from twenty-six to sixty-two years of age and demonstrated wide geographic diversity in terms of their country of origin, having immigrated to the U.S. from the Philippines, Nepal, Tibet, Mexico, Guatemala, Colombia, Peru, Uruguay, Barbados, Saint Vincent and the Grenadines, Trinidad and Tobago, and Jamaica. I conducted interviews in the following neighborhoods: Manhattan—Tribeca, the East Village, Midtown, Columbus Circle, Central Park, Morningside Heights, the Upper East and West Sides, and Harlem; Brooklyn—Fort Greene, Park Slope, Bedford-Stuyvesant, Prospect Heights, and Clinton Hill; Queens—Woodside, Elmhurst, and Jackson Heights; and the Bronx.

Interviews in Queens and Brooklyn were usually at the home of the respondent or in her neighborhood, while those conducted in Manhattan tended to be either while the domestic worker was working, or immediately before or after her shift. I shadowed my respondents at work if they were amenable, and so our interviews took place in a number of locales, including coffee shops, public parks, toddler sing-alongs, the New York Public Library's story hours, workers' homes, their places of employment, and on public transportation. Spending significant time tagging along with domestic workers and their charges gave me a chance to see the excellent care these children received and the fun that they had, as well as the adroit ways that domestic workers kept a close watch on their surroundings, while also holding lively conversations with me. I offered all my respondents a Metro card worth ten dollars for giving their valuable time, and I always met them at a location of their own choosing.[1]

Over the course of my fieldwork I was involved in conducting research for the UCLA-based research network, "Experiences Organizing Informal Workers Global Research Network." This opportunity enabled me to travel as an academic ally to the founding conference of the International Domestic Workers Federation (IDWF) in Montevideo, Uruguay, where I brought T-shirts, legislative materials, and informative pamphlets from New York City's domestic worker organizations with me to exchange with other countries' domestic worker associations. This research-network consultant position and the relationships established with the IDWF and the ILO also enabled me to attend a regional meeting of the IDWF the following year in Hong Kong where I engaged with many domestic worker leaders from across Asia. These comparative global experiences helped to shed light on my own project. And to provide social context to my research in New York, I also interviewed legal staff from immigrant-advocacy groups, domestic workers' organizations, and urban-justice groups.

Since my New York friends either didn't have children or didn't earn enough money to pay for a nanny or housecleaner, and because it looked and felt odd to visit the parks without children of my own or charges entrusted to my safekeeping, I regularly accompanied a longtime friend with her two young children, ages three and eighteen months, who lived in Brooklyn's Kensington neighborhood, to facilitate easier conversations with nannies and mothers. After each interview, meeting, and event, I took copious field notes. I then wrote longer analytical memos using these field notes each month, which allowed me to recognize patterns occurring in my observations and data. All of my recorded interviews were transcribed (and translated from Spanish, in three cases), for coding and further qualitative analysis.

It was significantly more difficult to talk with workers in New York City for a number of important reasons. The city is always moving, and there is a sort of momentum rushing through the streets and subways that appealed to me; I liked rushing with the city and following commuters, and I especially enjoyed accompanying domestic workers and their charges on their walks and commutes. I enjoyed my daily routine of commuting to the Worker Institute or heading to a park, library, or apartment to meet up with domestic workers. Yet the initial difficulties in New York surprised me, as I had expected an easier transition to my second field site because I know the city fairly well, I have several friends scattered throughout various boroughs, and I communicated mainly in English, rather than Spanish. However, by the time that I began this research in mid-2013, the several main domestic worker organizations were already stretched thin and burdened by what one journalist I spoke with called "researcher fatigue." This was a result of the heightened media coverage of the Bill of Rights, as well as a flurry of interviews with individual organizers. While in many ways the domestic worker organizations and domestic workers themselves saw this attention and interest as positive, they were also simply exhausted. I, thus, strategically tried to be useful by putting my skills to practical use however they might be of service; I wrote research reports for the National Domestic Workers Alliance (NDWA) and the International Domestic Workers Federation, and I filled in when the NDWA lost their intern and needed assistance with office tasks and odd jobs. I also volunteered at holiday benefits for Damayan and for the NDWA by working at the coat-check closet, checking in registered guests upon arrival, selling raffle tickets for their fundraisers, and cleaning up after these events. I also shared my growing findings throughout the course of my research with the organizations in both Lima and New York City by either doing informal presentations (New York) or roundtable-type workshops (Lima) with domestic workers, sharing patterns that arose within the fieldwork. This was especially effective when doing field revisits after the initial stage of fieldwork was completed in each site.

While based in Manhattan, I was fortunate enough to hold a visiting scholar position at Cornell University's Worker Institute. My affiliation there was key, as many Caribbean domestic workers from Domestic Workers United had completed the Nanny Training Program started by the Worker Institute in 2012 and, thus, had favorable impressions of the Institute's programs and dedicated faculty and staff. Additionally, those faculty and staff had long-standing relationships with many of the domestic worker organizations, and that connection allowed me greater access to archival research and to informal conversations with workers. Some of these organizations had held their early meetings at the Worker Institute before they were able to establish a formal presence and brick-and-mortar space in the city. Reading over meeting notes and planning discussions from the early 2000s with those organizations gave me a sense of recent context to the upsurge in domestic worker organizing as well as the chronology around organizing first for a citywide ordinance and, later, for the statewide Domestic Workers' Bill of Rights.

However, power dynamics are always inherent in shaping research interactions, and this never felt truer for me than in the Upper East Side, where I shared a 325 sq. ft. apartment with two roommates. My race, gender, and relative economic capital as a white, highly educated woman positioned me as part of the neighborhood and, thus, often mistaken as an employer. I, too, mistook many mothers with small children as domestic workers. Early on in my fieldwork in New York City, I tried walking the blocks of my new neighborhood and casually striking up conversation with people on the street with children, thinking that perhaps they were nannies. Not only were they too busy to stop and talk with me, but several bristled at the thought of being considered as such. In May 2013, I tried talking to two women in their mid-thirties, pushing upmarket strollers in the heat on Lexington Avenue. With the heat and the crowds up against us, the woman to my right flipped her brown ponytail over her shoulder and turned to face me, muttering under her breath, "Look, most of the nannies aren't white here! I mean, I hate to say that, but . . ."[2] She trailed off as she marched forward with her stroller and child, and I faltered in my step, mumbled a thank you, and then fell back into pace with the rest of the crowd.

Similarly, on a humid afternoon a couple of weeks later, on 81st and 3rd Avenue, a Caribbean nanny slowly navigated a large navy blue and pink stroller containing a drooling two-year-old with curly blonde hair around store displays in an overly air-conditioned shoe store. Halfway through my rehearsed skit of approaching her, introducing myself and the research, and asking if she had time to speak about her work experiences and the Bill of Rights, she cocked her head and started looking toward the ceiling. As she listened to me from the side, she nodded and then slowly murmured quietly, "I can't risk that right now, right here . . . but there are so many nannies with stories for you, I wish you could hear them and talk to them, ohhh, I do." Well aware that most of the other women in the store were potential or former employers and that it was thus an inappropriate location in which to talk openly, she and I both went our separate ways.

However, the other reason that it was initially challenging to speak with domestic workers in New York City stems from my standpoint and my positionality within the field. In Lima, I was and will always remain a cultural outsider in important, immutable ways, regardless of how long I might live there, or how much I learn about Peruvian history and politics, or how many interviews I conduct. Yet I embrace that status, as it allowed me to approach the field site with fresh eyes, and I have come away from the research in Lima with a strong sociological analysis of how class, race, gender, and power operate within the city. In New York, however, I very much blended in with the rest of the majority white, upper-middle- to upper-class residents of the Upper East Side, where I lived for the first nine months of fieldwork. Rather than an intriguing advocate, as I was generally understood in Lima, in New York City I was often perceived as a potential employer, or certainly on the "other" side of the employment relationship. While employers in Lima also assumed that I hired a worker to clean my apartment, the employer class is so ubiquitous that it did not matter that I actually did not hire anyone; the assumption was enough, and domestic workers in Lima were still more willing to speak with me precisely because of my outsider status. My access was slow and steady, and only thanks to word of mouth support from different NGOs and contacts at the Worker Institute. This process gave me a different understanding and particular view of the field as my sample was more heavily weighted with activist domestic workers and those most involved in their organizations. I accounted for this by also using snowball sampling with domestic workers and their own friends and contacts, and by including other workers in my sample who I spoke with at parks, libraries, and other public settings throughout the city.

COMPARATIVE LAW APPENDIX

THE NEW YORK DOMESTIC WORKER BILL OF RIGHTS, 2010

Current provisions of the law include the following (Gonzalez and Leberstein 2010):

Minimum Wage Coverage
- Domestic workers, including all babysitters who work on anything but a casual basis
- Live-out and live-in companions, employed privately by an individual employer and/or by an agency

The law understands *casual* as *irregular*, or that which does not follow a routine pattern. So, for instance, if a nanny works only for eight hours each Monday and Wednesday, but that schedule is fixed, regular, and repetitive, she is covered by the law and not considered a casual worker. A teenage babysitter who watches children intermittently on the weekends, for instance, is not covered. Family members are also exempt (29 CFR 552.5).[1] Also of note is an understanding of who, exactly, is categorized as a "companion." According to the law, companions are defined as workers who provide assistance, care, and protection for an elderly person. Their job duties may include household work as long as those hours do not exceed 20% of the total weekly hours worked, however (29 CFR 552.6).[2]

Overtime Rate Coverage
- Live-out domestic workers = 1½ x regular rate of pay after 40 hours/week
- Live-in domestic workers = 1½ x regular rate of pay after 44 hours/week
- Live-out companions employed by private individual in a household = 1½ x regular rate of pay after 40 hours
- Live-out companions employed by agency = 1½ x minimum wage after 40 hours
- Live-out companions employed by private individual in a household = 1½ x regular rate of pay after 44 hours
- Live-out companions employed solely by agency = 1½ x minimum wage after 44 hours

Additional Rights
- One day of rest (24 hours) per week, or overtime pay if workers agree to work that day
- Three paid days of rest each year after one year of work for the same employer
- Protection under New York State Human Rights Law
- Creation of a special cause of action for domestic workers who suffer sexual or racial harassment

THE PERUVIAN HOUSEHOLD WORKERS' LAW, 2003: LEY NO. 27986: LEY DE LOS TRABAJADORES DEL HOGAR

Article 1: *Ámbito de aplicación*: This law regulates the labor relations of household workers.

Article 2: *Definición*: Household workers do the work of cleaning, tidying, cooking, washing, assisting, caring for children, preserving the residence of the home, and developing the life of the home. This applies to those who do not run a business inside of the home.

Article 3: *Celebración del contrato de trabajo*: The work contract may either be in verbal or written format.

Article 4: *Reserva sobre la vida en el hogar*: Workers are obligated to be diligent and private about what goes on in the employer's home, unless required by law to do otherwise.

Article 5: *Monto de la remuneración*: The wage rate is to be decided by mutual agreement. The employer is obligated to pay for food and/or housing for the worker, according to the economic level of the employer. Housing and food should not be considered part of the salary.

Article 6: *Pago de remuneración*: Wages may be paid monthly, bi-weekly, or weekly. Workers must maintain a record of the payments they receive from the employer, which will serve as their proof of payment.

Article 7: *Terminación del contrato de trabajo*: Workers must give their employers 15 days of notice when ending the work contract/quitting. Employers must also give 15 days of notice when firing a worker, or 15 days of pay if there is no notice given.

Article 8: *Otras formas de terminación del contrato de trabajo*: Other causes for ending the work contract include death of one of the parties, mutual agreement, retirement of the worker, and serious, grave offenses.

Article 9: *Compensación por tiempo de servicios*: Compensation for time of service is equal to 15 days of wages per year of service, or the proportional amount. This will be paid within a reasonable timeframe after termination of contract, and at each year's end.

Article 10: *Descanso semanal*: Household workers have the right to 24 hours of uninterrupted rest per week.

Article 11: *Trabajo en días feriados*: Household workers have the right to paid holidays off in the private sector. If they do agree to work on those holidays, they will be paid time-and-a-half, or an extra 50% of their salary added to their daily salary.

Article 12: *Vacaciones*: Household workers have the right to 15 days of annual vacation.

Article 13: *Gratificaciones*: Household workers have the right to bonus pay twice a year. Bonus pay is 50% of their monthly salary, paid twice yearly—once in July for Peru's Day of Independence, and once in December for Christmas.

Article 14: *Trabajo para el hogar "cama afuera"*: Household workers who want to sleep in their own homes are still covered under the law and are classified as "cama afuera" and under no obligation to live in their employer's home.

Article 15: *Trabajo para el hogar "cama adentro"*: For workers who live in the home of the employer, their working hours are not meant to exceed 8 hours per day and 48 hours per week.

Article 16: *Obligaciones del empleador*: When a worker sleeps in, the employer must provide appropriate housing according to the economic comfort of the employer, as well as food.

Article 17: *Derecho a la educación*: Workers who serve in the house have the right to education. Employers must provide all that they need to make sure they regularly attend school outside of their workday.

Article 18: *Riesgos cubiertos*: Household workers have the right to a pension and social security coverage, and they may opt into either the public pension fund or a private pension fund. A percentage will be paid by the worker [9%], and a percentage will be paid by the employer [13%].

NOTES

Chapter 1

1. See the Comparative Law Appendix to read the text of each law in Chapter 6. The law governing domestic work in Lima is much more substantive than that of New York City, and so I reference its tenets in-text in Chapter 4 as well.

2. For instance, in the Arab states, more than 50% of domestic workers are men (ILO 2015), while Pariser (2015) found that 97% of domestic workers in the early decades of colonialism in Dar es Salaam were African men.

3. 2017 estimates regarding the demographic breakdown of the Peruvian population show 25.8% as Indigenous, 60.2% as mestizo (mixed Indigenous and white), 5.9% as white or European descendant, 3.6% as African descent, 1.2% as Japanese and Chinese descent, and 3.3% as unspecified (World Factbook 2024).

4. Names and identifying details of individuals have been changed in order to protect those interviewed for this project. The names of civil society associations and domestic worker organizations in Lima and New York City have not been changed, however, as they are recognized organizations with public visibility. In New York City, knowing the organizations' ethnic and cultural identity is important to understand the broader social context in which the industry is embedded.

5. To provide some context on Bastidas Aliaga's (2012) survey, the sample size was 433 and the survey was administered in the 10 most populous cities throughout Peru, with the cities of Lima and Callao included as one. The aims of the survey were to collect information on social protections, labor rights, employment data, and social dialogue from the perspective of women workers. In a more recent survey according to Ocampo and Arcondo (2021), 21% of domestic workers are between the ages of 15 and 29, 66% are between the ages of 30 and 59, and 12.3% are 60 years and older. This data comes from a report for the Ministry of Labor and Employment Promotion (MTPE),

"Domestic Workers in the Peruvian Labor Market 2015–2019," which uses data from the National Household Survey on Living Conditions and Poverty (ENAHO) of the National Statistics Institute (INEI). This survey has a probabilistic sample based on interviews that were conducted in 24 national departments across Peru.

Chapter 2

1. Janette responds, "A little. I cook meat stew, or with chicken or lamb."

2. Conversions are adjusted throughout according to the average exchange rate of Peruvian soles to U.S. dollars at the time.

3. Personal interview, November 11, 2012.

4. Personal interview, December 4, 2012.

5. Personal interview, April 26, 2013.

6. Due to the end of a number of international NGO grants and support paired with rising rent costs, La Casa de Panchita left Jesús María and relocated to a smaller but still centrally located spot in the district of Lince in recent years, and now (2025) has relocated to Magdalena del Mar.

7. Fraser (2013) importantly complicates this understanding, suggesting an ostensible alliance of interests between particular versions of feminism and neoliberal reforms.

8. Personal interview, October 30, 2012.

9. However, by only specifying hours of nightly rest rather than daily work, the decree stipulated a default sixteen-hour workday.

10. "Tupac Amaru lo prometió; Velasco lo cumplió," states the poster (Walker 2014).

11. Fujimori's forceful return to rule effectively eliminated any extant political proposals in process. The same was feared might happen during the 2016 elections with respect to amendments to the household workers' law in various stages of legal formation, as Fujimori's daughter Keiko was a close contender for the presidency and she is a strict *fujimorista*.

12. Personal interview, April 25, 2013.

13. Personal interview, April 25, 2013.

14. To a significantly lesser degree, a number of other NGOs contributed to this effort: CESIP (Centro de Estudios Sociales y Publicaciones), founded in 1976 to "work toward the development and participation of all social actors, including children, adolescents, and women"; Las Manuelas, el Movimiento Manuela Ramos, a feminist NGO founded in 1978 to "improve the situation and position of women"; APRODEH (Asociación Pro Derechos Humanos), founded in 1983 and dedicated to the defense, promotion, and diffusion of human rights; DEMUS, founded in 1987 by four lawyers who wanted to create a feminist political space in which to build sustainable strategies to end violence against women and push for political rights; Centro de Derechos y Desarrollo (CEDAL); Comité de América Latina y el Caribe para la Defensa de los Derechos de las Mujeres (CLADEM-PERU); Flora Tristán, the key feminist organization previously mentioned; and other civil society organizations (Mauricio 2015).

15. Personal interview, December 8, 2013.

16. "The workers. Us."

Chapter 3

1. While *empleada* technically means "employee," throughout Latin America it more specifically refers to someone who cleans and works in the home; a maid.

2. Decrees were passed in 1957 and 1970 which offered the most basic worker protections, but the 2003 law: Ley No. 27986: The Peruvian Household Workers' Law is notable as it was approved by Congress, signed into law by the first democratically elected Indigenous president, Alejandro Toledo, and covers the entire nation, though the majority of household labor is concentrated in Lima.

3. Between the years of 1898 and 1945, an estimated 27,000 Japanese people immigrated to Peru (Yamakana 2000).

4. Chinese immigrants mainly worked in Peru's sugar fields and silver mines in the nineteenth century (Gonzales 1989).

5. *Cama adentro* is a labor arrangement in which the worker lives and sleeps inside of the employer's home, as opposed to *cama afuera*, which means living and sleeping outside in one's own space.

6. *Chola* refers to someone of Indigenous heritage and is often used interchangeably with *empleada*. Its verb form, *cholear*, means to "classify someone in a derogatory manner as racially and socially inferior in a competition for *blancura* (whiteness)" (Vasquez del Aguila 2014:17).

7. "Ugly, little ugly ones," and "mixed race, close to Indians"; derogatory.

8. Personal interview, December 9, 2012.

9. See Mary Douglas (1966) and her work on dirt and pollution as a symbolic idea that reflects relationships around superiority, social disorder, and inequalities.

10. Personal interview, April 26, 2013.

11. Personal interview, November 18, 2012.

12. Personal interview, January 15, 2013.

13. Personal interview, October 30, 2012.

14. These signs state, "Uso Exclusvio para Socios, no Amas" and "SSHH de Amas," respectively.

15. Personal interview, March 12, 2015.

16. A friend living in Lima uses his "servant's room" to store his bicycles. "It's cement, it's damp, it's small—what else am I going to store in here? It's certainly not a place for someone to live!" he commented.

17. Note that the figure itself labels this space as a *walking closet* in the master bedroom, and that is the only word written in English in the blueprints themselves. The Peruvian architect labeled these blueprints as such, and I also heard other Peruvian friends mention that term when talking about their parents' homes. While the technical term is *walk-in closet*, this kind of slight linguistic adaptation with a shifted yet corresponding meaning happens often when technical or specialized words in English are adapted into Spanish.

18. Personal interview, November 11, 2012.

19. Personal interview, January 24, 2014.

20. Personal interview, April 25, 2013.

21. Personal interview, December 19, 2012.

22. Personal interview, October 30, 2012. Roselia is a pseudonym, used to preserve her anonymity.

23. Personal interview, January 22, 2014.

24. Personal interview, November 14, 2012.

25. Personal interview, January 14, 2013.

26. Personal interview, December 4, 2012.

27. Personal interview, December 9, 2012.

28. Personal interview, December 14, 2012.

29. Personal interview, December 12, 2012.

30. Personal interview, February 8, 2013.

31. Personal interview, November 18, 2012.

32. Personal interview, February 3, 2013.

33. The ILO survey used data from ENAHO (National Household Survey on Living Conditions and Poverty) and a rapid online survey aimed at domestic workers which was carried out between April and May 2021 and reached a sample of 203 domestic workers (ILO 2022).

34. In the ILO (2022) survey conducted more recently, the numbers were fairly consistent as only 23.5% of domestic workers reported receiving Christmas bonuses (meaning 76.5% did not receive this bonus), and 19.1% reported receiving national-holiday bonuses, leaving 80.9% without the holiday bonus.

35. Personal interview, March 10, 2013.

36. This number is adjusted according to 2012's average exchange rate of Peruvian soles to U.S. dollars.

37. In March 2016, then-President Ollanta Humala raised the Peruvian national minimum wage by 13% or PEN 100, from PEN 750 to PEN 850 (from USD 224.90 to USD 254.90 at 2016's average exchange rate of Peruvian soles to U.S. dollars).

Chapter 4

1. For a focused study on the organizing of African American household workers from the 1950s to 1970s, see Premilla Nadasen's *Household Workers Unite* (2015).

2. Other popular occupations included, by size: agricultural laborers; tailoresses and seamstresses; milliners; dressmakers; stenographers and typists; clerical and kindred workers; laundry workers; farmers, planters, and overseers; cooks; employees of hotels and restaurants; housekeepers and stewards; trained nurses; and telephone operators (1988:6–7).

3. The full text of the National Labor Relations Act (29 U.S.C. § 151–169) regarding this point is the following: "The term 'employee' shall include any employee, and shall not be limited to the employees of a particular employer, unless the Act [this subchapter] explicitly states otherwise, and shall include any individual whose work has ceased as a consequence of, or in connection with, any current labor dispute or because of any unfair labor practice, and who has not obtained any other regular and substantially equivalent employment, but shall not include any individual employed as an agricultural laborer, *or in the domestic service of any family or person at his home,* or any individual employed by his parent or spouse, or any individual

having the status of an independent contractor, or any individual employed as a supervisor, or any individual employed by an employer subject to the Railway Labor Act [45 U.S.C. § 151 et seq.], as amended from time to time, or by any other person who is not an employer as herein defined" (29 U.S.C. § 152(3); emphasis mine).

4. The text of the Occupational Safety and Health Act (OSHA, 1970) states: "Policy as to domestic household employment activities in private residences: *As a matter of policy*, individuals who, in their own residences, privately employ persons for the purpose of performing for the benefit of such individuals what are commonly regarded as ordinary domestic household tasks, such as house cleaning, cooking, and caring for children, shall not be subject to the requirements of the Act with respect to such employment" (29 C.F.R. § 1975.6; emphasis mine).

5. While much of New York is accessible by metro transit, several of my interviewees have discussed how needs changed within their employer's family as children grew up and started attending school. Parents preferring that their children be driven to school meant that non-driving nannies had to look for a new place of employment. For nannies without documents, licenses are beyond reach and thus these nannies cannot take jobs that require driving children around the city. However, for the majority of nannies and other residents of the city, the subways and buses are sufficient.

6. Personal interview, December 5, 2013.

7. At the time this research was conducted, immigrants made up 47% of New York City's labor force (Lobo and Salvo 2013).

8. It is worth noting that most immigrants (77%) are legally in the country, as data from 2022 shows: 49% (23.4 million) were naturalized U.S. citizens, 24% (11.5 million) were lawful permanent residents, 4% (2 million) were legal temporary residents, and 23% (11 million) were unauthorized immigrants (Moslimani and Passel 2024).

9. Personal interview, November 7, 2013.

10. According to the U.S. Department of Homeland Security, the U.S. issued 1,329 B-1 visas to personal or domestic workers in 2013. In 2020, the U.S. only issued 517 B-1 visas. This number reached 7,306 B-1 visas in 2022 and 4,987 by May 1, 2023 (Office of Strategy, Policy, and Plans 2023).

11. To gather this data, a total of 208 surveys were collected between the spring of 2004 through the summer of 2007. Surveys were completed in all five boroughs of New York, Jersey City, in the suburbs of New Jersey, and parts of Connecticut—close to where domestic workers work and live—and on buses, in the parks and subways, and in house meetings and Filipino restaurants (Caballes et al. 2010).

12. Personal interview, Brooklyn, New York City, December 15, 2013.

13. Personal interview, October 19, 2013.

14. *Companions* are defined as workers who provide assistance, care, and protection for an elderly person. Their job duties may include household work, as long as those hours do not exceed 20% of the total weekly hours worked (29 CFR 552.6; see also the Comparative Law Appendix).

15. Personal interview, December 4, 2013.

Chapter 5

1. Personal interview, October 19, 2013.
2. Personal interview, December 7, 2013.
3. Personal interview, December 4, 2013.
4. Personal interview, December 18, 2013.
5. Personal interview, December 5, 2013.
6. Personal interview, December 19, 2013.
7. Personal interview, December 7, 2013.
8. Personal interview, December 17, 2013.
9. Personal interview, December 15, 2013.
10. Personal interview, December 18, 2013.
11. Personal interview, October 19, 2013.
12. Personal interview, November 14, 2013.

Chapter 6

1. *Chicha morada* is a traditional, sweet, and non-alcoholic Peruvian drink made from purple corn and commonly served with lunch and dinner in restaurants.

2. Personal interview, December 18, 2013.

3. Domestic workers have long been organized in a large regional network across Latin America; the Confederación Latinoamericana y del Caribe de Trabajadoras del Hogar (CONLACTRAHO: Latin American and Caribbean Confederation of Household Workers) was founded in Uruguay in 1988, just three years after the country's return to democracy.

Methodological Appendix

1. At the time of my research, the Metro base fare was USD 2.50, so these cards would allow workers two free rides to their chosen destination, there and back.

2. Personal encounter during fieldwork, Manhattan, New York City, May 26, 2013.

Comparative Law Appendix

1. Code of Federation Regulations (CFR). Legal Information Institute, Cornell University Law School. 29 CFR § 552.5 "Application of the Fair Labor Standards Act to Domestic Service. Subpart A—Casual Basis." https://www.law.cornell.edu/cfr/text/29/552.5

2. Code of Federal Regulations (CFR). Legal Information Institute, Cornell University Law School. 29 CFR § 552.6: "Application of the Fair Labor Standards Act to Domestic Service. Subpart A—Companion Services." https://www.law.cornell.edu/cfr/text/29/552.6

REFERENCES

Albiston, Catherine. 2006. "Legal Consciousness and Workplace Rights." In *The New Civil Rights Research: A Constitutive Approach*, edited by Benjamin Fleury-Steiner and Laura Beth Nielson. Hanover, NH: Dartmouth/Ashgate Publishing.

Allen, Sheila. 1989. "Locating Homework in an Analysis of the Ideological and Material Constraints on Women's Paid Work." In *Homework: Historical and Contemporary Perspectives on Paid Labor at Home*, edited by Eileen Boris and Cynthia R. Daniels. Urbana, IL: University of Illinois Press.

Ally, Shireen. 2009. *From Servants to Workers: South African Domestic Workers and the Democratic State*. Ithaca, NY: Cornell University Press.

Althusser, Louis. 1971. "Ideology and Ideological State Apparatuses." In *Lenin and Philosophy and Other Essays*. New York: Monthly Review Press.

Alvarez, Sonia. 1999. "Advocating Feminism: The Latin American Feminist NGO 'Boom.'" *International Feminist Journal of Politics* 1(2):181–209.

———. 2009. "Beyond NGO-Ization? Reflections from Latin America." *Development* 52(2):175–84.

American Community Survey. 2019. https://www.census.gov/programs-surveys/acs/

Anderson, Bridget. 2000. *Doing the Dirty Work? The Global Politics of Domestic Labour*. London, UK: Zed Books.

Anderson, Elizabeth. 2017. *Private Government: How Employers Rule Our Lives (and Why We Don't Talk About It)*. Princeton, NJ: Princeton University Press.

Anzaldúa, Gloria. 2000. *Interviews/Entrevistas*. Edited by AnaLouise Keating. New York, NY: Routledge.

Arendt, Hannah. 1958. *The Origins of Totalitarianism*. Second enlarged edition. New York, NY: Meridian Books, Inc.

Auyero, Javier. 2012. *Patients of the State: The Politics of Waiting in Argentina*. Durham, NC: Duke University Press.

Ballantyne, Tony, and Antoinette Burton. 2005. *Bodies in Contact: Rethinking Colonial Encounters in World History*. Durham, NC: Duke University Press.

Banerjee, Swapna M. 2010. "Debates on Domesticity and the Position of Women in Late Colonial India." *History Compass* 8(6):455–73.

Bapat, Sheila. 2014. *Part of the Family? Nannies, Housekeepers, Caregivers and the Battle for Domestic Workers' Rights*. Brooklyn, NY: Ig Publishing.

Bartolomei, Maria Rita. 2010. "Migrant Male Domestic Workers in Comparative Perspective: Four Case Studies from Italy, India, Ivory Coast, and Congo." *Men and Masculinities* 13(1):87–110.

Bastidas Aliaga, María. 2012. *Protección social y trabajadoras del hogar en el Perú desde la visión de las protagonistas*. Centro Internacional de Formación de la Organización del Trabajo. Turin, Italy.

Beauvoir, Simone de. 2015. *The Second Sex*. London, UK: Vintage Classics.

Benson, Susan Porter. 1989. "Women, Work, and the Family: Industrial Homework in Rhode Island in 1934." In *Homework: Historical and Contemporary Perspectives on Paid Labor at Home*, edited by Eileen Boris and Cynthia R. Daniels. Urbana, IL: University of Illinois Press.

Bernardino-Costa, Joaze. 2011. "Destabilizing the National Hegemonic Narrative: The Decolonized Thought of Brazil's Domestic Workers' Unions." *Latin American Perspectives* 8(5): 33–45.

Berrey, Ellen, Robert L. Nelson, and Laura Beth Nielson. 2017. *Rights on Trial: How Workplace Discrimination Law Perpetuates Inequality*. Chicago, IL: The University of Chicago Press.

Bhabha, Homi. 1997[1984]. "Of Mimicry and Man: The Ambivalence of Colonial Discourse." In *Tensions of Empire: Colonial Cultures in a Bourgeois World*, edited by Frederick Cooper and Ann Laura Stoler. Berkeley, CA: University of California Press.

Blackett, Adelle. 2019. *Everyday Transgressions: Domestic Workers' Transnational Challenge to International Labor Law*. Ithaca, NY: Cornell University Press.

Blofield, Merike. 2009. "Feudal Enclaves and Political Reforms: Domestic Workers in Latin America." *Latin American Research Review* 44(1):158–90.

———. 2012. *Care Work and Class: Domestic Workers' Struggle for Equal Rights in Latin America*. University Park, PA: The Penn State University Press.

Blofield, Merike, and Liesl Haas. 2011. "Gender Equality Policies in Latin America." In *The Great Gap: Inequality and the Politics of Redistribution in Latin America*, edited by Merike Blofield, 278–309. University Park, PA: The Pennsylvania State University Press.

Blondet, Cecilia. 1987[1972]. *Mujer y sociedad: perspectivas metodológicas*. Lima, Peru: Fundación Friedrich Naumann, I.E.P. Ediciones.

Boesten, Jelke. 2010. *Intersecting Inequalities: Women and Social Policy in Peru, 1990–2000*. University Park, PA: The Pennsylvania State University Press.

Boris, Eileen. 1989. "Black Women and Paid Labor in the Home: Industrial Homework in Chicago in the 1920s." In *Homework: Historical and Contemporary Perspectives on Paid Labor at Home*, edited by Eileen Boris and Cynthia Daniels. Champaign, IL: University of Illinois Press.

Boris, Eileen, and Jennifer N. Fish. 2014. "'Slaves No More': Making Global Labor Standards for Domestic Workers." *Feminist Studies* 40(2): 411–43.

Boris, Eileen, and Jennifer Klein. 2012. *Caring for America: Home Health Workers in the Shadow of the Welfare State*. New York, NY: Oxford Press.

Boris, Eileen, and Premilla Nadasen. 2008. "Domestic Workers Organize!" *WorkingUSA: The Journal of Labor and Society* 11(4):41–437.

Boydston, Jeanne. 1994. *Home and Work: Housework, Wages, and the Ideology of Labor in the Early Republic*. New York, NY: Oxford University Press.

Bunster, Ximena, and Elsa Chaney. 1985. *Sellers and Servants: Working Women in Lima, Peru*. Austin, TX: University of Texas Press.

Burghgrave, Chase. 2017. "Where Despots Rule: An Interview with Elizabeth S. Anderson." *Jacobin*. June 29. https://jacobin.com/2017/06/private-government-interview-elizabeth-anderson

Burnham, Linda, and Nik Theodore. 2012. *Home Economics: The Invisible and Unregulated World of Domestic Work*. New York, NY: National Domestic Workers Alliance. https://www.domesticworkers.org/wp-content/uploads/2021/06/HomeEconomicsReport.pdf

Caballes, Ana Liza L., Alexa Kasdan, Terri Nilliasca, Linda Oalican, Leah Obias, and Ninotchka Rosca. 2010. *Doing the Work That Makes All Work Possible: A Research Narrative of Filipino Domestic Workers in the Tri-State Area: Executive Summary*. October 23. IssueLab.

Cahill, David. 1994. "Colour by Numbers: Racial and Ethnic Categories in the Viceroyalty of Peru, 1532–1824." *Journal of Latin American Studies* 26(2):325–46.

Campbell, Kristina M. 2014. "Rising Arizona: The Legacy of the Jim Crow Southwest on Immigration Law and Policy After 100 Years of Statehood." *Berkeley La Raza Law Journal* 21(1):101–38.

Carrillo, Teresa. 2014. "Translation and Transnationalization of Domestic Service." In *Translocalities/Translocalidades: Feminist Politics of Translation in the Latin/a Américas*, edited by Sonia E. Alvarez, Claudia de Lima Costa, Verónica Feliu, Rebecca J. Hester, Normal Klahn, and Mille Thayer. Durham, NC: Duke University Press.

Carstens, Andrew. 2012. "Quién es Panchita?" https://www.youtube.com/watch?v=-5pEYo7gFqo&t=117s. May 12.

Casanova, Erynn Masi de. 2013. "Embodied Inequality: The Experience of Domestic Work in Urban Ecuador." *Gender and Society* 27(4):561–85.

———. 2019. *Of Dust and Dignity: Domestic Employment in Contemporary Ecuador*. Ithaca, NY: ILR Press.

Castro, Chelsy. 2008. "Dying to Work: Osha's Exclusion of Health and Safety Standards for Domestic Workers." *The Modern American* (Spring 2008):3–9.

Chaney, Elsa M., and Mary Garcia Castro. 1989. *Muchachas No More: Household Workers in Latin America and the Caribbean*. Philadelphia, PA: Temple University Press.

Chang, Grace. 2001. *Disposable Domestics: Immigrant Women Workers in the Global Economy*. Boston, MA: South End Press.

Chen, Martha Alter. 2012. "The Informal Economy: Definitions, Theories and Policies." Working Paper 1. Women in Informal Employment Globalizing and Organizing. https://www.wiego.org/wp-content/uploads/2019/09/Chen_WIEGO_WP1.pdf

Childress, Alice. 1956. *Like One of the Family: Conversations from a Domestic's Life.* Brooklyn, NY: Independence Publishers.

Chopin, Kate. 1899. *The Awakening.* New York, NY: Herbert S. Stone & Company.

CIED (Centro de Investigación, Educación y Desarrollo). 2007. "Perú: características socio económicas de los hogares 1971–72 a 2003–04." November.

Coble, Alana Erikson. 2006. *Cleaning Up: The Transformation of Domestic Service in Twentieth Century New York City.* New York, NY: Routledge.

Coleman, Leo. 2016. "Inside and Outside the House." *Journal of Contemporary Ethnography* 45(6):692–715.

Colen, Shellee. 1995. "Like a Mother to Them": Stratified Reproduction and West Indian Childcare Workers and Employers in New York." In *Conceiving the New World Order: The Global Politics of Reproduction,* edited by Faye D. Ginsberg and Rayna Rapp. Berkeley, CA: University of California Press.

Collier, Ruth Berins. 1999. *Paths Toward Democracy: The Working Class and Elite in Western Europe and South America.* New York, NY: Cambridge University Press.

Collins, Patricia Hill. 1986. "Learning from the Outsider Within: The Sociological Significance of Black Feminist Thought." *Social Problems* 33(6):S14–S32.

———. 2001. "Like One of the Family: Race, Ethnicity, and the Paradox of US National Identity." *Ethnic and Racial Studies* 24(1):3–28.

Collins Cromley, Elizabeth. 1990. "Alone Together: A History of New York's Early Apartments." In *Housing and Dwelling: Perspectives on Modern Domestic Architecture,* edited by Barbara Miller Lane. Routledge.

Condiciones generales de diseño. 2012. "Título III.1 Arquitectura." https://transparencia .produce.gob.pe/images/stories/Repositorio/transparencia/proyectos-de -inversion/niveles-de-servicio/2021/PNDP/NS/Norma_A_010_CONDICIONES _GENERALES_DE_DISENO.pdf

Cook, Maria Lorena. 2008. *Politics of Labor Reform in Latin America: Between Flexibility and Rights.* University Park, PA: The Penn State University Press.

Cotler, Julio. 1978. *Clases, estado y nación en el Perú.* Lima, Peru: Instituto de Estudios Peruanos.

Covert, Bryce. 2013. "How to Include Domestic Workers in Immigration Reform." *The Nation.* February 12. https://www.thenation.com/article/archive/how-include -domestic-workers-immigration-reform/

Darian-Smith, Eve. 2004. "Ethnographies of Law." In *The Blackwell Companion to Law and Society,* edited by Austin Sarat, 545–68. Malden, MA: Blackwell Publishing.

Das Gupta, Monisha. 2008. "Housework, Feminism, and Labor Activism: Lessons from Domestic Workers in New York." *Signs: A Journal of Women in Culture and Society* 33(3):532–7.

Davidoff, Leonore. 2003. "Gender and the 'Great Divide': Public and Private in British Gender History." *Journal of Women's History* 15(1):13–15.

de la Cadena, Marisol. 1998. "Silent Racism and Intellectual Superiority in Peru." *Bulletin of Latin American Research* 17(2):143–64.

De Regt, Marina. 2010. "Ways to Come, Ways to Leave: Gender, Mobility, and Il/legality Among Ethiopian Domestic Workers in Yemen." *Gender & Society* 24(2):237–60.

Díaz Uriarte, Adelinda. 1989. "The Autobiography of a Fighter (Peru)." In *Muchachas No More: Household Workers in Latin America and the Caribbean*, edited by Elsa M. Chaney and Mary Garcia Castro. Philadelphia, PA: Temple University Press.

Dill, Bonnie Thornton. 1988. "Making the Job Good Yourself: Domestic Service and the Construction of Personal Dignity." In *Women and the Politics of Empowerment*, edited by Ann Bookman and Sandra Morgen. Philadelphia, PA: Temple University Press.

Douglas, Mary. 1991. "The Idea of a Home: A Kind of Space." *Social Research* 58(1):287–307.

———. 2002[1966]. *Purity and Danger: An Analysis of Concepts of Pollution and Taboo*. New York, NY: Routledge.

Drinot, Paulo. 2011. *The Allure of Labor: Workers, Race, and the Making of the Peruvian State*. Durham, NC: Duke University Press.

Duffy, Mignon. 2007. "Doing the Dirty Work: Gender, Race, and Reproductive Labor in Historical Perspective." *Gender & Society*, 21(3):313–36. https://doi.org/10.1177/0891243207300764

Earle, Rebecca. 2012. *The Body of the Conquistador: Food, Race and the Colonial Experience in Spanish America, 1492–1700*. New York, NY: Cambridge University Press.

El Comercio. 2014. "Plantean que empleadas del hogar no ganen menos de la RMV." August 13. https://elcomercio.pe/economia/peru/plantean-empleadas-hogar-ganen-rmv-175340-noticia/

———. 2017. "Accidentes de tránsito en Lima: dónde y cómo evitarlos." April 19. https://elcomercio.pe/peru/accidentes-transito-lima-evitarlos-415537-noticia/

Elias, Juanita. 2010. "Making Migrant Domestic Work Visible: The Rights Based Approach to Migration and the Challenges of Social Reproduction." *Review of International Political Economy* 17(5):840–59.

ESRI. 2016. "Wealth Divides." http://storymaps.esri.com/stories/2016/wealth-divides/index.html

Ewe, Koh. 2023. "She Left Home to Work 5,000 Miles Away But Was Killed and Abandoned in a Desert." *Vice*, February 1. https://www.vice.com/en/article/she-left-home-to-work-5000-miles-away-but-was-killed-and-abandoned-in-a-desert/

Ewig, Christine. 2010. *Second-Wave Neoliberalism: Gender, Race, and Health Sector Reform in Peru*. University Park, PA: The Pennsylvania State University Press.

Fakih, Farabi. 2023. "Colonial Domesticity and the Modern City: Bandung in the Early Twentieth Century Netherlands Indies." *Journal of Urban History* 49(3), 645–67.

Fanon, Frantz. 1952. *Black Skin, White Masks*. New York, NY: Grove Press.

Federici, Silvia. 2004. *Caliban and the Witch: Women, the Body, and Primitive Accumulation*. London, UK: Autonomedia.

Feldacker, Bruce. 1999. *Labor Guide to Labor Law*. Prentice Hall.

Feliu, Verónica. 2014. "Chilean Domestic Labor: A Feminist Silence." In *Translocalities/Translocalidades: Feminist Politics of Translation in the Latin/a Américas*, edited by Sonia E. Alvarez, Claudia de Lima Costa, Verónica Feliu, Rebecca J. Hester, Normal Klahn, and Mille Thayer. Durham, NC: Duke University Press.

Figueroa, Blanca. 2003. *Las leyes y la realidad: Trabajo infantil doméstico*. Lima, Peru: Asociación Grupo de Trabajo Redes (AGTR).

Fine, Janice. 2007. "Worker Centers and Immigrant Women. "In *The Sex of Class: Women Transforming American Labor*, edited by Dorothy Sue Cobble. Ithaca, NY: ILR Press.

Fineman, Martha A. 2009. "Evolving Images of Gender and Equality: A Feminist Journey." *New England Law Review* 43:437.

Fish, Jennifer N. 2017. *Domestic Workers of the World Unite! A Global Movement for Dignity and Human Rights*. New York, NY: New York University Press.

Ford, Michele. 2004. "Organizing the Unorganizable: Unions, NGOs, and Indonesian Migrant Labour." *International Migration* 42(5):99–117.

Fox-Genovese, Elizabeth. 1988. *Within the Plantation Household: Black and White Women of the Old South*. Chapel Hill, NC: The University of North Carolina Press.

Fraser, Nancy. 2013. *Fortunes of Feminism: From State-Managed Capitalism to Neoliberal Crisis*. London, UK: Verso Press.

García, Ana Camila. 2013. "Mujeres de servicio doméstico e intimidad familiar en Bogotá." *Revista colombiana de antropología* 49(2):111–30.

Genovese, Eugene. 1976. *Roll, Jordan, Roll: The World the Slaves Made*. New York, NY: Vintage Press.

Giddens, Anthony. 1984. *The Constitution of Society*. Cambridge, UK: Polity Press.

Gill, Lesley. 1994. *Precarious Dependencies: Gender, Class, and Domestic Service in Bolivia*. New York, NY: Columbia University Press.

Glenn, Evelyn Nakano. 1991. "Cleaning Up/Kept Down: A Historical Perspective on Racial Inequality in 'Women's Work.'" *Stanford Law Review* 43(6):1333–56.

———.1992. "From Servitude to Service Work: Historical Continuity in the Racial Division of Paid Reproductive Labor." *Signs* 18(1):1–43.

Glymph, Thavolia. 2008. *Out of the House of Bondage: The Transformation of the Plantation Household*. New York, NY: Cambridge University Press.

Goldberg, Harmony. 2014. "'Prepare to Win': Domestic Workers United's Strategic Transition Following the Passage of the New York Domestic Workers' Bill of Rights." In *New Labor in New York: Precarious Workers and the Future of the Labor Movement*, edited by Eileen Boris and Ed Ott, 266–88. Ithaca, NY: Cornell University Press.

Gonzales, M.J. 1989. "Chinese Plantation Workers and Social Conflict in Peru in the Late Nineteenth Century." *Journal of Latin American Studies* 21(3):385–424.

Gonzalez, Priscilla, and Sarah Leberstein. 2010. *Rights Begin at Home: Protecting Yourself as a Domestic Worker*. Domestic Workers United and National Employment Law Project: New York City.

Graubart, Karen B. 2007. *With Our Labor and Sweat: Indigenous Women and the Formation of Colonial Society in Peru 1550–1700*. Palo Alto, CA: Stanford University Press.

Gray, Brenda Clegg. 1993. *Black Female Domestics During the Depression in New York City, 1930–1940.* New York, NY: Garland Publishing.

Hall, Matthew, Emily Greenman, and George Farkas. 2010. "Legal Status and Wage Disparities for Mexican Immigrants." *Social Forces* 89(2):491–513.

Hayden, Dolores. 1981. *The Grand Domestic Revolution: A History of Feminist Designs for American Homes, Neighborhoods, and Cities.* Cambridge, MA: MIT Press.

Higgins, James. 2005. *Lima: A Cultural and Literary History.* Oxford: Signal Books.

Hochschild, Arlie. 1989. *The Second Shift: Working Parents and the Revolution at Home.* New York, NY: Penguin.

Hondagneu-Sotelo, Pierrette. 2001. *Doméstica: Immigrant Workers Cleaning and Caring in the Shadows of Affluence.* Berkeley, CA: University of California Press.

Hondagneu-Sotelo, Pierrette, and Cristina Riegos. 1997. "'*Sin Organización, No Hay Solución*': Latina Domestic Workers and Non-Traditional Labor Organizing." *Latino Studies Journal* 8:54–81.

hooks, bell. 1990. *Yearning: Race, Gender, and Cultural Politics.* Boston, MA: South End Press.

HRPM (Hudson River Park Mamas). 2025. https://www.hrpmamas.com/

Hufstader, Chris. 2010. "The Injustice of Racism." Oxfam. November 30. https://www.oxfamamerica.org/explore/stories/the-injustice-of-racism/

ILO (International Labour Organization). 2003. *Report V: The Scope of the Employment Relationship: Fifth Item on the Agenda.* International Labour Conference 91st Session. Geneva: International Labour Office. https://webapps.ilo.org/public/english/standards/relm/ilc/ilc91/pdf/rep-v.pdf

———. 2013. *Domestic Workers Across the World: Global and Regional Statistics and the Extent of Legal Protection.* Geneva: International Labour Office. https://www.ilo.org/media/458491/download

———. 2015. ILO *Global Estimates on International Migrant Workers: Results and Methodology.* Labour Migration Branch: Geneva. https://www.ilo.org/sites/default/files/wcmsp5/groups/public/@dgreports/@dcomm/@publ/documents/publication/wcms_808935.pdf

———. 2016. Ratifications of C189, Domestic Workers Convention, 2011 (No. 189). http://www.ilo.org/dyn/normlex/en/f?p=1000:11300:0::NO:11300:P11300_INSTRUMENT_ID:2551460

———. 2022. *Promoviendo el trabajo decente para las trabajadoras del hogar en Perú. COVID-19, cambios en el empleo, condiciones laborales y riesgo de trabajo forzoso de las trabajadoras del hogar remuneradas en Perú. [Promoting decent work for domestic workers in Peru. COVID-19, changes in employment, working conditions and risk of forced labor of paid domestic workers in Peru.].* Lima, Peru: International Labor Organization. https://www.ilo.org/es/publications/promoviendo-el-trabajo-decente-para-las-trabajadoras-del-hogar-de-peru

INEI (Instituto Nacional de Estadística e Informática). 2022. *Condiciones de vida de la población venezolana que reside en el Perú. Resultados de la "Encuesta dirigida a la población venezolana que reside en el país" II EMPOVE 2022. [Living Conditions of the Venezuelan Population Residing in Peru. Results of the "Survey Directed to the Venezuelan Population Residing in the Country" II EMPOVE 2022].* Lima, Peru: Instituto Nacional de Estadística e Informática. https://www.inei.gob.pe/media/MenuRecursivo/publicaciones_digitales/Est/Lib1886/libro.pdf

Ives, Mike. 2016. "After Window-Washing Deaths, a Debate Over Migrants' Rights in Hong Kong." *The New York Times.* November 23. https://www.nytimes.com/2016/11/23/world/asia/hong-kong-migrants-domestic- workers.html

Jaquette, Jane. 1994. *The Women's Movement in Latin America: Participation and Democracy.* New York, NY: Westview Press.

———. 2009. *Feminist Agendas and Democracy in Latin America.* Durham, NC: Duke University Press.

Jefferson, Ann, and Paul Lokken. 2011. *Daily Life in Colonial America.* Westport, CT: Greenwood Press.

Jiang, Zhe, and Mark Korcynski. 2016. "When the 'Unorganizable' Organize: The Collective Mobilization of Migrant Domestic Workers in London." *Human Relations* 69(3):1–26.

Johnson, L.L., and S.M. Socolow. 2002. "Colonial Centers, Colonial Peripheries, and the Economic Agency of the Spanish State." In *Negotiated Empires: Centers and Peripheries in the Americas, 1500–1820,* edited by Christine Daniels and Michael V. Kennedy, 59–78. New York, NY: Routledge.

Juravich, Tom, and Kate Bronfenbrenner. 1999. *Ravenswood: The Steelworkers' Victory and the Revival of American Labor.* Ithaca, NY: Cornell University Press.

Kasinitz, Philip, John H. Mollenkopf, and Mary C. Waters. 2013. "The Next Generation Emerges." In *One Out of Three: Immigrant New York in the Twenty-First Century,* edited by Nancy Foner. New York, NY: Columbia University Press.

Kelley, Wyn. 2001. "The Style of Lima: Colonialism, Urban Form, and 'The Town-Ho's Story.'" In *Melville Among the Nations: Proceedings of an International Conference, Volos, Greece, July 2–6, 1997,* edited by Sanford E. Marovitz and A.C. Christodoulou. Kent, OH: The Kent State University Press.

Kelly, Annie, and Hazel Thompson. 2015. "The Vanished: The Filipino Domestic Workers Who Disappear Behind Closed Doors." *The Guardian.* October 24. https://www.theguardian.com/global-development/2015/oct/24/the-vanished-filipino-domestic-workers-working-abroad

Kessler-Harris, Alice. 1981. *Women Have Always Worked: A Historical Overview.* Old Westbury, NY: The Feminist Press.

Krieger, Linda Hamilton, Rachel Kahn Best, and Lauren B. Edelman. 2015. "When 'Best Practices' Win, Employees Lose: Symbolic Compliance and Judicial Inference in Federal Equal Employment Opportunity Cases." *Law & Social Inquiry* 40(4):843–79. https://doi.org/10.1111/lsi.12116.

Krutsch, Emily and Javier Colato. 2023. "World Health Day: Celebrating Good Health and In-Demand Healthcare Jobs." *U.S. Department of Labor Blog.* April 5. https://blog.dol.gov/2023/04/05/world-health-day-celebrating-good-health-and-in-demand-healthcare-jobs

Kuznesof, Elizabeth. 1989. "A History of Domestic Service in Spanish America, 1492–1980." In *Muchachas No More: Household Workers in Latin America and the Caribbean*, edited by Elsa M. Chaney and Mary Garcia Castro. Philadelphia, PA: Temple University Press.

La República. 2007. "Empleadas ingresarán a playas de Asia." March 10. https://larepublica.pe/sociedad/260310-empleadas-ingresaran-a-playas-de-asia

———. 2011. "¿Otro caso de discriminación? Ahora el Lima Cricket & Football Club." October 25. http://larepublica.pe/25-10-2011/otro-caso-de-discriminacion-ahora -el-lima- cricket-football-club

———. 2015."Ciudadano español golpeó a empleada del hogar en Miraflores." April 15. http://redaccion.larepublica.pe/14-04-2015/ciudadano-espanol-golpeo-a -empleada-del- hogar-en-miraflores

Lautier, Bruce. 2003. "Las empleadas domésticas latino-americanas y la sociología del trabajo, algunas observaciones acerca del caso brasileño." *Revista mexicana de sociología* 65(4):789–814.

Leghtas, Izza. 2014. "Hidden Away: Abuses Against Migrant Domestic Workers in the UK." *Human Rights Watch*. March 30. https://www.hrw.org/report/2014/03/30/ hidden- away/abuses-against-migrant-domestic-workers-uk

León, Ramón, Juan José Tan Martínez and Kathia Murillo Siancas. 1998. *El país de los extraños: una encuesta sobre actitudes raciales en universitarios de Lima Metropolitana*. Lima, Peru: La Parola Editorial, Universidad Ricardo Palma.

Levenstein, Lisa. 2009. *A Movement Without Marches: African American Women and the Politics of Poverty in Postwar Philadelphia*. Chapel Hill, NC: University of North Carolina Press.

Ley Número 27986, Ley de los Trabajadores del Hogar. https://natlex.ilo.org/dyn/ natlex2/r/natlex/fe/details?p3_isn=66103

Lobo, Arun Peter, and Joseph J. Salvo. 2013. *The Newest New Yorkers: Characteristics of the City's Foreign-Born Population*. Population Division of the Department of City Planning. New York City Mayor's Office of Immigrant Affairs.

Logan, John R., Wenquan Zhang, and Richard D. Alba. 2002. "Immigrant Enclaves and Ethnic Communities in New York City and Los Angeles." *American Sociological Review* 67(2):99–322.

Luciak, Ilja A. 2001. *Después de la revolución: igualdad de género y democracia en El Salvador, Nicaragua y Guatemala*. San Salvador, El Salvador: UCA Editores.

Lugones, Maria. 2008. "The Coloniality of Gender." *Worlds & Knowledges Otherwise*. 1–17. https://globalstudies.trinity.duke.edu/wpcontent/themes/cgsh/ materials/WKO/v2d2_Lugones.pdf

Lum, Selina. 2021. "30 Years' Jail for Woman Who Starved and Tortured Myanmar Maid to Death." *The Straits Times*. June 23. https://www.straitstimes.com/ singapore/courts-crime/30-years-jail-for-woman-who-starved-and-tortured -maid-to-death

Lust, Jan. 2014. "Mining in Peru: Indigenous and Peasant Communities vs. the State and Mining Capital." *Class, Race and Corporate Power* 2(3). https://www.jstor.org/ stable/48645525

Martin, Linda, and Kerry Segrave. 1985. *The Servant Problem: Domestic Workers in North America*. Jefferson, NC: McFarland & Company.

Martínez, Julia and Claire Lowrie. 2009. "Colonial Constructions of Masculinity: Transforming Aboriginal Australian Men into 'Houseboys.'" *Gender and History* 21:305–23.

Massey, Douglas S. 2020. "Immigration Policy Mismatches and Counterproductive Outcomes: Unauthorized Migration to the U.S. in Two Eras." *Comparative Migration Studies* 8(1):21.

Mauricio, Sofía. 2015. Personal interview, December 15. Lima, Peru.

May, Vanessa H. 2011. *Unprotected Labor: Household Workers, Politics, and Middle-Class Reform in New York, 1870–1940*. Chapel Hill, NC: The University of North Carolina Press

Mendez, Jennifer. 1998. "Of Mops and Maids: Contradictions and Continuities in Bureaucratized Domestic Work." *Social Problems* 4(5):114–35.

Merry, Sally Engle. 1991. "Law and Colonialism." *Law & Society Review* 25(1991):889–922.

Mick, Carolyn. 2011. "Discourses of 'Border-Crossers': Peruvian Domestic Workers in Lima as Social Actors." *Discourse Studies* 13(2): 189–209.

———. 2016. "'Yo sé hablar, dije': The Conditions for Peruvian Domestic Workers to Speak Out for Their Rights." *Amérique Latine Histoire et Mémoire. Les Cahiers ALHIM* 31. http://alhim.revues.org/5437

Middaugh, Laine. 2012. "Lessons from the 'Unorganizable': Domestic Workers Organizing." *Kennedy School Review* 12(12):12–13.

Milkman, Ruth. 1987. *Gender at Work: The Dynamics of Job Segregation by Sex During World War II*. Urbana, IL: University of Illinois Press.

———. 2006. *L.A. Story: Immigrant Workers and the Future of the U.S. Labor Movement*. New York, NY: Russell Sage Foundation.

Minow, Martha. 1987. "Interpreting Rights: An Essay for Robert Cover." *Yale Law Journal* 96(8):1860–1915.

Monk, Ellis P. 2016. "The Consequences of 'Race and Color' in Brazil." *Social Problems* 63(3):413–30.

Morgan, Ronald J. 1998. "'Just like Rosa': History and Metaphor in the 'Life' of a Seventeenth-Century Peruvian Saint. *Biography* 21(3):275–310.

Morrison, Toni. 2017. "The Work You Do, The Person You Are." *The New Yorker*, May 29. https://www.newyorker.com/magazine/2017/06/05/toni-morrison-the-work-you-do-the-person-you-are

Mose Brown, Tamara. 2011. *Raising Brooklyn: Nannies, Childcare, and Caribbeans Creating Community*. New York, NY: New York University Press.

Moseley-Williams, Sorrel. 2014. "Lima's Mistura Food Festival: The Best Dishes in Peru Right Now." *Condé Nast Traveler*. September 10. https://www.cntraveler.com/galleries/2014-09-10/lima-s-mistura-food-festival-the-best-dishes-in-peru-right-now

Moslimani, Mohamad, and Jeffrey S. Passel. 2024. "What the Data Says About Immigrants in the U.S." Pew Research Center. https://www.pewresearch.org/short-reads/2024/09/27/key-findings-about-us-immigrants/#:~:text=Immigrants%20today%20account%20for%2014.3,the%20record%2014.8%25%20in%201890.

MTPE (Ministerio de Trabajo y Promoción del Empleo). 2012. "Conferencia del Convenio 189 del OIT." ["Conference on the International Labour Organization's Convention 189."] Ministerio de Trabajo y Promoción del Empleo. Lima, Peru. December 13.

Mullany, Gerry. 2014. "Injuries to Domestic Helper Cast Light on Abuses in Hong Kong." *The New York Times.* January 14.

Munro, Moira, and Ruth Madigan. 1999. "Negotiating Space in the Family Home." In *At Home: An Anthropology of Domestic Space*, edited by Irene Cieraad. Syracuse, NY: Syracuse University press.

Museo Larco. "Culturas y mapas de tiempo." Visited April 2013 and February 2014. https://www.museolarco.org/en/exhibition/permanent-exhibition/online-exhibition/introduction/peru-cradle-of-civilization/

Nadasen, Premilla. 2009. "Sista' Friends and Other Allies: Domestic Workers United." In *New Social Movements in the African Diaspora: Challenging Global Apartheid*, edited by Leith Mullings. New York, NY: Palgrave Macmillan.

———. 2015. *Household Workers Unite: The Untold Story of African American Women Who Built a Movement.* Boston, MA: Beacon Press.

Naples, Nancy. 2003. *Feminism and Method: Ethnography, Discourse Analysis, and Activist Research.* New York, NY: Routledge.

Navarro, Mireya. 2014. "'Poor Door' in a New York Tower Opens a Fight Over Affordable Housing." *The New York Times.*

———. 2015. "88,000 Applicants and Counting for 55 Units in 'Poor Door' Building." *The New York Times.*

NDWA (National Domestic Workers Alliance). 2024. New York City Domestic Work Factsheet. https://www.domesticworkers.org/membership/chapters/we-dream-in-black-new-york-chapter/nyc-care-campaign/new-york-city-domestic-work-factsheet

Nielsen, Laura Beth. 2004. "The Work of Rights and the Work Rights Do: A Critical Empirical Approach." In *The Blackwell Companion to Law and Society*, edited by Austin Sarat, 63–79. Malden, MA: Blackwell Publishing.

Nightingale, Carl. 2012. *Segregation: A Global History of Divided Cities.* Chicago, IL: University of Chicago Press.

NYCP (New York City Department of City Planning). 2017. "NYC's Foreign-born, 2000 to 2015." March. https://www.nyc.gov/assets/planning/download/pdf/planning-level/housing-economy/nyc-foreign-born-info-brief.pdf?r=1#:~:text=NYC%20Planning%20%7C%20March%202017%20%7C%20Foreign%2Dborn%20Info%20Brief&text=Latin%20Americans%20accounted%20for%2032,the%20olarg

NYDOL (New York Department of Labor). 2010. *Report on Outreach Efforts for Domestic Workers Legislation.* https://dol.ny.gov/system/files/documents/2021/03/report-to-governor-outreach.pdf

NYSS (New York State Senate). 2010. The Stenographic Record: Regular Session, July 1. Senator Andrea Steward-Cousins, Acting President, and Angelo Aponte, Secretary. https://legislation.nysenate.gov/pdf/transcripts/2010-07-24T10:00/

O'Brien, Rob. 2015. "Singapore's Domestic Workers Routinely Exploited and Often Abused in the Service of Rich Nationals." *The Independent*. July 28. https://www.the-independent.com/news/world/asia/singapore-s-domestic-workers-routinely-exploited-and-often-abused-in-the-service-of-rich-nationals-10422589.html

Ocampo, Ruben Alexis, and Zaida Guillermina Arcondo. 2021. *Trabajadores del hogar en el mercado laboral peruano 2015–2019. [Domestic Workers in the Peruvian Labor Market 2015–2019]*. Lima, Peru: Ministerio del Trabajo y Promoción del Empleo. https://cdn.www.gob.pe/uploads/document/file/1849631/Trabajadoras%20del%20Hogar%20en%20el%20Mercado%20Laboral%202015-2019.pdf?v=1619532945

Office of Strategy, Policy, and Plans. 2023. *Summary Data on B-1 Personal or Domestic Workers*. U.S. Department of Homeland Security. https://www.dhs.gov/sites/default/files/2023-11/2023_0920_dmo_plcy_summary_data_b1_personal_or_domestic_workers_fy23.pdf

Office of the New York State Comptroller. 2024. *New York City's Uneven Recovery: Foreign-Born in the Workforce*. 20–2024. Office of The New York State Comptroller. https://www.osc.ny.gov/files/reports/osdc/pdf/report-20-2024.pdf

Orlove, Benjamin S. 1993. "Putting Race in Its Place: Order in Colonial and Postcolonial Peruvian Geography." *Social Research* 60(2):301–36.

Ortiz, Daniela. 2012. *Habitaciones de servicio*. http://angelsbarcelona.com/en/artists/daniela-ortiz/projects/habitaciones-de-servicio/534

OSHA (Occupational Health and Safety Act). 1970. 29 C.F.R. § 1975.6 https://www.law.cornell.edu/cfr/text/29/1975.6

Osorio, Alejandra B. 2008. *Inventing Lima: Baroque Modernity in Peru's South Sea Metropolis*. New York, NY: Palgrave.

Osterman, Paul. 2017. *Who Will Care For Us? Long-Term Care and the Long-Term Workforce*. New York, NY: Russell Sage Foundation.

O'Toole, Rachel Sarah. 2012. *Bound Lives: Africans, Indians, and the Making of Race in Colonial Peru*. Pittsburgh, PA: University of Pittsburgh Press.

Palmer, Phyllis. 1995. "Outside the Law: Agricultural and Domestic Workers Under the Fair Labor Standards Act." *Journal of Policy History* 7(4):416–40.

Panamá America. 2009. "Multas por poner uniforme a empleadas domésticas van de 58 a 2.300 dólares en Perú." April 6. https://www.panamaamerica.com.pa/node/350605

Pariser, Robyn. 2015. "Masculinity and Organized Resistance in Domestic Service in Colonial Dar es Salaam, 1919–1961." *International Labor and Working-Class History* 88:109–29.

Parker, David Stuart. 1998. *Idea of the Middle Class: White-Collar Workers and Peruvian Society, 1900–1950*. University Park, PA: The Pennsylvania State University Press.

Parreñas, Rhacel Salazar. 2015[2001]. *Servants of Globalization: Women, Migration, and Domestic Work*. Palo Alto, CA: Stanford University Press.

Perea, Juan F. 2011. "The Echoes of Slavery: Recognizing the Racist Origins of the Agricultural and Domestic Worker Exclusion from the National Labor Relations Act." *Ohio State Law Journal* 72(1):95–138.

Pérez, Leda M., and Andrea Gandolfi. 2024. "From Dead Letter to Functional Policy? Domestic Workers' Rights and 'Disformality' in Peru." *International Labour Review* 163(3):455–76.

Pérez, Leda M., and Pedro M. Llanos. 2022. "Vulnerable Women in a Thriving Country: An Analysis of Twenty-First-Century Domestic Workers in Peru and Recommendations for Future Research." *Latin American Research Review* 52(4):552–70. doi: 10.25222/larr.67.

Perkins, Frances, and William H. Stead. 1939. *Job Descriptions for Domestic Service and Personal Service Occupations.* Washington, DC: United States Printing Office.

Perkins Gilman, Charlotte. 1892. "The Yellow Wallpaper." *The New England Magazine.*

Perú21. 2011. "El Country Club tiene 'baño para amas.'" October 13. http://archivo .peru21.pe/noticia/1317207/denuncian-discriminacion-country-club

Plöger, Jorg. 2007. "The Emergence of a 'City of Cages' in Lima: Neighbourhood Appropriation in the Context of Rising Insecurities." *European Journal of Geography.* Map of Lima, Peru, with Concentrated Housing Clusters. https://doi.org/10.4000/ cybergeo.6785

Poma de Ayala, Felipe Guaman. 2006[1613]. *The First New Chronicle and Good Government.* Translated by David Frye. Indianapolis, IN: Hackett Publishing.

Poo, Ai-jen. 2010. "Organizing with Love: Lessons from the New York Domestic Workers Bill of Rights Campaign." *Left Turn.* December 1. http://www.leftturn .org/Organizing-with-Love

Qayum, Seemin. 2002. "Nationalism, Internal Colonialism and the Spatial Imagination: The Geographic Society of La Paz in Turn-of-the-Century Bolivia." In *Studies in the Formation of the Nation State in Latin America,* edited by James Dunkerley. London, UK: University of London Press.

Qayum, Seemin, and Raka Ray. 2003. "Grappling with Modernity: India's Respectable Classes and the Culture of Domestic Servitude." *Ethnography* 4(4):520–55.

———. 2010. "Male Servants and the Failure of Patriarchy in Kolkata (Calcutta)." *Men and Masculinities* 13(1):111–25.

Quijano, Aníbal. 2000. "Colonialidad del poder y clasificación social." *Journal of World-Systems Research* 6(2):342–86.

Radcliffe, Sarah A. 1993. "The State and Peasant Women in Peru." In *"Viva": Women and Popular Protest in Latin America,* edited by Sarah A. Radcliffe and Sallie Westwood, 197. New York, NY: Routledge.

Ramírez, Tomás, Renato Carcelén, Carmen Roca, and Joann Vanek. 2023. "Informal Workers in Peru: A Statistical Profile, 2015–2021." WIEGO. https://www.wiego .org/wp-content/uploads/2023/04/WIEGO_Statistical_Brief_N34_Peru.pdf

Ray, Raka, and Seemin Qayum. 2009. *Cultures of Servitude: Modernity, Domesticity, and Class in India.* Palo Alto, CA: Stanford University Press.

Restall, Matthew, and Kris Lane. 2011. *Latin America in Colonial Times.* New York, NY: Cambridge University Press.

Riles, Dustin, and Emily Rolen. 2023. "Making a Career of Caring for Others." *U.S. Department of Labor Blog.* https://blog.dol.gov/2023/02/15/making-a-career-of -caring-for-others

Rivera, Fernando. 2016. "Peru: Words Under the Fog." In *The Palgrave Handbook of Literature and the City*, edited by Jeremy Tambling. New York, NY: Palgrave Macmillan.

Roediger, David, and Philip S. Foner. 1989. *Our Own Time: A History of American Labor and the Working Day*. New York, NY: Verso.

Rollins, Judith. 1985. *Between Women: Domestics and Their Employers*. Philadelphia, PA: Temple University Press.

Romero, Emilio. 1979. *Siete ensayos: 50 años de historia*. Lima, Peru: Biblioteca Amauta.

Romero, Mary. 1992. *Maid in the USA*. New York, NY: Routledge.

———. 2011. *The Maid's Daughter: Living Inside and Outside of the American Dream*. New York, NY: NYU Press.

Rosaldo, Manuel. 2021. "Problematizing the 'Informal Sector': 50 Years of Critique, Clarification, Qualification, and More Critique." *Sociology Compass* 15(3). https://doi.org/10.1111/soc4.12914

Rousseau, Stephanie. 2010. "Populism from Above, Populism from Below: Gender Politics Under Alberto Fujimori and Evo Morales." In *Gender and Populism in Latin America: Passionate Politics*, edited by Karen Kampwirth. University Park, PA: The Pennsylvania State University Press.

Rubiano-Matulevich, Eliana. 2023. "Five Pieces of Data about Poverty and Economic Growth in Peru." World Bank Blogs, October 16. https://blogs.worldbank.org/en/latinamerica/datos-pobreza-crecimiento-economico-en-peru

Ruiz, Vicki L. 1987 "By the Day or the Week: Mexicana Domestic Workers in El Paso." In *Women of the U.S.-Mexico Border*, edited by Vicki L. Ruiz and Susan Tiano, 61–76. Boston, MA: Allen & Unwin.

Rutté García, Alberto. 1973. *Simplemente explotadas: el mundo de las empleadas domésticas de Lima*. Lima, Peru: DESCO Centro de Estudios y Promoción del Desarrollo.

Said, Edward. 1994. *Culture and Imperialism*. New York, NY: Vintage Books.

Salazar Bondy, Sebastián. 1964. "Lima la horrible." Mexico City: ERA.

Sánchez Flores, Miguel Antonio. 2016. "Más allá del *pop achorado*: una propuesta de relectura de los afiches de Jesús Ruiz Durand para la reforma agraria del gobierno de Juan Velasco Alvarado." M.A. Thesis in Art History. Pontificia Universidad Católica del Perú (PUCP), Lima, Peru.

Santos, Boaventura de Sousa. 1987. "Law: A Map of Misreading. Toward a Postmodern Conception of Law." *Journal of Law and Society*. 14(3):279–302.

Sarat, Austin. 1990. "'. . . The Law Is All Over': Power, Resistance, and the Legal Consciousness of the Welfare Poor." *Yale Journal of Law & the Humanities* 2(2):343–80.

Sarti, Raffaella. 2010. "Fighting for Masculinity: Male Domestic Workers, Gender, and Migration in Italy from the Late Nineteenth Century to the Present." *Men and Masculinities* 13(1):16–43.

———. 2014. "Historians, Social Scientists, Servants, and Domestic Workers: Fifty Years of Research on Domestic and Care Work." *International Review of Social History* 59(2):279–314.

Sassen, Saskia. 2014. "Labor Migration and the Transnational Demand for Domestic Labor." (Panel #3, Justice in the Home, Bernard Center for Research on Women, October 16–18). https://bcrw.barnard.edu/videos/labor-migration-and-the-transnational-demand-for-domestic-labor-justice-in-the-home-panel-3/

Schönwälder, Gerd. 2002. *Linking Civil Society and the State: Urban Popular Movements, the Left, and Local Government in Peru, 1980–1992*. University Park, PA: The Pennsylvania State University Press.

Schultz, Vicki. 1992. "Women 'Before' the Law: Judicial Stories About Women, Work, and Sex Segregation on the Job." In *Feminists Theorize the Political*, edited by Judith Butler and Joan W. Scott. New York, NY: Routledge.

Seiffarth, Marlene, Florence Bonnet, and Claire Hobden. 2023. *The Road to Decent Work for Domestic Workers*. Geneva, Switzerland: International Labour Office. https://www.ilo.org/sites/default/files/wcmsp5/groups/public/%40ed_protect/%40protrav/%40travail/documents/publication/wcms_883181.pdf

Seligmann, Linda J. 1989. "To Be in Between: The Cholas as Market Women." *Comparative Studies in Society and History* 31(4): 694–721.

Siegel, Reva B. 1994. "Home as Work: The First Woman's Rights Claims Concerning Wives' Household Labor, 1850–1880." *The Yale Law Journal* 103(5):1073–217. https://doi.org/10.2307/797118

Silva-Peñaherrera, Michael, Amaya Ayala-Garcia, Erika Alferez Mayer, Iselle Sabastizagal-Vela, and Fernando G. Benavides. 2022. "Informal Employment, Working Conditions, and Self-Perceived Health in 3098 Peruvian Urban Workers." *International Journal of Environmental Research and Public Health* 19(10):6105. doi: 10.3390/ijerph19106105.

Skop, Emily H., and Paul A. Peters. 2007. "Socio-Spatial Segregation in Metropolitan Lima, Peru." *Journal of Latin American Geography* 6(1):149–71.

Slaughter, Anne-Marie. 2016. "The Work that Makes Work Possible." *The Atlantic*. March 23. https://www.theatlantic.com/business/archive/2016/03/unpaid-caregivers/474894/

Socolow, Susan Migden. 2000. *The Women of Colonial Latin America*. New York, NY: Cambridge University Press.

Spitta, Silvia. 2007. "Lima the Horrible: The Cultural Politics of Theft." *PMLA* 122(1): 294–300.

Staab, Silke, and Kristen Hill Maher. 2006. "The Dual Discourse About Peruvian Domestic Workers in Santiago de Chile: Class, Race, and a Nationalist Project." *Latin American Politics and Society* 48(1):87–116.

Stasiulis, Daiva K., and Abigail B. Bakan. 1997. "Regulation and Resistance: Strategies of Migrant Domestic Workers in Canada and Internationally." *Asian and Pacific Migration Journal* 6(1):31–57.

Stephen, Lynn. 1997. *Women and Social Movements in Latin America: Power from Below*. Austin, TX: University of Texas Press.

Stoler, Ann Laura. 2002. *Carnal Knowledge and Imperial Power: Race and the Intimate in Colonial Rule*. Berkeley, CA: University of California Press.

Stoler, Ann Laura, and Frederick Cooper. 1997. "Between Metropole and Colony: Rethinking a Research Agenda." In *Tensions of Empire: Colonial Cultures in a Bourgeois World*, edited by Frederick Cooper and Ann Laura Stoler. Berkeley, CA: University of California Press.

Su, Alice. 2017. "Slave Labour? Death Rate Doubles for Migrant Domestic Workers in Lebanon." *The New Humanitarian*. May 15. https://www.thenewhumanitarian.org/2017/05/15/slave-labour-death-rate-doubles-migrant-domestic-workers-lebanon

Swider, Sarah. 2006. "Working Women of the World Unite? Labor Organizing and Transnational Gender Solidarity Among Domestic Workers in Hong Kong." In *Global Feminism: Transnational Women's Activism, Organizing, and Human Rights*, edited by Myra Marx Ferree and Aili Mari Tripp. New York, NY: New York University Press.

Takenaka, Ayumi. 2004. "The Japanese in Peru: History of Immigration, Settlement, and Racialization." *Latin American Perspectives* 31(3):77–98.

Telles, Edward, and Tianna Paschel. 2014. "Who Is Black, White, or Mixed Race? How Skin Color, Status, and Nation Shape Racial Classification in Latin America." *American Journal of Sociology* 120(3):864–907.

Tizon, Alex. 2017. "My Family's Slave." *The Atlantic*. June. https://www.theatlantic.com/magazine/archive/2017/06/lolas-story/524490/

Tomei, Manuela. 2011. "Decent Work for Domestic Workers: Reflections on Recent Approaches to Tackle Informality." *Canadian Journal of Women and the Law* 23(1):185–212.

Tronto, Joan. 2002. "The 'Nanny' Question in Feminism." *Hypatia* 17(2):34–51.

Tuominen, Mary C. 2003. *We Are Not Babysitters: Family Child Care Providers Redefine Work and Care*. New Brunswick, NJ: Rutgers University Press.

Ungar, Mark. 2002. *Elusive Reform: Democracy and the Rule of Law in Latin America*. London, UK: Lynne Rienner Publishers.

Van Raaphorst, Donna L. 1988. *Union Maids Not Wanted: Organizing Domestic Workers, 1870–1940*. New York, NY: Praeger Publishers.

Vargas, Virginia. 1991. "The Women's Movement in Peru: Streams, Spaces, and Knots." *European Review of Latin American and Caribbean Studies* 50(June 1991):7–50.

———. 2013. Personal interview, April 25.

Vasquez del Aguila, Ernesto. 2014. *Being a Man in a Transnational World: The Masculinity and Sexuality of Migration*. New York, NY: Routledge.

Waldinger, Roger. 1999. *Still the Promised City? African-Americans and New Immigrants in Postindustrial New York*. Cambridge, MA: Harvard University Press.

Walker, Charles. 2014. "Peru: Reflections of Tupac Amaru." *Berkeley Review of Latin American Studies* (Fall). http://clas.berkeley.edu/research/peru-reflections-tupac-amaru

Wallace, James M. 1984. "Urban Anthropology in Lima: An Overview." *Latin American Research Review* 19(3):57–85.

Waters, Mary C. 2005. *Black Identities: West Indian Immigrant Dreams and American Realities*. Cambridge, MA: Harvard University Press.

Watson, Sophie. 1986. "Housing and the Family." *International Journal of Urban and Regional Research* 10(1):8–28.

Waze. 2016. *Global Driver Satisfaction Index*. https://benzinazero.wordpress.com/wp-content/uploads/2016/09/driver-satisfaction-index-2016.pdf

Weinbaum, Eve. 2004. *To Move a Mountain: Fighting the Global Economy in Appalachia*. New York, NY: The New Press.

Weitzman, Hal. 2012. *Latin Lessons: How South America Stopped Listening to the United States and Started Prospering*. New York, NY: Wiley.

Woolf, Virginia. 1989[1929]. *A Room of One's Own*. New York, NY: Harcourt Brace & Co.

World Factbook. 2024. "People and Society: Peru." https://www.cia.gov/the-world-factbook/countries/peru/#people-and-society

Wrigley, Julia. 1995. *Other People's Children: An Intimate Account of the Dilemmas Facing Middle-Class Parents and the Women They Hire to Raise Their Children*. New York, NY: Basic Books.

Yamanaka, Keiko. 2000. "I Will Go Home, but When?": Labor Migration and Circular Diaspora Formation by Japanese Brazilians in Japan." In *Japan and Global Migration: Foreign Workers and the Advent of a Multicultural Society*, edited by Mike Douglass and Glenda S. Roberts. New York, NY: Routledge.

Yashar, Deborah. 2005. *Contesting Citizenship in Latin America: The Rise of Indigenous Movements and the Postliberal Challenge*. New York, NY: Cambridge University Press.

Young, Iris Marion. 1997. *Intersecting Voices: Dilemmas of Gender, Political Philosophy, and Policy*. Princeton, NJ: Princeton University Press.

Zarembka, Joy M. 2003. "America's Dirty Work: Migrant Maids and Modern-Day Slavery." In *Global Woman: Nannies, Maids and Sex Workers in the New Economy*, edited by Barbara Ehrenreich and Arlie Russel Hochschild. New York, NY: Holt Paperbacks.

Zelizer, Viviana. 1994. *Pricing the Priceless Child: The Changing Social Value of Children*. Princeton, NJ: Princeton University Press.

———. 2005. *The Purchase of Intimacy*. Princeton, NJ: Princeton University Press.

Zheng, Chunyan, Jiahui Ai, and Sida Liu. 2017. "The Elastic Ceiling: Gender and Professional Career in Chinese Courts." *Law & Society Review* 51(1):168–99. https://doi.org/10.1111/lasr.12249

INDEX

abuse, 3, 57; of child domestic workers, 44; by colonizers, 47; coverage of, 26, 156; leaving situations of, 124, 125; low wages as, 102; protections against, 14–15t, 87; sexual, 48, 62, 94

activism, 37, 60, 64, 131, 169, 170; of Black domestic workers, 111; collective, 153; of domestic workers, 174; feminist, 63, 70; human rights, 83; Jennifer N. Fish, 27; Myrtle Witbooi, 106; Nepali, 71; political, 143

Adhikaar (organization), 22, 36, 169

African workers, 79

African/Black Americans, 21, 25, 90, 105, 106, 116, 122, 132; as activists, 26, 111; Caribbean workers racialized as, 133; David Patterson, 128; history as domestic workers, 39, 108, 112, 141, 145; labor rights of, 109; legislating around, 110, 130; migrate from Southern U.S., 107; nannies, 146. *See also* slavery

Afro-Caribbean workers, 133, 169

Agrarian Reform, 1968–1973, 65

Albany, New York, 32, 33t, 126, 127, 128, 129

Ally, Shireen, 17, 112, 113, 114

Amaru, Tupac, 65, 66

Ancash, Peru, 71

Anderson, Bridget, 21

Anderson, Elizabeth, 12, 160

Andes (Peru), 59, 70, 77, 78; during colonial times, 66, 76; community in, 56; highlands (Peruvian), 31, 44, 45, 51, 52, 80, 165; household labor practices in, 18; migration from, 53

apartheid (South Africa), 17, 112

Arequipa, Peru, 31, 52

Arequipeños, 52

Argentina, 53

Arizona, 109

armed conflict, 35, 43, 46, 53, 60, 63

Asia, 26, 121, 122, 171; China, 46, 78; Hong Kong, 3, 34, 127, 129, 156, 171; India, 46; Indonesia, 77; Japan, 78, 165, 179n3, 181n3; Singapore, 3, 156; South, 33t; Southeast, 127; Tibet, 36, 170

ARTICULATIONS STUDIES IN RACE, IMMIGRATION, AND CAPITALISM

EDITORS
Cedric de Leon
Pawan Dhingra

Change is afoot in sociology and related fields. Motivated by mounting social inequality and the latest groundbreaking research, a new generation of scholars is pushing for a more synthetic and empirically rigorous approach to race, immigration, and capitalism. This book series seeks work at the intersection of these three fields. The series is a space to push forward a positive research agenda that articulates immigration, race, and capitalism together as overlapping systems that are experienced in people's everyday lives. Such studies will allow us to offer more nuanced analyses on topics such as immigrant assimilation, the pervasiveness of white supremacy, and the governing economic structures that surround all forms of discrimination. With an emphasis on sociological and qualitative work, the series will also be interested in interdisciplinary work across the social sciences and humanities, with a range of methodological approaches.

Language Brokers: Children of Immigrants Translating Inequality and Belonging for Their Families
HYEYOUNG KWON 2024

The Borders of Privilege: 1.5-Generation Brazilian Migrants Navigating Power Without Papers
KARA B. CEBULKO 2024

Enduring Empire: U.S. Statecraft and Race-Making in the Philippines
KATRINA QUISUMBING KING 2025